RUSSIA

FROM RED TO BLACK

Experiences of Russia

Roderick Heather

Pen Press

First published in Great Britain

All paper used in the printing of this book has been made from wood grown in managed, sustainable forests.

ISBN13: 978-1-78003-284-9

Printed and bound in the UK
Pen Press is an imprint of
Indepenpress Publishing Limited
25 Eastern Place
Brighton
BN2 1GJ

A catalogue record of this book is available from the British Library

Cover design by Jacqueline Abromeit

About the Author

Following an honours degree in Economics from Sheffield University in 1967, the author spent almost 30 years working for various manufacturing businesses in the UK and overseas. In 1995 he moved to Russia, leading a team of international consultants at a large automotive company for 12 months. In 1997 he became an advisor to UK Foreign Office and later the Department for International Development covering Russia and Poland until 2002. He subsequently worked as a management consultant on various projects in Russia and Ukraine as well as running one of the UK's leading interim management companies. As well as Russia, the author has lived in Canada, Switzerland, France and the USA and has travelled to some 70 different countries. He is currently a Welsh Assembly Government appointee on the Environment Agency's Flood Risk Management Committee. The author is married with 3 adult sons and lives in Chester.

The author has also written 'The Iron Tsar' a biography of John Hughes, the Victorian inventor and entrepreneur who founded the city of Donetsk in Ukraine (Penpress 2010).

Contents

Preface		i
Introductory Notes		iv
Map of western Russia		x
Part One	**A Year in Tatarstan, May 1995 to June 1996**	1
Chapter One		2
Chapter Two		21
Chapter Three		36
Chapter Four		57
Chapter Five		77
Chapter Six		91
Chapter Seven		119
Chapter Eight		139
Part Two	**From the Black Sea to Siberia, 1997 to 2000**	155
Chapter One		156
Chapter Two		166
Chapter Three		185
Chapter Four		196
Chapter Five		212
Chapter Six		223
Chapter Seven		240

PREFACE

Russia experienced two traumatic revolutions during the 20th century, the first in 1917 bringing the Bolsheviks to power and ultimately ushering in the era of the Soviet communist state. The second in late 1991 saw the rapid dismantling of the Soviet empire, the demise of the communists as the dominating force in Russian and eastern European politics and the installation of Boris Yeltsin as the first elected Russian president. The 1991 Revolution was largely made possible as a result of the reformist programmes introduced by Yeltsin's predecessor Mikhail Gorbachev. His ambitious experiments of glasnost (open society) and perestroika (economic restructuring) were to have as great an impact on Russia and its people as the Bolshevik revolution or World War II, though happily without the same turmoil or bloodshed. The dramatic and far reaching consequences of these reforms and the 1991 revolution were still working their way through Russian society when I arrived in the country in 1995.

Earlier that year, I had set up my own management consultancy business and one of my first clients was Cummins, a US corporation manufacturing large diesel engines in various plants around the world. In May 1995, they asked me to go out to Tatarstan in Russia to assist them with a restructuring project for a company called KamAZ with whom Cummins had a joint venture agreement. This project was initially viewed as being for just a few weeks but eventually lasted for over one year. On my return to the UK in 1996, my experience in Russia led to my being asked to do other work in the region, both for private clients and later as an adviser to the UK Foreign Office and subsequently, the Department for International Development (DFID). The latter role lasted until 2002 and in carrying out my work I was a regular visitor to Russia during a period of over five years, travelling to most corners of this vast country. My book is largely based on diary notes that I kept during my stay in Russia and relates some of my experiences and observations while visiting the country during this fascinating period in its history.

For an outsider, Russia is an incredibly difficult country to get to know and understand. Churchill's often quoted but extremely apt phrase frequently came to mind during my travels there:

'Russia is a riddle, wrapped in a mystery inside an enigma.'

Churchill, who also later coined the phrase *'the iron curtain',* made the above comment in 1939. Even at the time of my writing, without any iron curtain, Russia and its political / economic culture remain hard to penetrate and comprehend for a foreigner. Indeed, on many occasions I felt that the Russians themselves didn't truly understand their own country and society. I mention all this as a kind of 'health warning' to readers, especially any Russians. There may be things described in this book that I have misunderstood or events where I failed to appreciate the full Russian context. If this causes indignation or offence, then it is not intended.

Although some things have changed since my early visits to Russia, generally for the better, much of the basic, day to day life remains largely the same, especially outside Moscow, St Petersburg and one or two other large cities. Living standards have generally risen with new shops, restaurants and leisure facilities now providing much greater choice for the consumer. New businesses have started up, especially in the service and distribution sectors, giving more career choice and employment opportunities, particularly for the young. Increasingly, there are long overdue improvements to the infrastructure – roads, airports and housing – but they are still relatively few away from the capital. Massive wealth has been created by a small group of oligarchs and politicians, mostly derived from large Soviet enterprises that were privatised and then restructured. In today's Russia, those that have money and influence can enjoy virtually all that modern life can offer. Sadly, for the vast majority of Russians, poor public services, widespread corruption, low incomes, questionable legal processes and a muzzled media combine to limit the quality of life and freedom of expression. Russia is still in transition and remains far from being an open, transparent society. However, the majority of its people seem willing to accept the situation, at least for the time being.

No momentous or dramatic single event features in this book and during my period in Russia I didn't meet any especially famous people. My experiences in Russia, whilst often interesting or amusing, at least to me, were largely ordinary, everyday events. The vast majority of the Russian people I mixed with were normal working people struggling to come to terms with a new political and economic system while trying to survive the upheaval and earn a living. By observing and understanding the ordinary lives of its people, we may have a better chance of comprehending the complex enigma that is modern day Russia.

Chester, England
August 2011

The present is in constant dialogue with the past. Understanding our past not only enables us to better comprehend the present but also to raise the curtain a little on our future.

Introductory Notes

Tatarstan

The Tatar region was first incorporated into what was then the Principality of Moscow by Ivan the Terrible when he defeated the Khanate of Kazan, sacking the city in 1552. This victory was the precursor for a massive expansion of Moscow's influence under Ivan who became the first Tsar of Russia. Since then Kazan has been something of a dividing line between Russian culture and interests in Europe and Asia. Tatarstan became an autonomous Soviet Socialist Republic in May 1920 and was granted the rights of religious freedom and the use of its own language alongside Russian. However, in the late 1920s the Soviet government under Stalin became increasingly repressive towards most of the cultural minorities within the Soviet Union and in Tatarstan the national culture and use of the Tatar language were increasingly restricted. The Soviets decreed that the Tatar alphabet should be changed first to Latin and then to Cyrillic and over the ensuing thirty years as the Russian language and culture were promoted, the Tatar language along with other national cultural institutions such as theatres and schools all but disappeared. The Islamic religion was also severely repressed.

During World War II, in the face of the advancing German invasion, the Soviets relocated many manufacturing plants and their workers to Tatarstan, along with the Soviet Academy of Sciences and this led to the increasing industrialisation of the region. More than half a million people from Tatarstan were drafted into the Soviet armed forces during the war and over fifty percent of them were killed. This significant loss of population had an important effect on the region's demographics as large numbers of Russians from other parts of the Soviet Union were then encouraged to migrate to Tatarstan to replace the lost workers. The discovery of large oil deposits during the war accelerated industrial development as well as providing the revenues to build and equip major new manufacturing facilities in the 1960s and 1970s. By then, Tatarstan had become one of the most important industrial regions of the whole Soviet Union.

With perestroika and the dissolution of the Soviet Empire in 1991, there was strong talk of independence from radical nationalists and relationships between the Tatars and Russians became strained for a time. Eventually a compromise was reached giving Tatarstan limited autonomy within the new Russia and its Tatar language and culture were once again officially recognised. In June 1991, a new Tatar president, Mintimir Shaimiev, was elected who retained this position until early 2010. Tatarstan's capital is Kazan and it has now developed into a relatively harmonious, culturally and racially mixed state and is politically stable.

Naberezhnye Chelny and KamAZ

The Tatars claim the first settlement in the Naberezhnye Chelny area dates from 1172. Located on the Kama River, a tributary of the mighty Volga, it was first given the status of a town in 1930. The name in Russian means 'riverbank boats'. Naberezhnye Chelny lies almost 600 miles (900 kilometres) east of Moscow and around 125 miles (200 kilometres) north east of Kazan. It expanded rapidly with the construction by the Soviet government of the KamAZ truck manufacturing facilities in the early 1970s – the population grew from 20,000 to over 500,000 in 15 years. KamAZ was built to serve the needs of Russia's growing military and industrial complex. The latest equipment was purchased from around the world, largely financed by Tatarstan's rapidly growing oil wealth (this was the time of the world's first oil crisis). Several thousand foreign specialists were brought in to construct the facilities and install the new machinery. Politburo members, artists, and poets came to visit. The workers enjoyed special privileges and food allocations but Naberezhnye Chelny was also designated a 'dry town' and the sale of vodka was totally forbidden. Construction workers took 'vodka flights' from Chelny to other cities on their days off in order to be able to enjoy a drink. The first KamAZ truck rolled off the production line February 1976. The name KamAZ is derived from the Kama river and the abbreviation AZ meaning an automotive factory in Russian. Internationally, the company is perhaps best known for winning the truck category in the Paris to Dakar annual rally ten times since 1996.

Today, forty percent of Naberezhnye's population are Tatars and close to fifty percent are ethnic Russians and it is now the largest city in Tatarstan after Kazan. Between 1982 and 1988, it was called Brezhnev City after the Soviet president Leonid Brezhnev who was an avid fan of vehicles. In the early 1990s, the leader of the Tatar independence party, Fauzia Bairamova, moved from Kazan to Naberezhnye Chelny and the city became a centre for the radical wing of the Tatar national movement. Demonstrations were held demanding independence, Russian flags were burned in the streets on numerous occasions and protests organised against the war in Chechnya. Tatar nationalists also organised meetings to demand the "Jewish bosses" of KamAZ be fired and that a Tatar be appointed to head the factory. For a while the civil unrest in Tatarstan generally and Naberezhnye Chelny in particular was viewed by the Russian government with great concern but the changes described earlier to the status of Tatarstan eventually calmed the situation down.

During the period covered by this book, KamAZ operated the largest single automotive plant in the world with over two square miles of vertically integrated facilities and was one of the largest companies in Russia. It designed and built a range of mid-size trucks as well as a small passenger car plus its own diesel engines and many other components. It also ran or had responsibility for the city's schools, hospitals, transport systems plus social assets such as theatres and sports facilities. At its peak in the mid 1990s, the company had some 130,000 employees in Naberezhnye Chelny with a further 40,000 in other factories and offices across the former Soviet Union and overseas. In 1990, largely at the instigation of the president of the company, Nikolai Bekh, KamAZ became the first major Russian company to be privatised and became a prototype model for the transfer of other former Soviet large enterprises out of complete state control. Bekh understood that the move away from Soviet central planning to a market economy in Russia would necessitate major changes to the way the business operated, especially in the areas of quality, sales and marketing and finance.

To modernise, the company needed to restructure and find new partners to invest money and technology. The reduction in military orders which previously had accounted for up to forty percent of production, had hit the company hard and it needed to significantly reduce its workforce as well as rid itself of responsibility for non-core assets without driving the city to economic and social ruin. Lastly, it had to find new markets and acquire modern financial, manufacturing and marketing skills. In these respects KamAZ was an early example of the problems facing hundreds of large former Soviet enterprises, mostly in mono-company towns, as the Russian economy struggled to evolve from a centralised command structure and reduced state control. The situation at KamAZ was dramatically worsened when in April 1993 a major fire mysteriously ripped through its main engine manufacturing facility, all but destroying it. There were rumours that the fire had been engineered by the KGB as a warning to Tatar nationalists. Sadly, the company was not insured and production and revenues were disastrously affected. KamAZ already had a joint venture deal signed with Cummins and after the fire, the two companies agreed to speed up their co-operation. Cummins then became a key part of the recovery plan at KamAZ and this led to the formation of a restructuring team of foreign experts that the author joined in May 1995.

Know How Fund & DFID

The Know How Fund (KHF) was a programme established by the UK government in the mid 1990s to provide bilateral technical assistance to countries of Central and Eastern Europe and Central Asia. Its objective was to support the process of transition to democracy and a market economy in a way that promoted the interests of all levels of society. Until the formation of the DFID, the KHF came under the wing of the Overseas Development Agency (ODA) and Lynda Chalker who was Minister of State for Overseas Development at the Foreign Office.

The Department for International Development (DFID) was set up by the Labour government under Clare Short in 1997 as a new government department, separate from the Foreign & Commonwealth Office (FCO). It replaced the ODA and incorporated the KHF. Prior to Short's arrival, the KHF staff was a mixture with most of the managers seconded from the Foreign Office or other government departments such as the Department for Trade & Industry. They had the option of either staying with KHF or eventually returning to their mother organisation. Short decided however, that her new department's staff must be permanent without links to other government departments. In essence, the staff had to choose – either 'swear an oath of allegiance' to DFID or go back to where they came from and sadly, several capable people chose the latter course of action. The KHF projects in Russia covered a wide spectrum of activity involving health (especially aids), civil society, broadcasting & media, youth training, military resettlement etc. The largest programme, for which I was responsible, covered enterprise restructuring and economic development.

Personal and Place Names

Where the names of the people I worked with or met are already in the public domain, I have used their actual names, or in the case of Russians, the currently accepted Anglicised version. In all other cases I have altered their real names to provide some anonymity. During my period in Russia, many towns and cities had recently or were in the process of changing their names, generally to ones used in pre-Soviet times and this practice was to cause me (as well as many Russians) occasional confusion. I have tried to use the place names and Anglicised spelling currently in use at the time of writing.

Map of Western Russia

PART ONE

A YEAR IN TATARSTAN

MAY 1995 – JUNE 1996

CHAPTER ONE

Feminine Persuasion

I knew before I took the telephone call that I didn't really intend to go. I had been to Russia twice before, in the early 1980's, during the communist era and definitely didn't enjoy the experience, although it had been fascinating to gain first-hand a very limited glimpse of the people and country. While waiting for the call to come through, I admit that I did fleetingly think it might be quite interesting to see how things had changed since the advent of 'glasnost' and 'perestroika' under Gorbachev and now Yeltsin. However, depressing memories of unfriendly people, long queues, empty shops and bad food quickly re-surfaced in my mind so going back for a third time was not exactly high on my list of priorities. Also, news headlines at the time were dramatic, hardly encouraging a return visit. The war in Chechnya jostled with stories about the Russian mafia, rising crime, nuclear disasters, political instability and headlines billing a chaotic Russia as the 'last frontier'.

It was mid-morning in early May when she called. I was sitting in my office at home kidding myself that I was dealing purposely with some paperwork but in reality I was idly staring out of the window at the pouring rain outside. It's interesting how the weather can affect us and set our moods. If she had called with her proposal on a bright sunny morning, I might have been more resolute and things might have turned out differently. However, the squally rain was depressing me with thoughts of another cool, wet English summer to come. So as we talked once the call came through, the possibility of a few weeks of warm Russian sunshine gradually didn't seem all that bad. I'm not saying that this was the main factor in my agreeing to go of course, but it certainly had an influence.

The principle reason for accepting the offer was that she proved to be very enthusiastic and persuasive – unsurprisingly perhaps. As a relatively young female director in a large US automotive company, an industry run almost exclusively by men, she had to be good at her job. Her company, Cummins, had a joint venture with a large Russian automotive company in Tatarstan, some 600 miles south-east of Moscow and they were putting together a small team of consultants to implement a company restructuring project. They wanted me to initially go out for a few days to evaluate the situation and draw up an action plan of what might be feasible. Recently privatised by the Russian government, with over one hundred thousand employees making trucks and cars plus their own engines, gear boxes, axles etc. and with a couple of farms and various social assets thrown in, KamAZ was a typical former Soviet state enterprise. They now faced the daunting prospect of adapting to the new Russian market economy. The challenge was complex and immense but therefore interesting from a consultant's viewpoint. After a long discussion, we agreed that I would fly out with a couple of Cummins' senior managers on a short exploratory visit and then see what I thought. It seemed a relatively risk-free decision – I would be paid for my time and get to visit somewhere new without any long term commitments. So a couple of weeks later at the end of May, I found myself on a flight to a place called Naberezhnye Chelny in Tatarstan – a town I'd never heard of before and none of us could even pronounce properly. We all soon learnt that is was much easier and quicker to simply refer to the city as Chelny.

The trip went well enough with no untoward problems, though, from what I was to experience later, this was deceptive. We stayed in a decent modern hotel and the few KamAZ managers we met seemed business-like and friendly, not at all like the people I met in the former Soviet days.

A quick tour of the manufacturing facilities indicated several significant problems – lack of modern equipment, poor state of repair, inefficient process flows and labour utilisation – but nothing totally unexpected. I also had the opportunity to take a good look at some of their trucks and although the design was perhaps twenty years behind that of equivalent vehicles in the west, they looked robust and well suited to operating conditions in Russia. Last but certainly not least, the weather during my short visit was gloriously warm with bright blue sunny skies, which always makes life feel better. Once back in England, Cummins told me they had already lined up a couple of US consultants to go out to Chelny and asked me if I would be willing to return to lead the team for an initial six week period to get the project underway. From a professional viewpoint I felt this short assignment would be stimulating and so I agreed to go back to Tatarstan. The terms for my project work were soon agreed, a new Russian entry visa was sorted out and the flight tickets were booked.

Back in the USSR

On a warm, early evening in late June I found myself once again in the international terminal at Sheremetyevo, Moscow's main airport, built to showcase the Soviet Union's modernity for the 1980 Olympics. So here I was back in the USSR, well almost, as the country was now officially called Russia, part of the CIS – the Commonwealth of Independent States. I remember arriving here on my very first visit to Moscow and was quite impressed by the airport's spacious, if quirky, layout but not by the long queues at passport control and customs. Things had changed and it was now much busier and the queues were even longer. The good news was that by being near the front of club class on the British Airways flight, I was able to beat the worst of the queues at passport control. No problems with my visa and fifteen minutes later I was through and on my way to collect my luggage. Too much good news however, is bad for you in Russia and this vast country constantly had many ways of getting even. Today's form of retribution was that I discovered one of my bags had been lost on the flight from London Heathrow – what a start to my month in Russia. I was told it should arrive on the BA flight the next day and would then be forwarded to me in Chelny. As it mainly contained my food supplies and other 'support equipment' – radio alarm, portable electric fan etc. plus my toilet bag, I was confident I could survive. Two other cases containing my clothes, work books and files were now both safely by my side, having been rescued off the creaking airport carousel.

The missing bag was one of those ubiquitous black Samsonite holdalls that I had tried to take on board as hand baggage. Unfortunately, an eagle eyed BA check-in girl spotted me hoisting it onto my shoulder, trying nonchalantly to appear as if it was half empty and obviously failing. She insisted on weighing it and was surprised to find it was some 25 kilos (I tried to emulate her surprise – probably unsuccessfully). She then firmly stated that it was too large for the overhead cabin lockers and would have to go in the hold. All this took place at the boarding gate and reluctant as I was to part with my bag, most of you will recognise that it's impossible to argue with those nice young ladies from BA – especially when there is a long line of people behind you waiting to board. Anyway, I was assured with one of those smiles that the world's favourite airline staff are trained to give, that she would personally make sure that it was loaded onto the flight. That evening, sitting watching the empty luggage carousel slowly rotate in Sheremetyevo, two conclusions rapidly came to mind. Never trust an airline smile and do some weight training in Russia so that next time I could make a better show of hoisting my overweight bag onto my shoulder.

I had flown out with one of Cummin's London-based managers working on the KamAZ project, who was coming out for a few days to help set things up. Having negotiated the lost luggage department and customs, a car met us for the transfer to the domestic terminal for our private charter flight to Chelny. On the way to the domestic terminal, we stopped off at the airport hotel to pick up another consultant who had flown in earlier from the USA. While the driver loaded his luggage, I darted off to the hotel shop to buy replacements for my toothbrush, razor and soap that were presumably sitting somewhere in Heathrow. Two surprises were in store at the hotel – the £10 price tag for my few toiletries (a welcome to Moscow prices) and the discovery that I was not alone in losing luggage. My new US colleague, Roy, was without his clothes – other than those he was fortunately wearing – his main suitcase having also gone missing somewhere en route to Moscow. Even if he was willing to pay Moscow prices for some replacement clothes, at that time of night there was little that he could do except to hope, like me, that the missing bag would quickly catch up with us in Tatarstan.

We arrived at the domestic terminal and were gratefully guided through the worst of the swirling, anarchic chaos to check in and board our chartered plane. The flight itself in a Russian Yak jet was relatively smooth and mercifully without problems. However, despite its three engines, the plane was slow, taking two hours twenty minutes to cover the 500 or so mile journey from Moscow to Chelny. We could have taken a commercial flight with Aeroflot, but it would have required a tiresome ninety minutes transfer to another airport to the south of Moscow. There were however, more important considerations than the potential dangers of a taxi ride across Moscow. The news media at the time was full of lurid stories about the poor maintenance practices and safety record of the former Soviet airlines in general and Aeroflot in particular. Our charter company, although running with Russian crew and equipment, was US-owned and therefore, we were reassuringly informed by the Cummins security people (who were paid to know about these things), had an acceptable maintenance and safety system. Although we didn't know it then, this was something we were to put to the test at a later date.

VIP treatment

Curiously, despite being well to the east of Moscow, Tatarstan operates on the same time zone – unlike the surrounding region. This was to make communications easier with the capital we were later told in Chelny. From our limited experience of the Russian telephone network and postal system, we weren't sure whether this remark was to be taken seriously or not. Later attempts to communicate with Moscow were to make us seriously doubt that Tatarstan would have been any worse off if they had opted to be one hour ahead like the rest of that part of Russia. We touched down around 21.30 and were greeted by pleasant, balmy night air and Misha who would be our friendly guide and minder for the duration of our stay. He was from the KamAZ foreign affairs department and had a couple of smart Volvo cars – a rare sight at the time in Chelny – waiting for us on the tarmac by the plane. With our bags quickly loaded, we set out for the city about thirty minutes drive away, where we presumed we would be taken to our hotel. As we headed away from the runway and past the terminal building, a Russian Lada police car pulled out in front with blue flashing lights and led our convoy at high speed through the night all the way into the city.

If you have never experienced this type of VIP treatment, I can assure you it is a real pleasure – at least if you have any inclination towards thinking you are more important than you really are. Any unfortunate local driver ambling along in the road in front was quickly eased over into the gutter. Pedestrians thinking about risking their life with an attempted street crossing in front of our convoy were similarly persuaded of the relative security of the pavement and the possible benefits of a longer life. As we were later to see time and again, pedestrians often appear almost oblivious to oncoming vehicles which seemed foolhardy if not fatalistic, given the poor standard of driving and almost universal absence of insurance in Russia. One regularly sees advertisements in the west for Red Letter Days; that 'special present with a difference' – driving a racing car, skid pan courses, mud slugging in a 4x4 for a day etc. But for me, the man who can organise rides through a major city with a police car in front with blue flashing lights should make a fortune. This was an experience not to be missed and one that I was to enjoy very occasionally again in the future.

Having survived the journey but now feeling very tired, we found ourselves not at the hotel as expected but outside the KamAZ international business centre – known as the InterClub – where we were told a dinner awaited us, hosted by several senior Russian managers. Now a good meal in Russia is not something that one should easily pass up. As a seasoned traveller, I was well aware that you should always try to eat when food is offered, not only out of politeness to your host but just as importantly you never know when the next meal will materialise. But as we had already eaten on both the BA and charter flights and it was now approaching 10.30pm, the thought of a third dinner in the same evening was not something that any of us wanted. Polite excuses were gently made by our group, the hour was late, we had important meetings the next day, we had eaten on the plane, bags had been lost, we didn't speak Russian (interpreters had thoughtfully been laid on), we were not dressed for the occasion but to no avail. All our protestations were gently, but firmly brushed aside and the three of us were ushered upstairs for yet another dinner.

Somehow, we managed to do sufficient justice to the very substantial spread that was laid on and to make enough polite conversation through the interpreters to earn our ride back to the hotel. Honour and etiquette was served by both sides. It was close to midnight when we finally reached our hotel. By the time I had completed check in formalities, handed over my passport, carried my luggage upstairs and briefly inspected my new 'home', I was too tired to unpack. After three flights and just as many dinners, I was ready for sleep.

The Dialog hotel

We were fortunate to have rooms reserved at a modern, privately owned hotel – the Dialog. It was on the outskirts of the city but only some ten minutes drive from the InterClub and the sprawling KamAZ factory complex was in full view across the fields. Outside of Moscow and St. Petersburg, Russian hotels mostly come in one of two categories – those to avoid (but are survivable, if you really have nowhere else to go) and those that are in need of a complete refurbishment (which includes the staff as well as the building) and should be closed immediately. I was to have the dubious pleasure of staying in both kinds of hotel during my time in Russia. As well as needing a lot of patience when staying at a Russian hotel, there are also three key words or phrases that the intrepid foreign traveller must know. First, you need to be able to explain when something in the room isn't working, which is often the case – no hot water, toilet broken, room lights and telephone or television not functioning etc. Second you need the word for the floor lady or concierge who, in the larger hotels, resides on each floor and is responsible for your general well being (sic), including giving out the room key. She is the person you complain to when things aren't working, although she is usually disinterested, powerless to do anything or simply doesn't understand your frantic gestures and pathetic Russian. She's seen it all before and what can she do about it anyway and there's no point changing rooms, they all have the same problem. Although any complaint to the floor concierge will usually be met with indifference, at least you might feel better afterwards and the concierge will definitely remember you for the rest of your stay. Lastly, it's useful to know the word for cockroaches and even more impressive if you can couple this with a few numbers at the same time – five, ten, twenty etc. Cockroaches are understandably an unpublicised feature in Russian buildings and the Russians seem to treat them in much the same way as we might feel about say the pigeons in London. They are dirty, a health hazard and a nuisance but are an accepted part of the scenery. The main difference for me however, is that the pigeons are polite enough to stay outside whereas the cockroaches get everywhere inside. That first encounter with one of these shiny brown insects scuttling across your bathroom floor when you turn on the light or, worse still, on your bed just when you are dropping off to sleep, can be very unnerving and unpleasant.

On my first trip out to Chelny a couple of weeks before, I had been pleasantly surprised at the quality of the hotel and my room, perhaps partly because I had expected much worse from past Russian experiences. The Dialog hotel, with around twenty rooms set on three floors, had only been completed the year before – so everything was clean and relatively modern. This hotel was to become my home and base for the rest of my time in Chelny and although my rooms changed as I came and went, I was generally fortunate to have a small suite – a sitting room with a single bedroom and shower / toilet. The furnishings were simple but adequate. So as I unpacked my things late that night, I felt some familiarity with my surroundings and looked forward to a good sleep in preparation for the busy day to come. But my hopes of a quiet rest were quickly shattered. It was a hot night and with no fan or air conditioning, the temperature in my room rose steadily to an uncomfortable level. Opening the window was pointless since the outside night air was just as humid and stifling as that in my room and would undoubtedly usher in swarms of hungry mosquitoes. This was a conundrum that I frequently encountered during my time in Russia and one to which there was no easy solution. So I tossed and turned patiently waiting for sleep. I can't exactly remember when I realised that I had indigestion, probably due to the late 'welcome' meal we had with KamAZ. But I do recall that the double discomforts of excessive heat and indigestion combined to delay my much desired sleep until close to dawn.

Initial Meetings

Inevitably, our first few days were taken up by introductory meetings and briefings with the various Russian managers with whom we were to work over the coming weeks and months. First impressions for me are always important and I felt that most of the senior people we met were genuinely happy to see us and enthusiastic about our joint project. They were positive and appeared to understand well their problems and the priority areas where our assistance would be most useful. Previous business experience in the Soviet days had led me to feel that Russian managers were a pretty dour group, difficult to get through to and impossible to establish any personal relationship with. So I was pleasantly surprised by the openness and evident good humour that came through during these early meetings. To paraphrase Maggie Thatcher's remarks about Mikhail Gorbachev, these were people that I felt I could not only do business with but with whom I would enjoy working. There was also no doubt about their stamina and capacity to work long hours. Most of the senior managers were working 12 to 14 hours daily, with no real break for lunch and would often put in at least a half day on Saturday with Sunday morning meetings being common. If quantity of work was the answer to their problems then these KamAZ managers deserved success. This was particularly true of the company president, Mr Bekh, who was the size of a Russian bear and occasionally displayed a temperament to match, although he was almost always polite and very patient with us foreigners. He was the first I met of the three senior KamAZ directors with whom I was to spend a lot of time over the coming months. Each of their surnames began with the letter 'B' – Bekh, Borisov and Belenyenko and this trio soon became known to us as the three bears. The remaining senior director, Ivan Kostin, who was in charge of engineering, was not at these initial meetings but I had already met him on my initial short trip to Chelny.

There were plenty of things during those early days that we didn't understand or found strange. I well remember my first formal discussions with Oleg Belenyenko, the sales and marketing VP. We met in his office at the KamAZ head-quarters and I soon found myself listening to a thirty minute lecture on the company and how things were generally going well and my help was not really needed. All this delivered in a hectoring manner of which old style Soviet politicians would have been proud – no discussion, no time for questions and few pauses for translation. This was not an auspicious start and left me wondering whether I might be flying back to the UK earlier than planned. As I sat there waiting for him to finish, both his appearance and mannerisms somehow made me think of photos I had seen of Trotsky. I subsequently discovered that Oleg, who was Ukrainian, had been a senior company member of the communist party and was used to giving orders. I soon came to understand that this haranguing and dismissive style was used constantly with all his staff and was endemic throughout the company and indeed many other sizeable Russian enterprises. A very different approach compared to the current western management style of team building and empowerment.

Having patiently survived Oleg's initial salvos, we finally got down to business and sorted out a preliminary plan of work. Although it was to take some time to build up a good level of mutual understanding and trust, I believe we eventually developed a solid working relationship. I later discovered he had a decent sense of humour (like most Russians) that occasionally emerged, especially in one on one situations. As with all the KamAZ senior management we met however, there was strangely no social inter-action. Unlike Europe or North America where in similar circumstances one might be invited home to meet the family or to a local restaurant for dinner, this never occurred during our stay. One day I asked my interpreter about this and she indicated that the managers felt awkward about inviting us back to their small flats and anyway there weren't any decent restaurants in Chelny to take us out for dinner. I suspect there was an element of truth in this but given the relatively luxurious life style of the senior managers – high disposable income, country dachas etc. – I was not entirely convinced. It was probably more to do with work being kept totally separate from the very limited time left for home life due to the long hours worked.

The pressures and risks for senior managers in these large former Soviet enterprises were very high. Working hours were long, project deadlines often arbitrary or unrealistic, with usually no coherent or sustainable strategy, cash shortages and always hovering in the background, political pressures and interference. But if you could stand the heat, the jobs at senior level were not without rewards. Although the basic salary was just that, extra cash payments (often in foreign currency) were available and the company covered or contributed towards the cost of most other day to day living expenses – housing, health, car and driver, dachas, accommodation in Moscow, overseas trips etc. Nonetheless, even with the benefits, the pressures and dangers were very real for these senior managers. Additional risks relating to corruption, both political and criminal, were often present. At the KamAZ HQ building, there were always armed security guards on duty checking out all who arrived. A couple of years later, after I had returned to the UK, I learnt that Oleg had left KamAZ following some internal problems and joined another automotive company in the Urals. Then one day in 2001 I met by chance Andrei, one of Deloitte's Russian consultants who had worked with us at KamAZ, on an Aeroflot flight from Siberia to Moscow. Inevitably, we sat and chatted about what had happened over the past few years and Andrei told me that Oleg had recently been shot dead outside the Urals factory gates – apparently in some Russian mafia related incident. It was very sad news and shocked me to think that someone with whom I had worked so closely should die in this way.

That evening, I also met with two consultants from Deloitte, the US consulting giant who were staying in the Dialog hotel. The company had been appointed as auditors at KamAZ a year or so earlier and had a small team of western and Russian consultants regularly visiting Chelny to carry out this work. With our arrival, they had been asked to look more at the financial operations of the company and some of their team had now been assigned to this task and would work alongside us at the InterClub. Over the coming months, we were to become a close knit group, spending most of waking hours together.

The Factory Tour

The main manufacturing complex of KamAZ was so immense that it was difficult to take in at one go and even harder to describe. Acre after acre was covered by a vast array of concrete and brick-built buildings in a variety of shapes and sizes. As a vertically integrated manufacturer, virtually all the components and processes needed to build their vehicles were located on this one site. Built mainly during the 1970's with large quantities of modern foreign tools and equipment, the huge investment was funded from the rapid increase in oil revenues enjoyed by Russia at this time and hundreds of skilled foreign workers were brought in to install the new equipment and train the locals. But by the 1980s, thinking in the automotive industry in the west was moving away from this type of manufacturing behemoth. Japanese methods – lean and mean, just in time inventory planning, manufacturing flexibility etc – were the new trends challenging the previous 'big is beautiful' concept. Handicapped by a relatively inflexible manufacturing system and facilities that had seen little new investment or serious maintenance since they were built, KamAZ' problems were seriously worsened by a major fire in their main engine factory a couple of years before our arrival. This had all but burnt the building and equipment to the ground, almost putting the company out of business. Sheer guts and Russian determination had kept them going so far but the post perestroika changes in the market place now presented an unfamiliar challenge, which was largely why we were brought in.

Roy's first day was a little more problematical than mine, since without the clothes in his missing suitcase he was struggling to make the right kind of first impression on the Russians. Jeans and T-shirt would obviously not convey the right message. Between us, we managed to get him dressed in a reasonable manner, though as I am a little taller, the borrowed clothes didn't fit too well. 'Hang loose' came quickly to mind as the right approach for Roy that day. Back in the hotel that evening, our first priority was to find out whether our lost bags had turned up. The word from BA was that mine had been found to be still in London but it would definitely be on tomorrow's flight to Moscow and should be in Chelny in a couple of days. Roy's bag appeared to have been put on the wrong flight and was now lost in a European Bermuda triangle somewhere between Moscow, Germany and Greece. No one was saying when he would see it again. The seriousness of the temporary loss of my bag began to sink in that night. It contained both my portable electric fan and my plug-in mosquito killer and another hot, sleepless night lay ahead. There was one other problem to sort out – my sleeping arrangements. The bed looked comfortable enough but after a few minutes in it, I found that the mattress began to sag more and more in the middle. Unfortunately, the cause of my sagging mattress problem and its eventual solution were not immediately apparent. What were to become my regular Russian bedroom gymnastics – open the window, try to sleep; close the window, try to sleep; hunt the mosquitoes, try to sleep – initially took priority over sorting out the bed. Finally, sometime in the early hours, I yanked off the bedding and mattress in desperation to investigate the problem. I discovered the mattress was supported underneath by four or five horizontal wooden slats – a simple, normally effective idea. Unfortunately, the Russian craftsman who had constructed my particular bed had obviously been a little short of wood – one of the central slats was not quite long enough to fully bridge the frame under the weight of my body in bed. I realised that if I exchanged the central short slat with a good one from the foot of the bed, where weight was less critical, I would eliminate the sagging. With my quick fix in place and a thousand and one thoughts buzzing through my mind, exhaustion finally took over and I slept.

The next morning, Roy and I were collected from our hotel and driven to the InterClub which was now to become our second home in Chelny for the duration of our stay. It was a relatively modern, two storey building located in a primarily residential area that had originally been built as a centre for hosting international visitors to KamAZ. Why the InterClub had been sited here was never clear to me as it was a good fifteen minutes by car to both the main manufacturing complex and the head offices of KamAZ. The InterClub building contained a large theatre style conference room, various offices and meeting rooms as well as a kitchen, small bar and restaurant. The offices were furnished in a fairly conventional manner; however, the bar and restaurant were a fascinating eclectic mixture of styles, colours and materials. Copious amounts of black plastic mixed uneasily with decorative red or orange diaphanous curtains and wall coverings in ethnic Tatar swirling patterns, mostly brown, beige and black in colour. I don't know what concept was in the mind of the interior designer that put this together but I always found it to be rather funereal and depressing. As I later came to travel more extensively around Russia, I often came across similar weird interior design mixtures in their hotels, offices and restaurants. Although not to my taste, such decorative choices certainly gave Russian buildings a unique if somewhat old fashioned style. Surprisingly, at one end of the InterClub there was a large room equipped with a full size billiard table – Russian style. Although the table was the same size as that used for conventional western billiards or snooker, the rules of Russian billiards are different and the balls are larger and heavier. As neither we nor our InterClub staff knew how to play, the novelty of this facility soon passed and the room soon became just another meeting area. We were assigned an office on the first floor and were introduced to the Russian staff that had been drafted in by KamAZ to provide the communication, translation and general support services we would need for our work. Initially, on a typical working day, there would be around ten Russian employees here, including the security and catering staff. With an office base sorted, I soon settled into a regular pattern of daily life that was to vary little during my stay in Chelny.

Cards and Wine

By the end of our first week in late June, both missing bags had been retrieved and forwarded to us in Chelny. Roy was finally able to change into some fresh clothes and I now had my electric fan, radio alarm and mosquito zapper – sleep now came much easier. I did ask in the hotel about the possibility of air conditioning for my room and was amazed when reception told me that a new unit was already on order and would be here in a few days. Sure enough, a couple of days later, two units arrived and were installed in Roy's room and mine. One thing I had forgotten to bring with me to Chelny was the traveller's essential pack of playing cards. Several of us enjoyed bridge and this gave us our first excuse for a foray to the Chelny shops, accompanied inevitably by one of our translators. Yes, the Russians play cards and we were assured it would be no trouble finding a couple of packs. Reality was very different. What would seem an easy purchase in the UK was, however, to prove very different here and we scoured the few shops within easy walking distance of the InterClub without any success. We moved on to a local open air market where we did eventually find a couple of continental style short decks containing 36 cards which had garish nudes in a variety of revealing poses on the backs – not at all what I was looking for. The stall holder was a local Tatar woman and presumably therefore, Muslim so I found it a little surprising that she would stock such cards. She said that she usually sold normal playing cards but was 'temporarily' out of stock.

'No problem – I would definitely find what I wanted at the local market at the weekend' our translator cum shopping guide said. But I didn't and so eventually bought a couple of packs on my next trip back to England. This was my first experience of the difficulties of finding in Chelny what for me seemed quite normal articles to buy. There was no doubt that the choice and variety of goods in the shops and markets was substantially better than under the old communist regime, especially in Moscow. But availability of many things in the regions was still variable and often seemed dependant on the next truck load coming in.

We had an enjoyable dinner that evening in the InterClub with Yuri Borisov, deputy to the company president and his assistant, neither of whom spoke much English. It was a bit of a struggle with only one interpreter on hand. But we managed, with an enthusiastic mixture of broken Russian, German, English and appropriate hand signals, eased as is always the case on such occasions, by the flow of alcohol. White wine was available plus beer and of course the ubiquitous vodka but strangely, red wine was not. Quite reasonable red wine is produced in several parts of the former Soviet Union, though it was always hard to find in Chelny – why, I never found out. To compensate, we later took to organising our own regular shipments from Moscow, along with other 'essential' supplies. In many ways Yuri was typical of the old style Russian managers, impatient, follow my orders, don't ask questions and do it now. Tall, silver haired and patrician-like, he certainly didn't take any prisoners. But he was intelligent, well travelled and could be very charming with a dry sense of humour. He reminded me of the deputy head at my old grammar school in England – capable, forceful and direct but without the finesse to take the top job. Like many senior managers of the large former state enterprises across Russia, he had done relatively well from perestroika and the new market economy. They retained much of their power but now enjoyed more freedom, including the ability to travel overseas freely plus a significantly higher disposable income. During my time in Chelny, Yuri was in the process of building a large new dacha on the outskirts of the town; I was told it was very impressive but never had the opportunity to see it. A year or so later, I heard that there was a fire at his dacha and it had burnt down. I never found out whether the fire was accidental and simply bad luck or the result of some more sinister criminal action. But Yuri not only lost the house but all the furniture and possessions inside, which, as he would not have been insured, must have been a very sad blow. I believe he then had something of a mental breakdown, brought on no doubt by this catastrophe plus the unrelenting pressure at work and he retired. I truly felt sorry for him.

An Invitation to Dance

On the first Sunday in July I took my first opportunity to visit the much spoken about local market. As in most Russian cities, the few conventional shops had a relatively limited selection of products and the outdoor markets proved to be the main focus of most people's shopping activity. There were in fact several scattered strategically round the city, usually open from Friday through Sunday. We were lucky to have a large market less than ten minutes walk from the hotel. It combined both an indoor area – mainly filled by fresh meat, fruit and vegetable stalls – together with an extensive outdoor array of clothes, shoes, dry goods, carpets, household items, car parts, tools, flowers etc. Like most people, I always find it interesting to explore foreign markets; wandering around the stalls gives an excellent insight into the habits and way of life of the local community. Although it had rained heavily overnight, the weather by mid morning that Sunday was warm and sunny and there were large numbers of people milling around the stalls by the time I arrived. Superficially, this market looked like most others around the world but despite the crowds, the normal hustle and bustle of a market strangely seemed absent. I put this down to two things. Firstly, the low levels of disposable income meant that most people were only shopping for essentials and spent the rest of their short time in the market looking rather than buying. Secondly, the stall-holders displayed none of the sales banter that normally greets you in markets in other countries. There were no special offers, 'get your bananas here, two for the price of one' type of approach that one might have expected in an open air market and it seemed to me that the people manning the stalls weren't very sales oriented at all. On my initial market excursions I tried negotiating prices with some of the stall holders, only to be met by stony stares or uncomprehending looks, partly due no doubt to my poor Russian. Bartering in this market was clearly not done. However, perseverance and desperation eventually paid off and despite the attitude of the stallholders I arrived back at the hotel with my few precious purchases. Today, these turned out to be a treat. Not only did I succeed in snatching the last bunch of bananas in the market before a woman who was pushing me in the back could reach them but I also found raspberries, one of my favourite fruits. These locally grown raspberries were in plentiful supply and I mean plentiful. Here they were being sold by the bag or bucket full – not the tiny punnets or little plastic containers you find in western supermarkets. I tried asking for just a small amount but in vain and ended up having to buy a huge bowlful plus a plastic bag in which to carry my fresh fruit back to the hotel.

That evening, together with a couple of the other consultants, we decided to try dinner out in a restaurant not far from the hotel. The meal was not particularly memorable but I had my induction into a standard Russian tradition. As in many Russian restaurants there was a live band playing and a few people were dancing. I was sitting with my back to the dance floor and so was generally unaware of what was happening behind me. Then I felt a hand on my shoulder and heard a female voice speaking to me in Russian and as I turned to see what she wanted, it was clear she was asking me to dance. As I later learnt, it's quite normal for Russian women to ask the men to dance. But this was the first time I had ever been asked to dance by a stranger and I wasn't sure what local protocol demanded. Could I politely try to refuse or was I expected to accept this invitation and try at least one dance. With the encouragement of my colleagues, I decided the latter course of action was the right thing to do and so followed my newly acquired partner out onto the large dance floor. She was probably in her mid-forties, of medium height with short, wavy blond hair and wearing a long, dark blue dress. She was not unattractive and had a pleasant smile but her make-up was a little heavy plus she was somewhat overweight, carrying a few more pounds than either of us would have liked. I freely admit that I'm not the best dancer in town and was happy that it was a 'slow' which allowed me to shuffle around without treading too much on my partner's feet. The music was loud and conversation difficult – I think I managed to convey the fact that I was English and working for KamAZ but I couldn't understand what she was saying and was grateful when the music stopped and I was able to say thank you and politely take my leave. Thankfully, I wasn't asked to dance again that evening.

CHAPTER TWO

New Faces

Roy and I had now been joined by another American consultant, Chuck. He was from the mid-West and had been brought in to concentrate on the truck production process at KamAZ. Chuck was short with thinning, slicked back dark hair and older than Roy and I, probably aged around sixty. Although well experienced in his field, this was his first time in Russia and he was clearly surprised both with the living conditions in Chelny and the poor state of the KamAZ factories. He actually arrived on the morning of US Independence Day. Even though we now had several US citizens in the Cummins and Deloitte consulting teams in Chelny, the day passed just like any other workday, except for enjoying a few beers and a game of cards back in the hotel later in the evening.

A couple of new elements were now added to the agenda of my daily routine. Each weekday I was now asked to meet with the president and senior directors of KamAZ at 3pm for a one hour meeting on selected urgent issues. This necessitated a twenty minute drive across the city from our base in the InterClub to the company's headquarters near the 'old town'. Although this was a fixed daily event and transport theoretically reserved, we frequently had problems obtaining a car at the right time. The drive across town then became more of a race, which I think the drivers secretly enjoyed, if we were not to commit the sin of sins – arriving late for the president's afternoon meeting. This event was then often followed by a daily telephone conference call with the company's financial advisors and partners in the USA and England, usually at 4pm (8am USA east coast time). Although it was useful for the various partners to talk to each other regularly and to check progress on outstanding issues, I increasingly felt these long (everything had to be translated) transatlantic calls to be of limited value and they often failed to progress or clarify the issues in hand. Exchanging faxes would have done the job better in many cases. There was one hilarious occasion later in August when a group of half a dozen KamAZ directors and consultants were huddled over the phone in the president's office on a conference call to the USA. One of our group was asked by the Americans to explain some financial information recently prepared and he spoke animatedly on the subject for over thirty minutes without any queries or comments from the other side. This was not necessarily unusual but it wasn't until he finished talking, with still no response, that we suddenly realised someone had punched the wrong button and the phone had been dead all along. Despite having asked the question initially, no-one from the States had felt it necessary to call us back in the meantime to tell us the line was dead.

Two new faces appeared for the first time today at the InterClub joining our Russian support team. The first was a young woman called Tanya who, as she proudly told me, had recently qualified as an engineer and was therefore definitely not to be regarded as a lowly interpreter. It seemed there was no work for her in her own discipline, so she had been 'temporarily' assigned to help look after us. This might have been regarded as a reasonable expedient, given the employment problems at KamAZ except that she spoke no English and since most of us spoke little or no Russian, she was clearly going to have communication problems. She did in fact speak some French, though not as well as she claimed and since I spoke it well, we were able to understand each other after a fashion in the early days. She eventually picked up a little English and as we steadily acquired a basic Russian vocabulary, things became a bit easier. But we frequently had to call on one of the other InterClub staff to speak with her and this occasionally caused some frustration on all sides.

Tanya is a fairly common girl's name in Russia so she inevitably became known as 'French Tanya' to distinguish her from the other Tanyas that we gradually met at KamAZ. Her husband was away studying at university and seemed to be rarely home and she lived with her mother. Tanya was clearly frustrated (emotionally and sexually) with her life in Chelny – absentee husband, few friends, a part time job that she clearly felt was beneath her and which she had difficulty doing. Sometimes she appeared a little snooty or stoically remote, which I found to be unusual in Russian women. Generally however, she quietly got on with her work and with a little prompting, could normally be relied on for a brief smile. After a couple of months, she hooked up with one of the Russian consultants from Deloitte and that seemed to brighten her up a little more. We never fully understood why she was given this job with our group but the temporary assignment turned out to be permanent since she was with us right through our stay in Chelny. It was yet another of those puzzling Russian mysteries.

The second new face was a tall, brown haired young woman with long legs and a figure to die for, though she was not particularly pretty. She well understood her main attributes and was usually to be seen in a tight mini-skirt, summer and winter but she was a quiet person and kept herself to herself, usually hiding behind large tinted glasses. Olga as she was called inevitably became known as 'legs Olga' to our team. She only worked part time and her main function was to provide us with flasks of hot water for our tea and coffee during the day and generally keep the office tidy. Hardly a demanding or interesting job but Olga was a single mother and working as our tea lady was probably the only income she had. The arrival of new faces at the InterClub – interpreters, office staff, cleaners, catering staff, chauffeurs etc. – became a permanent feature of our working routine. They all worked part time, usually three days a week; some were on early shifts and some on late to cover our long working day, with cover maintained over the weekend, although at a reduced level. I was surprised by the evident depth in both the numbers and capability of the KamAZ interpreters and technical translation department. I never found out how many there were because we mostly only met the English speakers (there were others for German, Italian etc.) but they were an obvious credit to their local language training institute.

It was hard sometimes to cope with this lack of staff continuity, especially with the interpreters. Having established a relationship in one meeting, explaining the relevant vocabulary or terms, follow up action etc., it was difficult to then take up with another person for the next session. Some interpreters were inevitably better than others and this led to some scrabbling between us for the person we each wanted for our various activities. I also noticed that there were very definite stresses and strains amongst the staff at the InterClub. There were four main categories, the translators, the support staff (responsible for sending faxes, making phone calls, photocopies etc.), the catering staff and the office supervisors. The latter, who organised our daily schedules, were often largely and openly ignored by the other staff. The translators reported into a different department in another building and therefore felt they were not directly under the orders of the office supervisors. The male translators were often lazy, obviously resented taking orders from any of the women and would try to leave as much dirty work as possible to them. Both male and female translators would avoid helping out with general office duties since that was the duty of the support group and therefore felt to be beneath them. The lowest echelon of support staff were at everyone's beck and call and conflicting instructions often led to chaos or jobs not being done at all.

One thing I was never to fully understand or explain was the apparent suspicion of the InterClub by all the KamAZ junior employees. It was the only location available to us to hold meetings and apart from our hotel, the only place to which we could invite someone for a drink or a meal. But almost invariably whenever we suggested meeting at the InterClub, there was always a reluctance usually followed by the offer to meet somewhere else. Although this gradually improved over time, there was always this subtle feeling of awkwardness about the place. When I asked one of our translators about this problem, I was told that the building was bugged –

a left-over from Soviet times – and so KamAZ staff felt it difficult to open up or relax at meetings there. I never fully accepted this explanation – most of our meetings were innocuous enough and given the state of most of the technical equipment in the building, I doubted that any bugging system would have been working long. One other unusual situation developed at our meetings during the first couple of weeks. At every meeting that we held, whether at the InterClub or in one of the KamAZ offices, a young man would turn up and take notes. Disconcertingly, none of the Russians seemed to find this strange or unusual and often they weren't even introduced to us. They were just there at every one of our meetings, obviously being totally familiar with our schedule. It took me some time to get to the bottom of this – which department these men came from and why they were present. It all turned out to be on the orders of Borisov, the deputy president. The reason we were eventually given was that by attending our meetings, these young men would learn and thus contribute to the company's future development. Yet it was obvious there was no pattern or rhythm to which young man attended which meeting and so there was not the remotest chance of them learning anything worthwhile. It became clear that senior management simply wanted to check up on what we and the Russian managers we met were discussing. After a few weeks as trust steadily built up (and a carefully worded request from me to the president), this shadowing practice suddenly stopped.

Our Contracts are Extended

The initial reaction at KamAZ to our work had been very positive and Cummins now asked Roy, Chuck and I whether we would extend our contracts for a further period of two months. Agreeing to this extension was a difficult decision for me. The work at KamAZ was certainly stimulating and although the general living conditions were far from ideal, they certainly bearable for another couple of months. But I was worried about the impact of another two months away from my business and of course I missed my family. Communication with home was extremely difficult – it was a far cry from today's world of instant contact by cell phone and email. In the end, we all agreed to continue our work in Chelny until September and this news seemed to be welcomed at KamAZ. The decision to stay on brought my first encounter with the intricacies of the local visa system. We had arrived in Russia on single entry visas and when we checked in at the hotel on the first night, the visa document was retained prior to returning our passports the next morning. We had innocently assumed that the visa would subsequently be handed back in time for our return home. Doubts and concern started to surface when I was asked to go with Tanya to have my photo taken for my new visa. But I already have an exit visa I carefully tried to explain and therefore don't need photos. Anyway, I can organise my next visa through our London office, as I did with the first one. This style of conversation went on in various stages through the rest of the morning with clearly neither side getting through to the other. By the afternoon, it was clear that arrangements had been made for me to have my photo taken, a car was waiting outside to take me and it seemed clear there would be a major undiplomatic incident if I didn't go.

So I set off with 'French Tanya' just as a heavy summer thunderstorm broke over the city. Our car whisked us off at high speed through the torrents of rain to a group of high rise buildings about five minutes away. They were typical 1970's Russian style, high rise blocks of flats grouped together in a semi-circle, purpose built to provide shops and offices on the ground floor, though most of these were vacant and shuttered. Tanya had great difficulty finding the photographer's studio and we were thoroughly soaked by the rainstorm as we searched up and down outside the buildings. Unsurprisingly, there was no-one around to ask for directions but finally she recognised a small sign in a window and we went in. It turned out we had already walked past the entrance twice. Inside was a small reception with a desk and in the back a studio into which I was duly ushered for my photo session. The set up was basically like any other photographer's studio – a tripod camera and a chair set in front of a white screen. What was of immediate interest though was the age and style of the camera. It was a real collector's piece and looked as if it been taking photos since the early days of Lenin. I tried to make a joke to this effect but my English thoughts spoken in French to Tanya for her to translate into Russian did not seem to produce the expected smile from the lady photographer. Maybe Tanya's translation wasn't very good or just possibly this lady really had been taking photos since Lenin's time and felt I was being unnecessarily flippant. The session over, I was told the required number of passport sized photos (black and white), together with the negatives, would be ready the next day and was presented with the bill. I had difficulty making out the amount at first on the tiny scrap of paper but after confirming with Tanya, realised that the total was less than 5000 roubles – roughly one US dollar. To me, it seemed incredible value, even cheaper than using the photo booths that are endemic to railway stations or shopping malls in the west and it was worth every rouble just to see the old camera in action.

The photos and negatives actually arrived early the following week at the InterClub and this event finally brought about an explanation as to why they were needed. Apparently, our original exit visas, issued in London, were to be retained by the authorities until we finally left Russia on completion of our contract. We would now operate on local visas, issued in the provincial capital Kazan, which would provide us with a single exit and re-entry visa each time we returned overseas on home leave. This, we were assured, was the normal system and would operate smoothly with the new visas usually being issued within a week of application by the InterClub, each time they were required. The Kazan authorities only worked with the old style black and white photos – no colour for them – which explained the special photo session last week. On the surface, this simple procedural change should not have been unreasonable – or at least that is what our hosts believed. However, when the reality of what was happening had sunk in, it caused tremendous concern and unease in our team. We were now effectively under the complete control of the KamAZ visa staff and the authorities in Kazan. We would be unable to leave Russia unless or until they agreed to issue a new departure visa.

Our concerns were twofold. First, if there was any political emergency which required our immediate evacuation from Russia and second, if there was any serious domestic crisis involving either our own health or that of our families overseas. In either case, we might not be able to leave for several days. We tried to explain our worries to the visa people, even requesting a meeting with the chief of police in Chelny but all to no avail. Everyone kept passing the buck and we were forced to accept the 'modus operandi Ruski'. This was one part of the old Soviet control system that had definitely not yet been dismantled. Ultimately, the only way round this was to apply for a new multiple entry visa but these were hard to come by and only issued when there was a clear need. Eventually, a couple of us managed to obtain multi-entry visas after a lot of lobbying towards the end of the year. But it meant that the intervening months saw repeated visa problems for all of us, resulting in nail biting frustration and arguments with KamAZ staff. Indeed, on several occasions the problems became so acute that we were unable to leave or return as scheduled, causing additional costs and wasted resources for both the Russians and ourselves.

Dachas and Tennis

That evening at dinner in the InterClub we were told that as tomorrow was Sunday, a visit had been organised for us to one of the KamAZ dachas by the Kama river a few kilometres outside the city. The river, which runs through Chelny, rises in the northern foothills of the Urals and flows south to join the mighty Volga near Kazan. It's already a very broad river by the time it flows through Chelny and as it meanders through the region, it provides some quite attractive scenic views. The company dacha turned out to be an extensive complex of various shapes and sizes of buildings, mostly constructed of wood in a neo-Alpine style, strung out along the north bank of the river. In its heyday this must have been an impressive rest and recuperation facility for the workers of Chelny, owned and fully funded by KamAZ. Set in attractive woodland, most sports and recreations were catered for. There were outdoor courts for volleyball and basketball; centres for horse riding and sailing, with motor boats and pedalos for hire; cross country skiing in winter; the inevitable saunas and even a sandy beach area with a couple of kiosks selling drinks and snacks. In some ways it reminded me of photos of a Butlin's holiday camp in the 1960's. However, the cash problems at KamAZ and the city in general were unfortunately clearly having an impact. The whole complex now had a rundown, rather seedy atmosphere, with most of the equipment either not working or in a poor condition. We were told that employees now had to pay to use the facilities. This meant that fewer people could afford to use these dachas so with falling revenues, an inevitable pattern of decline was setting in. Over the coming months we were fortunate to have the opportunity to visit this area quite often and on most occasions there were relatively few people around. Good for us but not for the inhabitants of Chelny and I suspected not a good omen for the city's wellbeing.

On arrival around noon, our group of four foreign consultants were escorted to a pleasant small dacha equipped with a sauna, nestling in the shade under some large birch trees. Our hosts were two Russian men, neither of whom spoke English. Through our ever-present interpreter, we understood that the plan was for us to have a sauna and then relax over a picnic lunch on the veranda of the dacha. I am not a particular fan of saunas and was on the point of deciding whether to take a walk through the woods to the river instead or open up a bottle of wine for a pre-lunch drink when one of the Russians asked me if I wanted to play tennis instead. I thought at first there must be some mistake. Since I enjoy the occasional game, when I had first arrived in Chelny, I had asked at the InterClub about the possibility of playing tennis, only to be told that there weren't any courts. Yet, here in the woods I was being asked to play and as if to emphasise that it was indeed possible, my would be opponent produced a couple of rackets (made in Bulgaria, I think) and a can of new balls. The fact that I was at a dacha with apparently a court, rackets and an opponent to play with was clearly no coincidence – this had been carefully arranged by KamAZ.

Fortunately, I had brought along a pair of shorts and trainers so I quickly changed and while the rest of our group went off to the sauna, I followed the Russian a hundred metres or so through the woods to the tennis court. It was an all weather surface in fairly good condition with floodlights, although the net had clearly seen better days. We introduced ourselves and knocked up for ten minutes or so, establishing that we were about the same playing standard. The Russian was maybe a couple of years younger than me, in his late forties but was shorter with a tanned, wiry build and obviously very fit. With neither of us speaking the other's language, it was difficult to communicate, although I did manage to understand that he played regularly. I lost the first set 6-2, blaming my poor score on the fact that I hadn't played for some time and a general lack of fitness. I did better in the second but still lost 6-3. As I felt I was now becoming more familiar with the court and my borrowed racket and in a determined effort to wear down my opponent, I doggedly suggested a third set. This was now a matter of upholding some British pride on the Chelny 'international' circuit in front of the crowd (the rest of our group had emerged from the sauna by now to watch). The games all went with serve to a tie break at 6-6 which I was lucky enough to win after some fine rallies – both of us determined not to lose. At that, honour and stamina were satisfied and we retired to enjoy some lunch and a few welcome beers with the others. I now learnt from my opponent through the interpreter that he was in fact the current veteran tennis champion of Chelny and had been invited out to the dacha today specifically to give me a game. He certainly did that; I enjoyed meeting him and resolved to bring my own racket out on my next trip home.

A Day in Moscow

Having completed my initial six week stay and with my new style exit visa safely in my pocket, I now left Chelny for Moscow en route to England for a much anticipated week-long break. Along with two other members of our team, I took the KamAZ shuttle – they operated their own morning return flight to Moscow, supplementing the daily Aeroflot service. The plane left Chelny airport at 6.30am which meant an unwelcome, 5am start from the hotel with no breakfast and it was an uncomfortable two hour flight to Moscow. Uncomfortable for two reasons of which, this being my first trip on KamAZ airways, I was blissfully unaware but shortly to confront. First, because the seats were set close together with no leg room for a six footer like me, unless you were fortunate enough to get the front row. If senior KamAZ managers were on board, they would usually take these seats. If not, there was an undignified scramble by us lesser mortals to board the plane first. Second, because there was no in-flight service – only water – which made the lack of a breakfast at the hotel very serious as far as my rumbling stomach was concerned.

The KamAZ shuttle operated out of Beikova, a small, rather rundown airport on the south side of Moscow, presumably because the operating costs there were cheaper. We landed in the middle of a heavy summer rainstorm at around 8.30am. Cummins had organised a car to take us to their Moscow office, about an hour and a half's drive across the city, where we were due to spend the day until it was time to leave for the British Airways evening flight to London. It was clear the urgent desire for food or at least a decent cup of coffee and a bread roll was fast becoming an overwhelming force in each of our minds. There was nothing at the airport so when we set off in the car, we asked the driver to stop at a café somewhere convenient en route. He agreed and said he would find somewhere on our way through Moscow. As we looked out at the Moscow suburbs, dreary in the morning rain, the thought of imminent hot food kept us going – there must be a café close by. There wasn't, or at least not one to which the driver felt he could take us. After an hour – it seemed like three – and several impatient reminders to the driver of our simple need for nourishment, we finally pulled up outside one of the large, expensive western style hotels close to the centre of the city. The driver had clearly over-rated our importance and our needs but now was not the time to quibble. After my six weeks in Chelny, the thought of a real western style buffet breakfast drove me through the front doors and quickly on to the restaurant where we found seats immediately – hang the expense. I have to admit that we gorged ourselves that morning, the temptations were too much to resist and we ate enough for both breakfast and lunch. The sizeable bill when it came was only a minor irritant; this kind of enjoyment is worth paying for and the way we felt, it would have been cheap at twice the price.

After our extended food break, we got back into our car and pressed on across the city. Cummins' driver in Moscow, Victor, turned out to have an interesting background. Of slim build, with bright eyes and an intelligent manner, he clearly wasn't the usual Moscow chauffeur type. Due to the security and crime problems currently prevalent in Moscow, they were normally stocky, moustachioed characters in black leather jackets, often ex-military. As we drove along, Victor and I chatted about his former life. Apparently, Victor had previously been a ballet dancer with the Bolshoi and had enjoyed the good life, travelling extensively around Europe under the old regime. With perestroika however, many of the former cultural elite found that either their services were no longer required or their pay dropped significantly – if they were paid at all. Victor decided it was time for a change and had taken this job as a driver. As he told me, at least he was paid regularly and still had the chance to meet interesting people. Not surprisingly, we were late in reaching the Cummins offices and the British manager had been quite concerned about what might have happened to us. The offices were situated on the eastern side of Moscow in a modern complex that would sit well in any western city. Various developments were underway in this area to provide new homes and offices to meet the rapidly expanding demand. Opposite however, by way of total contrast to this thrusting progress, was one of those awful grey concrete tower blocks so typical of the 1960's and early 1970's architectural design. This we were told was the Patrice Lumumba building, named after the Angolan socialist leader and erected to provide accommodation for African and other foreign university students. In its day, this may have been a residence to impress the newly arrived third world communist neophytes. Looking at it today though, it was hard to imagine that any of the current residents could be happy there. Neglected and run down, .the outside of the building was dirty and stained, parts of the concrete structure had fallen away and most windows displayed a selection of student underwear optimistically hung out to dry. Appropriately in a way, it all looked very third world. I wondered whose name would be used for its eventual replacement now that communism had gone capitalist. As I worked on my laptop computer, Bill Gates of Microsoft came to mind and seemed particularly appropriate.

One of my most poignant memories of my stay in Russia occurred as we drove across town in the torrential rain. We had pulled up at some traffic lights and several pedestrians were crossing the road in front of us. One of them, a man probably in his late fifties, was scurrying across, cradling in his arms a large, heavy brown paper parcel. Just as he reached the pavement on the other side, the brown paper, soaked through from the rain, decided that it could no longer contain its burden. In what seemed like slow motion as I watched from the comfort of my car, a large blue porcelain wash basin eased out from the bottom of the parcel and the safety of the man's arms. The inevitable happened when the basin hit the pavement below – it smashed into several large pieces. As we pulled away from the lights, I looked back to watch the man staring forlornly at the blue ceramic bits now lying at his feet. After a few seconds he obviously realised there was nothing he could do and slowly moved on, leaving his shattered wash basin where it now lay in the gutter. I still have a mental picture of this man who had probably saved for many months to buy the new basin, proudly carrying it home and then suddenly left with nothing. What would he say to his wife when he reached his apartment and how long would it take them to save for a replacement? Somehow this sad little incident seemed to me to encapsulate the difficult day to day struggles of many ordinary Russian people; working hard to achieve the goal of a better life but then, due to a quirk of fate beyond their control, left with unfulfilled dreams.

The rest of my journey was comparatively uneventful. We left the office and arrived at Sheremetyevo in good time. BA flew me (and my suitcase) to London safely and I then shuttled up to Manchester where my wife collected me. It had been a long day – it was now close to 1am Chelny time but it felt good to be back home, even if only for a few days. After six weeks of eating much the same food for lunch and dinner in the same place, day after day, the delights of home cooking and a choice of good local pubs and restaurants provided a much needed culinary change. I had particularly missed fresh fish and vegetables, which were rarely available to us in Chelny and treated myself through an all too brief week. With a clearer idea now of the kinds of foods available locally, a major objective on this visit back to the UK was to stock up with supplies for my return trip to Russia. I bought as much as I thought I could sensibly carry back from the local supermarket – breakfast cereals, UHT milk (we had been advised not to drink the local fresh milk), cans of tuna, tea bags and coffee, cheese, mixed nuts, pasta meals etc. and a couple of bottles of good wine. We had originally been promised a regular 'comfort pack' shipment from the Moscow office (most western goods were available there) but for reasons we never understood, this took many months to organise. So the UK shopping run became an important part of my periodic trips home.

Back in Beikova

Since my outward journey to the UK had been relatively trouble free, it was therefore time for Russian fate to intervene on the return. I had flown into Sheremetyevo the previous night, staying at the airport hotel and planned to take the KamAZ morning shuttle to Chelny. I had telephoned from the hotel to check arrangements for the shuttle; all was OK and I was told to be at Beikova airport for 7.30am for an 8.30am flight departure. Cummins' driver, Victor, collected me from the hotel at 6.30 the next morning and drove me safely to Beikova arriving on schedule. There was no-one around in the tiny KamAZ airport office and Victor's enquiries at the public information desk only produced the usual Russian shoulder shrug and 'no information' response. By 9.00 the in-coming flight from Chelny had not appeared and it was clear that things were not running smoothly. After several attempts, Victor managed to call the Moscow office of KamAZ and they confirmed that there were delays and we were told the flight was now re-scheduled to depart Moscow at 4pm.

Beikova airport is very small and not a place to while away several hours of delay. The facilities are very limited and probably hadn't changed much since the airport was built at least thirty years ago. Like many others in third world countries that I have had the misfortune to visit over the years, it certainly wouldn't appear on any of those lists of the world's top airports that are occasionally compiled by glossy travel magazines. The small ground floor departure area contained a shop selling the usual newspapers, sweets, soft drinks and black instant coffee. A couple of ready-made snacks sat forlornly on a glass counter looking quite unappetising and even though it was early in the day, had clearly not been freshly made. A few desultory and uninhabited airline offices filled most of the remaining space in the terminal. Smelly lavatories in the basement completed the feeling of decay and dilapidation. I stared at a fading old picture on the wall of an Aeroflot passenger jet flying above the clouds in clear azure skies. It seemed to represent a different world, a dream far from the seedy reality of Beikova airport on that day in late July. I had already spent almost two hours hanging around this miserable facility and Victor and I seemed to be the only people left in the building, apart from the three ladies manning the shop, the information office and the basement lavatories. The idea of being stuck there until 4pm was simply too much to contemplate, so I asked Victor to drive me back to the city to do a few hours work in the Cummins' office. We returned later that afternoon and I did finally leave Beikova shortly after 5pm, arriving back in my Chelny hotel some twelve hours after setting out that morning. As I was to confirm the next day at the InterClub, these kinds of problems were normal with the KamAZ shuttle – it was definitely not to be relied on. To be fair, the Aeroflot flights were not much better, always subject to delays or diversion and with a safety reputation that made you check your insurance policy each time you flew. Indeed, over the year of travel in and out of Russia, I can't recall a single round trip that was without some kind of hitch, regardless of the carrier.

CHAPTER THREE

Russian Drinking

The Russians – at least the men – had an international reputation for excessive, heavy drinking and I had seen some of this on my previous visits to the USSR. Under Gorbachev, attempts had been made to reduce alcohol consumption. The health risks and anti-social nature of heavy drinking were promoted and many of the vodka distilleries were closed in a move that was reminiscent of prohibition in the USA. This was not a new idea however, as both the Tsar and subsequently the Bolsheviks had done much the same thing during the First World War. Gorbachev's action had arguably disastrous results, both for ordinary Russians and the economy. Inevitably, illicit stills were set up, some making dangerously unhealthy vodka and then as the drinking lobby regained power under Yeltsin, there was insufficient capacity to meet the market's requirements. Although production was starting to recover by the time of my arrival in Russia, amazingly, a significant proportion of the vodka consumed in Russia was imported. Regular travellers through Moscow airport in 1995 will remember that it was usually impossible to buy domestically produced vodka in the duty free there. The ongoing shortages simply reinforced the demand for homemade moonshine.

Although not a fan of vodka, at least on its own, I do enjoy a drink and certainly would not wish to judge the Russians on their drinking habits. Given the hard life that many of the ordinary people lead (and have led for generations), without much hope of improvement to their daily lives, it would be odious to point a criticising finger. Yet, the damage that excessive drinking does, especially amongst the young was plain to see. It was quite common to see drunks in the streets, as well as the bars, both day and night, especially after pay day (an unpredictable event for many in Russia). The good news was that generally they did not seem to become violent or abusive – at least they never gave me any problems. Indeed, often in the bars these young men would insist on sharing a bottle of vodka with us foreigners, usually accompanied by the frequent toasts of which the Russians are so fond.

Drinking and driving was against the law in Russia as in most countries but the law was frequently disregarded and the local police derived extra income from catching people who did drink and drive. At the various social and business functions I attended, drinking was the norm, even though many of the men would be driving home. For the elite few whose position justified it, the benefit of a company car and driver was very obvious. For the great majority of Russians who have to rely on crowded public transport, the antics of the frequent drunks provided much needed light relief and entertainment for their more sober fellow passengers. Although there could be some tut, tutting from the older women, there was usually a helping hand to get the drunks on and off the bus or tram and to keep them more or less upright during the journey. However, excessive drinking was a serious problem, as a casual walk around any Russian city during the weekend regularly revealed with cast off drink cans and bottles littering the streets. In a country where street litter was generally not yet a problem this detritus was all the more obvious. For me, the broken glass bottles in the gutters symbolised the broken dreams of those who had consumed the alcohol. I felt that until the Russian government met the basic aspirations of the ordinary man in the street, the excessive drinking would not significantly improve. Although it was a very serious problem, sadly, it rarely seemed to be treated that way by much of the general public. The Russians used to quip that when you see toddlers staggering around, their unsteady movements are similar to those of drunks and they are simply practising for when they grow up. This lax attitude towards heavy drinking was something I would see much more of when later working for the Foreign Office.

Security and Escorts

Wherever we went in Chelny, we always had to be escorted by one of the Russians from the InterClub. During the week, the basic escort job fell mostly to our regular support team at the InterClub. For the weekend social activities however, they quite understandably wanted their time off so it was often a scramble for management to persuade anyone to be our minders and occasionally we were stuck with staff that spoke little or no English. This was both awkward and embarrassing for us as we understood their reluctant presence and we weren't really convinced of the need for their attendance in many cases. But it did at least give us the opportunity to get to meet a wider group of local people and so learn more about Russia and Tatarstan. There were sound reasons for this escorting, especially in the early days – we spoke little or no Russian and we didn't know our way around the city. In addition, we had been advised early on in our stay in Chelny that there was a possible security threat against our small group. The reality of this was difficult for us to assess as we were never sure who it might be that threatened us and no-one at KamAZ would ever say. I quickly discounted the Russian mafia who had shown no inclination to intentionally harm foreigners. It seemed to me the only possible local threat would come from the Tatar independence movement but the ongoing troubles in the south of Russia around Chechniya were an alternative potential source of concern. When we had first arrived, we were told that KamAZ had arranged a triple level of security protection for us foreigners – their own office support staff, the local police and a third more shadowy group that I assumed were the special security people at KamAZ and we occasionally saw them around when we were at public events in the city. Although though none of us ever had any real problems in this respect in Chelny, occasional stories of serious events elsewhere in Russia made the possibility seem more real. I had recently read about a British businessman who was killed during a mafia shoot-out in a St Petersburg cafe – he was sadly in the wrong place at the wrong time – as well as a German who was seriously injured during a shooting outside a Moscow factory. Such stories made us wary and kept us on our toes.

A Neptune Show

On the final Sunday of July another visit was organised for us to the KamAZ riverside R&R complex. A coach picked our team up from the hotel around 10.30 and we were taken to the dachas and beach area that we had visited a few weeks before. Once there, we were told all the various activities were available to us and we could spend our day as we wanted. Walking around, it was soon apparent that some of the facilities and equipment had mysteriously further deteriorated or disappeared since our original visit. The tennis net was sagging broken across the court. The racquets we used before were not available and a very poor excuse for a football was produced only after considerable pleading with our InterClub escorts. I have to assume that for our first visit, we were given VIP treatment and now KamAZ was more accustomed to us, things were being run on more normal lines. We did, however, see something new – a 'Neptune show' on the river. This was a rather weird event involving mostly a few young girls in bikinis and a man with a long false beard (presumably Neptune) parading around the beach and then moving onto a motorboat moored to a jetty, all accompanied by music broadcast over a tinny loudspeaker system. It wasn't clear whether the motor boat actually worked and as no-one asked if we would like to go for a ride in it, I assumed it was just decorative. It all became a bit embarrassing. We stood there on the sand watching but not understanding what was happening or whether we were expected to participate in some way. I never discovered whether this 'show' had been specially organised for us or whether it was a regular event at this dacha complex. If it was the latter case, the word had certainly spread amongst the locals that this was something definitely to be avoided. Apart from our group, there couldn't have been more than a handful of Russians who had come to watch and they were probably friends of the performers. It was a pity really because those involved had clearly gone to a lot of effort to organise the show. However, it gave us a laugh and with pleasant weather the rest of the day passed enjoyably enough.

It is hard for a non Russian to comprehend the full meaning of the word dacha to a Russian. At its most basic level, it describes a simple wooden hut on a small plot of land in the countryside, similar to an allotment in the UK. Over the years, many of the original huts have been extended and enlarged into effectively small cottages, habitable over a weekend. But there is much more to the word than this. As we have already seen, a dacha can also refer to a significantly larger building like the KamAZ ones we visited at weekends as well as the fancy country homes being increasingly built by the rich. But for the Russians the word not only has a physical dimension but also encompasses a deep underlying emotional feeling. To the urbanised Russian, the dacha has long represented a place of private sanctuary or escape from the pressures of city life and the economic system at weekends and holidays. It also provided a tenuous but tangible link to the soil of mother Russia and the long gone old peasant ways when every serf had his own plot of land to tend. In a country where property ownership has always been impossible or only for the elite few, a dacha was somewhere that a Russian could own and pass down to future generations; a personal space where he and his family could feel free and be themselves. For the city dweller, the small garden that came with the dacha also provided the important opportunity to grow fresh food during the summer months, much of which was preserved as a vital supplement to their diet during the extensive winter.

Russian Markets

The open air markets or free markets as the Russians called them, were an important part of the day to day commercial life. At this time, other than in the very largest cities, there were relatively few retail centres or even a main street or two with a decent parade of shops. In Chelny, each district had its own food store, together with a couple of other shops but the quality and choice was often limited. Thus the only way to have any choice or find a variety of items was to criss-cross the city, a time consuming and difficult process. The local free markets however, provided easy access to a wide range of products at reasonable prices all in one place. As well as all the things that you find in any outdoor market worldwide, the larger markets also offered building materials, tools, used cars, spare parts and replacement doors or windows. I noticed that usually the older people tended to wander through the markets, patiently ambling along with the press of the crowd, looking at the goods for sale, occasionally buying something they needed and then heading home. For the young, the visit to the market was often part of the social scene, somewhere to meet friends and chat, sharing a fruit juice or a cigarette – it was a day out for them.

Virtually no handicrafts or locally produced souvenirs were on sale in the Chelny markets or shops. The only exceptions that I could find were Russian fur hats (Chelny actually had a long established small company that made them that I later visited) and some handmade fine woollen shawls. The latter were unfortunately, only available in plain beige and brown colours which I found unattractive but they proved to be the closest I came to genuine local craftwork in the city. As I discovered later with more extensive travelling across Russia, the situation was much the same everywhere else. There were always the usual displays of garish modern paintings and occasionally one would find the traditional wooden nesting dolls or a few small painted boxes. With low disposable incomes and very few visitors outside of Moscow and St Petersburg, it seems there just wasn't a big enough market to support much handicraft production.

Apart from the official stalls, there were always many private individuals, mainly older women, lined up in the street at the edges of the market trying to sell a wide variety of things. Many of them were selling fresh seasonal fruit and vegetables, presumably from their dacha gardens in the country. There were always a couple of women offering the traditional dried and roasted black pumpkin seeds in little paper cones which many people chewed as they wandered around. I tried them once but found they were not to my taste. The men were mostly touting some kind of carpentry service, usually new kitchen cabinets or replacement windows, with a photo album of kitchens already installed from which customers could choose the design, colour and type of wood they preferred. Clearly, there were some people with money to spend on new kitchens in Chelny, despite the economic problems. There was always a cluster of older women (babushkas) trying to sell sweets and cigarettes or an assortment of Communist era badges and military paraphernalia or other oddments of clothing, usually spread out on a small table or cloth on the ground. Occasionally one of them would be standing there holding a puppy or kitten that was for sale. During the bitter winter months, these unofficial stall holders tended to relocate to the numerous pedestrian underpasses around the town. Although providing protection from the worst of the weather, these underpasses were dimly lit, claustrophobic and often smelly places in which to do business. But for these poor women, many presumably trying to supplement the constantly declining value of their fixed state pensions, there weren't any real alternatives. I felt sorry for them and would always try to buy a pack of cigarettes or chocolate bar from them on my way back from the market. Such people were to be seen at the markets and in the streets all over Russia. One of the things that also fascinated me in the markets was the subject of plastic shopping bags which seemed to be a relatively recent innovation in Chelny. As none of the food stores provided free bags, they were quite scarce and if you needed one you had to buy it. There were usually a couple of women selling them in the markets – all in the same colour and pattern. Then a few weeks later, the colour of the bags would change as a new supply arrived and it seemed to be a mini status symbol to acquire the latest style plastic bag and to be seen walking around with it in the market.

At the end of July, I needed a haircut and knew I couldn't last out until my next trip home so I asked the InterClub office manager to arrange for me to go somewhere suitable in Chelny the next day. This innocuous request caused great amusement at first, which rapidly changed to consternation – who would take me and where should I go? By the following morning, someone had evidently taken the necessary decisions, a hairdresser had been selected, an appointment made, a car booked to take me together with a female translator. Although we had difficulty finding the place – it was hidden away on the ground floor of an older apartment block – all went well. The salon was clean and well equipped and the staff courteous. With the translator hovering in the background, I was able to explain how I wanted my hair to the woman who had been entrusted with this important task. The only problem was when I was given the bill I didn't know whether to tip or not.

'Should I tip the lady and if so, how much?' I asked my translator.

'I'm not sure', she said. 'I don't know what men in Russia usually do'.

I tipped. If I was going to upset local feelings, I figured better to do it by giving a tip than not. The price was 33,000 roubles, about the same as I would pay for a trim back home. It seemed expensive for Chelny and at the time I couldn't help wondering if the locals paid that much – I somehow doubted it. I subsequently found out that the hairdresser I had been taken to regularly cut the hair of at least one of the KamAZ directors so the price of my haircut presumably reflected its position as the premier establishment in the city.

My daily meeting with the president of KamAZ finished early one afternoon so on my way back in the car to the InterClub, I asked the driver to take a short diversion to have a quick look at the old town. I knew there wasn't much to look at but had been told there were a few older buildings. We turned off the main road and drove a short distance along a small street that ran parallel with the river. I could now see two or three small brick buildings on the river bank that my driver told me were part of the old port of Chelny and dated from the late 19th century. Apart from a couple of other rather ramshackle, wooden cottages that didn't look as if they were still inhabited, there really wasn't anything else to see. On the other side of the road, a small mosque with a green minaret poked up between several brick and concrete buildings but they were all distinctly 20*th* century. After a short distance, we veered down a dirt track and soon dodged back onto the main road, quickly accelerating out of the way of a KamAZ truck that was bearing down on us. That was my tour of the old town, it didn't take very long and I was rather disappointed that there wasn't more of the original Chelny left to see. When I arrived back in the office, I let Roy know that it wasn't worth taking the tour of the old town.

Too Much Sun

It was now early August and Roy was due to return to the USA for his first home leave today – after eight weeks he was definitely ready. Having left the hotel early this morning to catch the KamAZ shuttle to Moscow, I was amazed to see a very dejected Roy appear mid-morning in the InterClub.

'What happened?' I asked, as he stormed in and flung his bags down on the floor.

'The flight's been cancelled! I've been told that I can either risk Aeroflot tonight or try again in the morning' he continued. 'Either way I'll miss my connections to the USA and will have to try to re-book everything.'

Despite the serious look on Roy's face, I couldn't help laughing. The Russian factor had struck again. This was something we were all to experience over the coming months but that never made it any easier to accept. There's no one to blame and there's nothing you can really do except wait. Roy was so keyed up for this trip home that he was inconsolable for the rest of the day, but he did finally get away the next morning, arriving home safely, if a day late.

The weather in Chelny generally remained hot and sticky – on most days the temperature rose above thirty degrees centigrade and there were frequent rain showers. The evenings were more pleasant and we regularly walked back to our hotel from the InterClub after dinner for some exercise and fresh air. The streets would usually be busy with lots of people out enjoying a stroll like us. It was quite normal to see families ambling along with young children or babies until quite late into the night. Their rooms in the tall apartment blocks with no air conditioning would have been hot and stuffy, making it difficult to sleep. So they wandered around until the temperature eased a little. This almost gave the city a continental European air except that there weren't any lively pavement cafes or decent bars to be enjoyed.

Since today was a Sunday, we were off to the KamAZ dacha area again for a shashlik or Russian barbecue. When we arrived at the entrance to the complex in our bus, there was clearly some problem. The security guards on the gate didn't want to let us in, despite the strong protests of our escorts. Apparently, the problem was a double booking with a local wedding party that was inevitably over-running its allocated time. We decamped from our bus and sat patiently around the entrance, enjoying the warm sunshine and waiting for them to drink up and leave. After forty minutes or so, we were finally ushered in as the Russian wedding party merrily staggered by in the opposite direction. We were back where I had played my first game of tennis several weeks before. There were no rackets available today but someone borrowed a worn football from the security guards and the tennis court was pressed into alternative service. It was fine for us as the court fencing kept the ball in play and a lively game started. We soon found ourselves joined by some of our security guards and a high scoring Russia versus the foreigners match developed which was played in excellent spirits. A generous lunch with copious beer, wine, vodka and brandy had been set out for us on trestle tables under the shade of a couple of large silver birch trees. We were all hungry and thirsty and tucked in, joined by the guards and our KamAZ escorts. Luckily, we had a couple of Russian speaking young American interns with us who had recently joined our team for the summer months. This helped the conversation, which remained lively until, after innumerable toasts, most of the Russians along with our young interns steadily became too drunk to remain sensible. One by one, they gradually collapsed, stretching out in the hot sun to snooze. The rest of us settled back to read a book or wandered off for a quiet walk down by the river. Our two InterClub escorts – Larissa and Ivan – staggered off together into the trees.... We all enjoyed the afternoon in our different ways.

Returning to the hotel later, the combination of football, sun and alcohol had made us all very thirsty and we asked at reception for our usual litre bottles of mineral water (no-one drank the tap water, including the locals, unless it was boiled). Much to our surprise, there was none in the hotel and no cartons of fruit juice either; the receptionist told us their next delivery wouldn't be for a couple of days. As it was late on Sunday evening, the shops were now all closed and so we made do with large quantities of tea. Shortages like this turned out to be a regular occurrence, both at the hotel and the InterClub and it always surprised me how the hotel and indeed the shops could run out of basic things so easily. No water, no bananas, no beer, no fruit juice – unhappy customers and lost profit opportunities. Evidently, the distribution systems for anything not locally produced were still very fragile and we seemed to be the last link in the supply chain from Moscow via Kazan to Chelny. You could always tell when a truck had arrived as the hotel display cabinet would suddenly be bulging again with vodka, beer, juice, cigarettes, nuts and chocolate – almost like Christmas, only more frequent.

Going Bananas

After the first couple of months it became obvious that we would need to supplement our food diet – there was little in the way of fresh fruit or vegetables at either the hotel or InterClub restaurant. The only exception was a seemingly unending supply of under-ripe tomatoes and cucumbers that were relentlessly presented with every meal. We regularly pointed out to the staff that we would appreciate a more varied diet but things never really changed much. I remember at one point wondering in desperation whether I could purchase some seeds to grow lettuce in the hotel yard. But enquiries about whether I could buy seeds anywhere in the local shops met with such a negative response that I dropped the idea. We had enjoyed the local soft fruits when we first arrived but these were now fast disappearing from the street stalls and the markets. There were some vegetables in the markets but we didn't have cooking facilities. Apples and oranges were available but of variable quality so the popular choice became the banana. In typical consultant fashion we analysed the position. Bananas come in their own protective wrapper, with no inherent pollution or contamination risks; the money we spent on them would help both third world countries as well as Russia; once imported, they are distributed by trucks so good for our industry and lastly, they are a real convenience food, easy to eat at any time. Buying our supply of team bananas became an indispensable event of our daily routine. During the week, we would take it in turns to make a sortie to the local stalls to see what was available. At the weekends, we usually bought in the local market where the choice and quality were better. It was a sad day when there were no bananas to be bought.

Although the vagaries of the Russian supply chain persisted throughout my year in Chelny, the variety of western consumer goods on sale erratically but inexorably increased. It was most obvious in the choice of chocolate bars, sweets and biscuits on the street stalls – Mars, Twix, Kit Kat, Wrigleys – all became common names, clearly enjoyed by the Russians. Breakfast cereals and savoury biscuits started to occasionally appear, some of them made in former Soviet bloc countries like Hungary or Latvia. In the local soft drinks war, Pepsi were easy winners for most of my stay. Coca Cola was impossible to find in Chelny until the last couple of months, despite having several plants in the CIS. Just as persistent was the growth in more expensive consumer products – white goods, cars, computers, cosmetics, imported wine and food. The only downside in all this progress was the need to carefully check the 'sell by' dates on everything one bought. It was common to find imported goods on sale well past their expiration date, even in Moscow. Of course, most Russian products conveniently omitted such useful consumer information, though there was talk of government legislation to introduce this as well as other consumer rights. It was impossible to establish whether this situation was the result of a lack of interest or awareness by the customer, the dumping of old stocks into Russia from adjacent, more demanding economies (though there was never any differentiation in prices) or simply due to an inadequate stocking and distribution system. The other obvious sign of growing wealth in Chelny was the increasing number of Mercedes, BMW and US or Japanese 4x4s on the streets. Despite the problems at KamAZ and the low wages for many, some people were clearly making a lot of money.

A Time Share Scam

One other curious sign of the developing consumerism in Chelny was the sale of overseas time share holidays. Around this time I discovered that there were a couple of other British men staying in our hotel occasionally. They seemed quite mysterious, we never saw them at breakfast or generally around the hotel but occasionally we clearly heard English voices in the corridors late at night. The pair turned out to be time share salesmen based in Moscow and they organised periodic evening presentations in the hotel conference suite for locals. I eventually found out who they were through one of the InterClub interpreters who also worked as their translator, supplementing her KamAZ pay. It seems they were quite successful for a while but like many of these operations around the world, it was mostly a scam. The money disappeared and the Russians didn't get the overseas holiday homes they thought they were buying, although it took several months before this was discovered. I never met these shady characters but from what I was told, they soon moved on to find new victims elsewhere in Russia, leaving a lot of Chelny residents to rue the day they had heard about time shares..

A Weekend in Moscow

In mid August, an urgent business meeting had brought me back to Moscow, giving me the unexpected chance to spend the weekend sightseeing. I was staying at the Aerostar, a western owned hotel, on the way into the centre from Sheremetyevo airport and giving convenient access to both. That evening, as I was walking through the lobby to reception to check for messages, I passed by the usual rank of wall-mounted hotel telephones. I couldn't help overhearing part of the conversation of a loud voiced American who was obviously flying home the next day after an extended stay in Russia and presumably calling his wife.

'And when I get back home, I don't want to see another god-dammed tomato or cucumber for at least a month' shouted the voice. 'No, I really mean it. It's all we ever get out here and make sure there aren't any left in the refrigerator as well.'

I understood exactly how he felt and it was comforting to know that others found the Russian vegetable scene as monotonous as I did. I mentally promised myself not to eat another tomato or cucumber while I was in Moscow, where there is a wide culinary choice, even if very expensive. I enjoyed every mouthful of my dinner, a seafood pasta in a creamy sauce – though I suffered later as my body struggled to digest this unaccustomed rich food. Sleep did not come easily that night.

Wandering around Moscow that weekend brought back memories of my previous visits more than ten years ago. The Lubyanka building no longer seemed as mysterious or threatening. I passed the Cosmos hotel where I had stayed during my very first visit. We called it the Cocmoc then due to its Cyrillic spelling (the Russian letter 'S' appearing as a 'C' on the hotel sign) and an unsubtle tribute to the large number of prostitutes who managed to gain entrance to what was supposed to be a Westerners only hotel. I also stopped for a coffee at the National hotel, just off Red Square. When I stayed there, it was a typical, old style Soviet warren of a building, where I was convinced my room was bugged. Now modernised, it's one of the most exclusive places to stay in Moscow. On to Red Square itself and the Kremlin – the queues today outside Lenin's tomb being a mere shadow of the long, patient, shuffling lines of the Soviet era. It's possible now to tour inside the previously forbidding walls, which were formerly only penetrated by the large black limousines of the communist party elite. To one side of the outer Kremlin walls is the Russian memorial to the unknown soldier – a simple but strikingly poignant monument. I was intrigued by the large epaulettes of one of the soldiers who were on silent guard duty. Russian military always seem to wear these gaudy over-sized epaulettes and when I returned to Chelny I asked about them. Apparently, they were first used in the time of the Tsars for officers but after the Bolshevik revolution they were regarded as badges of privilege and rank and so abandoned. However, in World War II the Soviets reintroduced them to try to improve troop morale in the face of constant losses to the Germans and the tradition has hung on. Opposite the Kremlin on the other side of Red Square I went into the world famous Gom store – the largest in Russia. My recollections were of an imposing building, which had large plate glass windows looking sadly across the Square, with little on display apart from a few tinned goods and the odd item of undesirable Soviet clothing, all supervised by large numbers of surly assistants. I was glad to find that much had changed since my last visit. The building, which has an interesting internal galleried design, is now a thriving complex, split into a bustling cornucopia of individual shops and boutiques, filled with products from around the world. Not everything has changed though. In a couple of the shops that I tried, the old familiar, surly attitude and lack of interest by the staff were still on display. But hopefully, there was probably some enterprising foreign consultant setting up a shopkeeper's charm school at the time of my visit to change all that.

Staying a couple of nights in Moscow not only gave me the chance to eat good food but also the opportunity to catch up with world events through daily English language newspapers plus US and British television programmes. Admittedly, there were TV's in our hotel rooms in Chelny. They received two Russian channels, which were of no value until our language capability improved, plus the local Tatar language station. The latter reminded me of past glimpses of early Welsh television broadcasts in the UK, rather amateurish and low budget, inevitably limited in scope. We also had access later to a satellite TV in one of the hotel rooms, installed I believe for the occasional times when Tatarstan's president stayed at our hotel. However, the selection of channels was most peculiar – a hotchpotch of Polish, Italian, German, Dutch, Spanish and Arabic from Dubai in the Gulf. Obviously, these choices had been made by someone with vastly superior language skills than any of us. One channel did however, provide limited English language coverage with a few programmes from NBC, the US broadcaster which were full of advertisements, US style and frequently repeated. Later, we discovered the half hour of so-called 'international' news from ITN broadcast every evening at 8pm Chelny time. This became our nightly mainstay for keeping up with the rest of the world, at least if we were back at the hotel in time to catch it. We became increasingly critical of this programme however, and would happily have shot the ITV editor if we had ever met him. I recognise that it must be difficult to select from the day's world news the stories to feature in a half hour slot. Paramount in that choice should surely be the potential audience, most of whom were likely to be English speaking ex-pats, similar to ourselves, mainly interested in major world events and news related to our home countries – the USA or Britain. For major international stories there was headline coverage – bombs, hi-jackings, natural disasters etc. The remainder of the programme however, contained an arcane mixture of snapshot reports from around the world which very rarely included the places or items of interest to us. I was fast becoming an expert on topics as diverse as Argentinean wild life, railway privatisation in Mongolia, political developments in Malaysia, Bengali agricultural reform and so on. Educational – yes, informative – possibly, of general interest outside the immediate country involved – definitely not. We were often left at the end of the programme feeling that there must have been more consequential news items than those selected for broadcast.

I had the same criticism, only more so, regarding BBC Radio's world service. On my previous trip back to the UK, I had purchased a small portable radio that I brought back to Chelny with the intention of listening to BBC short wave broadcasts. I thought I would be able to listen to the news and the occasional play or comedy programme in the evenings and at weekends. The listening experience however, proved very disappointing. As I discovered, BBC overseas broadcasts were geographically zoned and the only signal that I seemed to be able to pick up was the one for central Asia which meant that the news programmes were predominantly related to India, Pakistan or Sri Lanka. There was very little coverage of events in the UK, Europe or the USA which I thought would have been of prime interest to the audience, whether ex-pat or local. The selection of light entertainment programmes on offer was also limited and I soon gave up tuning in to the BBC. Why would a Russian want to listen to a broadcast in English of say, a Tchaikovsky concert, when he can do the same with ease and better reception on Russian radio? Or an Indian tune in to a programme on cooking curries? These may have helped them improve their English but I could think of a wide range of alternative programmes that would be just as useful in this respect as well as being more interesting, relevant and serving a wider audience.

Squats, Shuffles and Shoes

If you travel much around Russia, there are two things you are bound to come across. The first is the Russian squat, mostly practised by men. Instead of standing or sitting, they will drop down on their haunches as naturally and easily as blinking. They appear to be able to hold this position for minutes or hours on end and do it almost anywhere. Along the side of the road, in railway stations, in public buildings and offices, in fact, wherever there's nowhere to sit – including I suspected in the Russian lavatories (more on this later). Indeed, many Russian men seemed to prefer this squatting position to that of sitting on a convenient low wall or even the floor. It looks very uncomfortable and I'm not sure how or where this habit originated. Maybe with the cold winters it was too dangerous to perch anywhere without risking haemorrhoids or being frozen to the spot. The second phenomenon is what I call the Russian shuffle, commonly observed in winter across the country. Due to the almost continuous sub-zero winter temperatures and the absence of street gritting, any snow that fell was quickly trodden into hard ice making the pavements extremely slippery. To compensate for this, the Russians have evolved a unique style of winter walking which essentially involves trying to keep both feet on or near the ground at all times. By shuffling along this way, if one foot slips on the ice, they still retain some grip and can balance on the other and in these conditions it is rare to see a local fall over completely. Whereas until we foreigners watched, learnt and emulated this peculiar gait, we were frequently flat on our backs on the ice. But there was more to being street-wise on the treacherous compacted ice than the shuffle. Having the right type of sole on one's shoe is also vitally important in these conditions. As I was to discover later, most of my English shoes were simply not up to the job of keeping me on my feet in winter. Leather soles are downright lethal but even rubber or composites need careful selection if you want to stay upright. The best are those that are soft and 'grippy', similar to the crepe soles I remember on my sandals as a child.

But of course I was blissfully unaware of all this in August when I realised one day that a pair of my leather brogues needed new soles. A chat with one of our interpreters soon revealed there was a shoe-mender not far from the InterClub that would no doubt sort me out and she agreed to take me there. I showed the man my problem shoes and he asked what kind of soles I wanted. I naturally asked for leather to match the originals which immediately produced a sharp intake of breath and a look of surprise on the face of the cobbler, though I didn't understand why. I conferred with my interpreter.

'He does have leather doesn't he?'

'Yes,' she replied 'but he's not sure where he put it.' The cobbler then disappeared into the back of shop, no doubt to look for 'it'. After a while, he reappeared with a triumphant smile on his face. In his hands was a dusty, thick piece of leather about the size of a large cushion.

'Not much demand here for this' he said according to my interpreter. Indeed the leather looked as if it hadn't seen the light of day since the Bolshevik Revolution. However, it seemed very similar to the English leather of my worn out soles so I happily confirmed my order and returned to collect my newly repaired shoes an hour or so later. They looked and felt fine, giving me good service until winter arrived. Then I quickly discovered why the leather was gathering dust in the shop and rued my summer decision.

As the warm August weeks ticked by, there were two clear status symbols that I increasingly became aware of in Russian offices. The first was the array of telephones arranged on a manager's desk and / or that of his secretary – I frequently encountered offices with more than half a dozen. If you really wanted to make a powerful statement in this respect, you had multi-coloured phones instead of the more ordinary black or grey ones. Some of this excess reflected the endemic Russian problem of actually getting through on the phone and the feeling that if you had enough handsets you might stand a better chance of eventually speaking to someone. However, no human can speak and listen sensibly into more than a couple of phones at the same time and so most of them must have been for show. The other frequent, very visible display of power was the number of people waiting outside a manager's office. It was a very rare event indeed for me to attend a meeting anywhere in Russia without seeing at least two or three people – frequently more – patiently waiting outside the office, rather like petitioners to some Middle Eastern potentate. The thought came to my mind that here was an interesting opportunity for an enterprising individual to set up a rent a crowd business to more fully satisfy this market. The most important people had, of course, multiple phones and large ante-rooms filled with numerous hopeful supplicants.

A Growing Team

Our work load at KamAZ steadily increased through the summer and both the Cummins and Deloitte ex-pat consultant teams steadily expanded. The rise in consultant numbers caused increasing problems in various areas such as office space at the InterClub and translator support. It also meant that our hotel, the Dialog, was unable to provide sufficient accommodation for everyone. As a result, Deloitte decided that their team of consultants would relocate entirely to the so-called KamAZ Hilton. During construction of the KamAZ factories in the 1970's, a large part of the equipment and tooling installed came from overseas. At the peak there were apparently several hundred foreign specialists working in Chelny and to provide accommodation for them all KamAZ built a large hotel, soon nicknamed the KamAZ Hilton. At the time, it was probably an impressive facility, constructed in four multi-storey blocks around a large garden square, with its own restaurant and shops. Since then, KamAZ had converted most of the complex into offices for their own staff, with the remaining hotel accommodation split into two – one part for foreign specialists and another separate section for Russian visitors and workers.

Being less than a ten minute walk from the InterClub, the KamAZ Hilton was more convenient than the Dialog and much cheaper so I arranged a visit to the building to assess whether we should also relocate there. Yuri Borisov met me at reception and showed me round the complex, accompanied by an armed KamAZ security guard. I was somewhat surprised at the presence of the guard but didn't give it too much thought at the time. However, on later reflection, it was clear this was a symptom of a growing unease and concern by KamAZ senior management about security. As we were to subsequently discover, there was some corruption inside the company with associated threats from criminal elements as well as some disaffected former employees. Coupled with various backstage, unhelpful political manoeuvrings, it was no wonder that the directors felt worried and security around the KamAZ sites was steadily increased over the next few months. My short tour of the foreigners' section was enough to confirm that our group was much better off in the Dialog. Although the rooms were large, mostly suites, with a bedroom, sitting room, shower / toilet and kitchenette, the badly worn furniture and decor looked all too original and untouched for twenty five years and we had already heard that the plumbing left much to be desired. There was also no air conditioning in the building and the typically hot, sticky August afternoon as I walked around simply emphasised its absence. I was not allowed to see the Russian part of the hotel but assumed it was even worse. Although Yuri said that things would be updated soon, given the cash problems at the company, I knew this was very unlikely to happen. Also, an earlier inspection by Cummins security people was very critical of the place, so my team stayed on at the Dialog. More expensive, yes; but as a home away from home much more acceptable and it allowed us to escape a little from what was fast becoming almost a twenty four hours a day work environment.

In late August, we had to say goodbye to Chuck who was returning early to the USA. Although very experienced in truck manufacturing, he didn't settle very well into Chelny or the KamAZ culture and had very fixed ideas about how to sort out the Russians. This inevitably caused friction with some of the production managers with whom he worked and I was receiving complaints from the KamAZ directors. Sadly, I had to recommend to Cummins that his contract be terminated and asked them to find a more flexible replacement. Together with the Deloitte team, we organised a small but lively farewell party for Chuck on his final night in our hotel which went on until the small hours. At breakfast the next morning, we all had hangovers but Chuck seemed to be suffering the most and was still a little unsteady on his feet. We loaded him and his luggage into the car for the airport and waved him goodbye, hoping that he sobered up before landing back home in the USA

Chapter Four

Pictures from Yelabuga

I was alone in the hotel this weekend, the other members of our team being away on home leave and there didn't seem to be any Russian guests. It looked like the weather would be fine so I decided to do some sight-seeing. Just half an hour from Chelny, across the Kama river lay a small town called Yelabuga which I'd been told was an interesting place to visit. So I booked a car and driver for the Sunday afternoon and set off with Svetlana, one of the support staff from the InterClub. She had been to Yelabuga before, spoke good English and agreed to act as my guide. The driver had also brought along his daughter Julia, a student at one of the local colleges. She was an attractive, lively girl, with long auburn hair and proved to be a charming additional escort. It was a chance for her to have a day out as well as practice her English. Svetlana was also a student but was studying at a Moscow university. Back home for the summer, she had been drafted in by KamAZ to assist with general support duties in the InterClub. Being low on the pecking order, she was usually asked to work the late shift till 8 or 9 pm during the week and provide cover at the weekends. The pay was probably poor but she seemed happy to be able to improve her English and was insatiably curious about all aspects of our life in the west. Svetlana's family were originally from Moscow and had moved to Chelny when she was young. When I asked her what she thought about Chelny, she was quite dismissive, saying it was a backwater and she clearly couldn't wait to finish her studies and find a job in Moscow.

It proved to be a fascinating afternoon. Yelabuga sits on a bluff overlooking the Kama river and is well known in Tatarstan for being the birthplace of Ivan Shishkin, a leading Russian painter in the latter part of the 19th century and for its extensive original old town, with many wooden buildings dating from the eighteenth and nineteenth centuries. We visited Shishkin's former house, a large, relatively plain two storey building, which is now a museum. Most of the rooms had been refurbished in period style and his studio, with a large, covered balcony that looked out across the bluff to the river, contained an interesting display of his work. His best original paintings (mostly landscapes) now fetch six figure sums on the international market. Svetlana told me one of those apocryphal stories of when two senior KamAZ directors visiting New York on business a few years before, came across one of Shishkin's paintings for sale in an art gallery for $250,000. One of them said it would be wonderful to be able to buy this painting and take it back to its home in Chelny but of course that isn't possible since we don't have the money. The other, more senior manager said it's not the money that's the problem, it's deciding in whose office we should hang such a valuable work of art.

Close by the museum was a large, imposing old Orthodox church, painted white with green cupolas. We walked around the now seemingly unused building which unfortunately was suffering badly from abandon and decay. Neither of my two young guides seemed to know much about its history, though our driver later told us he thought it was possibly a convent before the Bolsheviks turned it into a school. I did see later, another smaller Orthodox church in the old town which, happily, did appear to be in use. Also nearby, we came across a block of brick apartment buildings that I was told had been constructed by German prisoners from the Second World War. I wondered what they had thought of Tatarstan and how many ever returned to their own distant homes. During my later time with the Foreign Office I was shown similar buildings erected by German POWs in many Russian towns. Several hundred thousand German prisoners were held by the Russians after the war in order to provide free labour for reconstruction projects. Many died in Russian prisons or labour camps and the last ones were not released until some ten years after the war's end.

Yelabuga was also home for a while to the tragic Russian poet Marina Tsvetaeva. After many years of living abroad, she returned to Russia in 1939 with the outbreak of World War II but like all Russians who had lived abroad, she was treated with great suspicion by Stalin's government and effectively ostracised. She was eventually sent here by the Soviet authorities in 1941 but with no family, friends or means of support, sadly committed suicide a few months after arriving. My main interest that afternoon was to wander round the old town, which spreads in a grid pattern over several blocks and try to take in the atmosphere. Thankfully the town was very quiet on this sleepy summer Sunday afternoon and there was hardly anyone to be seen. Apart from a few cars, the streets and houses appeared much as they must have been one hundred years ago. Scenes from the film Doctor Zhivago could easily have been shot here. The houses were mostly made of wood and built in a variety of fascinating styles, both single and two storeys. Many boasted intricate detailed wooden carvings and paintwork around their small windows and doors or on their fascia boards beneath the roof. Simple as their log cabin construction had been, the original inhabitants clearly had sufficient pride and interest in their homes to produce these decorative finishes. Although most now had electricity, I was told some still had no mains water and relied on wells, which was confirmed just a few minutes later. As we rounded a corner, there was an old babushka, struggling up the middle of the road shouldering a yoke with a bucket of water at each end – a picture that I will always remember.

I can still recall several other rustic images from that walk. The old man with a long white beard pushing an old, rusty pram along the street laden with chopped wood – it was hard to tell which was older, the man or the pram which looked as if it was the one his own mother had wheeled him around in. The woman dressed all in black but wearing a brightly coloured headscarf feeding crumbs to the geese in her back yard. A small row of eight or nine idyllic little cottages spread crescent shaped in front of a reed-filled duck pond. I couldn't help thinking that in Europe, homes like these would long ago have been converted into bijou residences by trendy young couples and artists or modernised as weekend retreats. For the moment, the Russians preferred the more modern apartment blocks in Chelny with their running water and central heating. But as disposable income and leisure time increased, I was sure that Yelabuga would become one of the smart places to live for some of the half million people down the road in Chelny.

Yelabuga had a population of around 70,000 and at the time of my visit was a town of two parts. In the small old town centre there were a few quite attractive classical style stuccoed buildings that quickly give way to streets lined with quaint little cottages stretching out along the bluff. The more modern suburbs built some twenty five to thirty years ago to house workers for an adjacent industrial estate sloped awkwardly down from the old centre. The contrast between the two could not be greater. The largely dilapidated 'modern' concrete apartment blocks looked more like prisons and jarred both the eye and the landscape. No attempt was made to harmonise with the old, either in terms of materials or style. There was one other site worth visiting a few minutes' drive from the centre of Yelabuga. Located on a high bluff, with magnificent views over the broad Kama river and the surrounding countryside, stood an old stone ruin, known as the Devil's Tower. This was the crumbling remnant of a small hill fort with a history going back several centuries which local legend associated with black magic, river pirates and as a base for Ivan the Terrible. Now, it was an understandably popular picnic spot and as we stood admiring the vista, a Russian wedding party drove up for a photographic session. The group's chattering and laughter echoing off the tower's stone walls soon broke the peaceful silence that we had been enjoying but I didn't mind, I was glad to see people happy and enjoying themselves. I hope that their memories of that day in Yelabuga remain as pleasant as mine.

Them and Us

As we began to travel more, both to Moscow and elsewhere in Russia, we started to discover the dual price systems which operated for things like air and rail tickets, hotel rooms etc. Although largely super-ceded now, at that time there was one price for the Russians and another, much higher, price for foreigners. Indeed, I was also told that there was even a third tier of prices which were those charged to residents from certain former Soviet bloc countries such as the Baltic States and the Ukraine. Whether this was revenge for their audacity in becoming independent or simply due to vagaries of exchange rates was never made clear to me. Although the rouble during my stay in Russia remained relatively stable – around 5000 to the US$ or 7500 to the pound – and the inflation rate was much better than in the recent past, we also encountered the pay now or the price will be higher tomorrow syndrome. The local offices of Aeroflot were particularly adept at this and the US$ price for a ticket could rise by ten percent overnight. A couple of times I tried to pay in roubles thinking I would get a lower price but it was obvious that I was a foreigner and I was always required to pay in US dollars.

Driving in Chelny

Each of the drivers at KamAZ was responsible for the maintenance of his car and generally, they did a good job, given the problems caused by the age of many of the cars and lack of cash to buy parts. I learned one day much to my amazement that there were over 3200 vehicles in the company fleet, cars, buses and trucks. As far as we were concerned, all requests for local transport, either by car or bus were controlled by the KamAZ 'dispatcher' – the Russians actually used this English word. Although much of the time, the InterClub organised our transport, the location and telephone number of the dispatcher's office became a vital piece of information for us when the InterClub was closed in the evenings or at weekends. Although we complained whenever a car didn't show up on time or wasn't available when we wanted, the dispatcher's job wasn't easy, trying to control all the company vehicles and meet everyone's needs. Overall, I thought they did a decent job of looking after us. One of the frustrating things about travelling in the various KamAZ pool cars was the fact that the window winders rarely worked. In the heat of the summer, it was often impossible to fully open the windows to improve air circulation and cool down. In the winter, it always seemed that the windows were not quite fully closed, allowing a draft of freezing air to come rushing into the car. Whether window winders are the Achilles heel of Russian car design or the cars had previously been used for more clandestine purposes requiring the isolation of the passengers, I never found out. More serious was the pervading odour of petrol fumes inside the cars. Due to the variability of petrol supplies in the city and the shortage of petrol stations between towns, the cars often carried large spare cans in the boot which like the windows never seemed to seal properly. The potential hazard from a rear end collision coupled with the risks from the chain smoking drivers did not bear thinking about. Along with the bald tyres, cracked windscreens, loose steering and general rattles, this always made for an interesting journey.

Vehicle drivers never give way to pedestrians or show any courtesy and the latter are definitely second-class citizens here. But in some respects they only have themselves to blame. I was constantly amazed at the way some pedestrians wanting to cross the street would walk blithely into the road without ever looking for any on-coming traffic. You find this in any urban environment of course but it was particularly prevalent in towns across Russia. At times it seemed as if they still hadn't fully adapted to the automobile age. Being a pedestrian was not easy however, as a walk along many Chelny streets could become an obstacle course, trying to avoid the potholes, cracked or missing paving slabs, uncompleted road works etc. As people weaved about in the streets, it was sometimes hard to tell whether they were drunk or just normal and simply trying to avoid the potholes. One of the control systems from the communist regime that I was surprised to still find operating was the roadside police checkpoint.

These were to be found in all cities as well as on main road exits on the edge of most conurbations. Certainly as one entered or left Chelny on each main road, there was a police post manned twenty four hours a day checking the traffic and the occupants' papers. Not all vehicles were stopped by any means but as they approached the checkpoint, drivers automatically slowed to a crawl in case they are pulled over for inspection, inevitably causing jams at peak times. The majority edged past and sped on, relieved to have avoided the loss of time if they had been stopped. I was told that these checkpoints are retained now mainly as a crime prevention measure. With vehicle theft and stolen goods such big business in Russia, the checking of occupants and their papers could possibly help. As far as I could see however, it was usually the small Lada or beaten up Volga that was stopped. The big black Mercedes and BMWs (the mafia's preferred modes of transport) invariably seemed to sail through. I was also sure that the criminals were smart enough to know the location of the checkpoints and when they were operating and so made appropriate arrangements. Trying to control the rising level of crime in Russia was no easy task and it was a difficult situation for the underpaid police. The checkpoints may have been there simply as visible proof that the police were doing something to try to reduce crime. The fact that they also provided the police with an income supplement by pocketing some of the fines extracted from those unfortunate to be stopped was of course incidental.

Linguistic Barriers

Like most of the others in our team, I arrived in Chelny equipped with a Russian phrase-book and an elementary teach yourself Russian. Whilst these proved useful in learning the Cyrillic alphabet and a basic vocabulary, the complications of the Russian language were such that I decided after the first couple of months that lessons were needed. I duly arranged a weekly session through the help of one of our interpreters and supplemented this by setting myself the objective of trying to learn two or three new words every day. This worked fine for a while but increasingly I found that cramming new words into my head was like trying to squeeze more clothes into an already full suitcase. You can't fit more in without removing some of those already there. Russian is not an easy language to master and I found it inordinately complicated in that everything appeared to have to agree with everything else in some kind of verbal collectivism. No wonder communism started in this country. Those that know these things tell us that Russian belongs to the European family of languages. If like me, you have struggled to come to grips with the complexities of this means of expression, you will forgive me if I cast some doubt on this apparent fact. Certainly, if you dig deep enough you will eventually find some vague connections with German or Latin-based languages and even a little shared vocabulary. But the grammar, sentence construction and use of the Cyrillic alphabet immediately marks the language out as being different. Certainly the eponymous Greek monk who invented their rather illogical script didn't do the Russians any favours. I believe Russian should be in a class of its own and those that master its intricate grammar and speak it fluently have my complete admiration and envy.

Perhaps recognising our limited linguistic abilities in trying to come to grips with Russian, no-one had troubled us by mentioning the existence of the Tatar language in Chelny. Officially, it had a dual status in Tatarstan alongside Russian but is a completely different language and at different times has been written in Arabic or as now in Cyrillic script. Without this important piece of knowledge, I became quite confused in my first few weeks. One day I was trying to find a government office building. I had been given the street address by the InterClub but wasn't sure exactly which building to go into. Walking up and down the street, I attempted to decipher the words of signs on the doors but no matter how hard I tried, I just couldn't make any sense of them. I knew my abilities in Russian were poor but this was ridiculous – I couldn't understand a word. I finally asked a passer-by who pointed me in the right direction. I didn't give this any further thought until a couple of weeks later, I ran into the same situation. So when I arrived back at the InterClub I asked about my problem and was told that all government buildings have their signs in Tatar with Russian underneath. A couple of the KamAZ managers I regularly met with were Tatars and they now started to teach me a few words but I didn't take it very far as I had enough of a struggle with Russian. But as I found out later, the fact that I had even bothered to learn a few words of Tatar and occasionally tried to use them was appreciated by those Tatars with whom I worked.

Old Friends

In late August I returned to Moscow for a couple of days to attend Russia's annual automotive show – not big by European standards but an interesting window onto the Russian market nonetheless. KamAZ had a large outdoor stand, which was undoubtedly the busiest of the show and luckily the weather was good. I was again staying at the Aerostar hotel and in the evening had arranged to meet up in the hotel with a couple of old friends and former colleagues who were visiting the exhibition. We had all previously worked for a British truck manufacturer and they were still with the same company, coincidentally now responsible for export markets including Russia. It seemed strange that after several years our individual career paths had brought us back together here in Moscow. We had an enjoyable evening together, reminiscing over old times in England and sharing our experiences of working in Russia. I looked out the next morning from my bedroom window over the car park and the area to the rear of the hotel. My friends had told me the previous night that the hotel had been a base for Russian special forces during the October 1993 constitutional crisis when President Yeltsin had ordered the army to shell and then storm the nearby Soviet parliament building. The conflict lasted more than one week and saw the deadliest street fighting in Moscow since October 1917 with more than 140 people killed. I well remembered watching the dramatic scenes on television at the time. Now on a quiet Sunday morning, it seemed hard to believe that such pivotal events had unfolded here just a couple of years before. As I took in the scene, I could also see beyond the hotel grounds what initially looked like a railway goods yard with dozens of large blue metal containers stacked in rows but no connecting railway line in sight. It was a bright sunny morning and I needed some fresh air so I left my room and wandered off to investigate and discovered that this was yet another large outdoor market. The containers, all originally the property of the Soviet railways, had been removed here and were now rented out to individual stall holders as very practical, secure lock-ups. How so many perfectly sound (and presumably valuable) containers came to be here, laid out in neat, long rows was uncertain but there was no doubt that they performed their new function excellently in Russia's market economy.

Basketball Match

Back in Chelny, the late August daily weather continued its warm, sunny but very humid pattern. On Sunday, I headed off towards the river to explore part of the eastern suburbs of Chelny. There wasn't really much of any interest to see, mostly row after row of apartment blocks lining the long broad streets. For me, simply observing the people proved to be the most interesting thing during these weekend excursions around town. Groups of men idly standing or squatting at street corners smoking a cigarette, couples with young children ambling along enjoying their own Sunday morning walk, teenage girls giggling and flirting in the morning sunshine with the boys and babushkas slowly treading their lonely route home from the market with laden shopping bags hanging heavily from their arms. Each one was a human picture that held my eyes for a moment or two as we passed each other by. It took about half an hour to walk to the broad Kama river from the hotel. The riverside area was pleasant enough with sandy tracks winding shadily through stands of tall leafy trees. It was popular with the locals who would come to picnic here or just to wander around like me. On my way back to the hotel I tried my first Russian ice cream cone, bought from a street stall. Staff at the InterClub had told me that the local ice cream was very good but so far I had avoided it due to concerns about the water. However, today was so hot that I couldn't resist buying one. The claims were justified; it was creamy and soft, the cup cone was fresh and crisp and excellent value at 1000 roubles and moreover, I didn't suffer any bad after effects. Unfortunately the good weather didn't hold. It rained that evening and the temperature dropped ten degrees overnight so the following day felt quite autumnal. Indeed, that was almost the last good weather we had in Chelny; little did we know that winter was just around the corner.

As the largest employer by far in the region, KamAZ funded various local social activities and sports teams. One was the football club, which was professional and played in the national league, not too successfully at the time I'm afraid. Another was the Chelny women's basketball team, which also played in a national league as semi-professionals. Basketball is a very popular sport in Russia and throughout the former Soviet Union for both men and women. We had been told that KamAZ actually sponsored the local women's team and one day in late August we were invited to go and watch them during a training session. As we had several keen players among our younger consultants, the InterClub told us that we were welcome to actually play a match with the women. We duly met up with them on a warm Saturday afternoon in a large municipal indoor stadium not far from the InterClub. Dreams of the men beating the women were quickly shattered as we watched them practice – they were very fit, skilful and professional. Despite frequent substitutions, the men couldn't really stand the pace and brawn plus muscle didn't equal skill and regular practice – we lost, heavily. After the game, as we joined the women for tea and cakes (no alcohol in sight), their intentions in inviting us to play became clear; they wanted money. Predictably, the financial support from KamAZ had fallen well below what was needed to meet the team's wages and travelling costs (being in a national league meant matches were played all over Russia and even abroad). The team coach had clearly done some homework and she made a beeline for me as the leader or elder statesman figure of the consultant group. She was quite short and portly with brightly dyed auburn hair, quite a contrast to the tall, lithe young women in the team and I couldn't help wondering how she came to be team coach – surely she was too short to have ever played serious basketball. She was also a very domineering and determined lady (it was she, the girls later explained, who strictly enforced the ban on all alcohol during the season). Cornered over a cup of tea, she gave me the full pitch about their problems and resultant need for new sources of money. I would rather have chatted to the attractive, dark-haired young woman recently recruited from St Petersburg, who was one of their new star players but I couldn't escape the coach. It was hard not to be touched by their situation; they had an excellent team (that went on to do very well in the league that year) and their needs were really quite modest. But women's basketball did not attract much attention or support and in any case, women came fairly low in the pecking order at KamAZ, as in Russia generally. As I considered the position, I thought there might be a chance of persuading Cummins to provide some limited sponsorship, especially as they had a woman in charge of the joint venture project. I promised the coach that we would try to raise a little money to help, which seemed to pacify her sufficiently so that I was allowed to move out from my corner and have another cup of tea. We did in fact obtain some money for them and I handed over $150 a few weeks later and subsequently a little more, all courtesy of Cummins. However, this was not the last I was to see of the women's basketball team and their coach.

In early September, a new colleague arrived to replace Chuck, a Dutchman named Henk. In his forties, slightly portly with receding hair and glasses, he looked quite serious but actually turned out to be a very affable, easy-going person who fitted into our team very well. When we arrived at the InterClub this morning we discovered that apparently there was no hot water in the town today. It seemed this was a periodic problem that occurred when work was being done on Chelny's central power and heating system and usually lasted for a couple of days. Luckily our hotel had its own generator and so we never suffered this problem. However, our Deloitte colleagues at the KamAZ Hilton were not as fortunate and so we offered evening showers to the rest of the team – for the small price of a beer of course. The full name of the company for which our colleagues worked was actually Deloitte and Touche but as a result of these problems it rapidly became known as Toilette and Douche to us. With the passing of summer, there was a noticeable decrease in the availability of good fresh fruit in both the local shops and the InterClub restaurant. Pears were now unobtainable and the apples and grapes were starting to look very indifferent. Tomatoes and cucumbers however, remained firmly on the daily menu at the InterClub, at least for the time being.

A Little Russian Humour

The Russians are always able to laugh at themselves and have an excellent sense of humour, even if it comes largely from adversity and a good understanding of their shortcomings. Although most of the KamAZ business meetings in which I participated were quite ordinary and normal, many were very serious, given the difficult state of the company. But even on such occasions, there were often glimpses of the Russian's pervasive humour. I well remember one day sitting with a couple of senior managers in the president's office waiting for him to arrive for one of our regular crisis meetings. We were casually chatting about various things and had moved onto the subject of skill levels and training in the company when one of the Russians leaned towards me with a serious look on his face and said 'You know part of our problem in Russia is due to the fact that half the people are below average intelligence, maybe even more'. This was duly translated for me, also in a serious tone and it wasn't until the Russian started to smile at his own joke that I fully realised what he had just said. On another occasion, during one of our Saturday morning sales review meetings, one of the KamAZ managers asked me 'How do you think we beat Napoleon in front of the gates of Moscow?'

'I've no idea, tell me' I answered.

'Everyone knows an army marches on its stomach, the French in particular. Well, they had got as far as they could on French food but when they saw how bad the Russian food was, they turned back!'

I later thought that it was a pity the French didn't stay and improve the Russian cuisine. Incidentally, the Russians claim that the word 'bistro' meaning 'quick' in Russian passed into the French language at the time of the Napoleonic invasion. The French soldiers were apparently looking for 'quick food' (was this because they knew they wouldn't be around very long?) and the word 'bistro' came to be used for places where such food was available.

Cockroaches Again

Their history on this earth goes back three million years; there are over three thousand known species; they exist on every continent and the female can lay half a million eggs each year. They are apparently radiation proof and the Russians used to joke that after the nuclear holocaust, these would be the only creatures to survive. I refer, of course, to the cockroach and no book about Russia would be complete without a comment on the ubiquitous cockroaches, or as the Russians call them takrani. They seem to be everywhere in Russia and as such are more accepted than in England, where the sight of one usually evokes a feeling of revulsion. My first encounter with them was in the InterClub office when sending a fax one day in the early summer. First one and then a whole family appeared from inside the machine, where, presumably attracted by the extra warmth, they had made their home and multiplied. As time went by, I came across them more and more in both the offices as well as on my travels to other parts of Russia but fortunately never once in the Dialog hotel rooms. At the InterClub this morning, we were told that we would have to vacate the building for the afternoon as it was de-bugging day. Not as we initially thought an attempt to rid the offices of any surreptitious electronic devices but the day of death for all takrani – allegedly. After lunch as we packed up our things and left for our hotel, we saw the death squad arrive and start work. For this annual event each of the rooms was sealed and a white powder sprayed everywhere which was then left overnight to do its fatal job. When we returned the next morning, the cleaners had removed most of the mess and although there were still remnants of powder in various cracks and crevices, there were no immediate signs of any cockroaches. However, a little later in the morning when the fax machine suddenly erupted into life, spewing out the first of the day's incoming messages, a large repulsive takrani could also be seen emerging. Apparently, during the de-bugging operation all equipment such as computers and fax machines were covered in plastic to prevent the ingress of powder, thereby severely limiting the effectiveness of the process. I remain convinced that the cockroaches knew this which is why they congregated in the relative safety of the machines in the first place.

A New Winter Coat

One of the most serious situations facing KamAZ and the city was the rising unemployment as the company scaled back its own payroll, a problem faced by most other towns and cities across Russia. Like many of the large previously state run enterprises now facing the harsh realities of the new economic system, KamAZ was under pressure to reduce their substantial over-manning and try to conserve cash and become profitable. This meant there was a desperate need to create new jobs in what was otherwise a 'one horse town'. Yet, the history of the Russians is one of dependence on a strong central authority, whether under the Tsars or the communists, controlling economic activity down to the last detail. The establishment of smaller, privately owned businesses had started with perestroika but this entrepreneurial culture, especially the concept of self employment, did not appear to come easily to the majority of Russians. The whole situation was worsened by the lack of disposable cash in the economy. Many workers did not receive their pay regularly, the tax regime effectively penalised the generation of cash profits and any redundancy payments, which could otherwise help fund new business ventures, were minimal. On top of all this was the negative impact of the Russian mafia which very effectively tracked the start up of any new business – probably more efficiently than the tax authorities – as a target for their 'squeeze'. The mafia was particularly active in Moscow and St. Petersburg, where the almost daily violence at the time was well publicised in the press but they were spreading their tentacles throughout the country and represented a major drag on economic regeneration. The young were especially vulnerable to recruitment, with promises of easy money and the 'good life' and this was a growing problem in Chelny. The concern about future employment prospects was evident from many of the conversations I had with local people and this was presumably an influence in the government elections, which took place later in 1996. The swing to the former communists under Gennady Zyuganov would be much stronger here than in many other parts of Russia.

The Tatarstan and Chelny authorities were well aware of the problems facing the local economy and were active in trying to do something about it. Indeed, part of our consulting brief was to provide advice in this area and for a few weeks Cummins sent out a consultant to provide specialist help to KamAZ and the city. Towards the end of his stay, we were both invited to attend an exhibition organised by the city and local Chamber of Commerce to show what Chelny private enterprise had already achieved. I met the organisers and was very encouraged by what was on show. There was a wide variety of business activities, with around fifty companies present, many of them displaying considerable design skills and the use of modern techniques and technology. These people have sound ideas about how to encourage business start ups and are drawing on the experiences of former eastern bloc countries as well as the west. Indeed, there were several small business assistance programmes financed from the west. Although start up finance could be a problem, what they need above all however, was a growing economy and less hindrance caused by the government or mafia crime. As I wandered round the exhibition stands, I came across one displaying a range of men's clothes on a rack and at one end I noticed a couple of thick padded winter coats, one in black and the other in a mustard colour. On closer examination, I saw they were actually like long thick duvets but well made with large poacher pockets and a double fastening zip-up front. I decided to try on the black one and although it looked quite smart it was too small for me. I then tried on the mustard yellow one which fitted very well but I wasn't sure about the colour. The woman on the stall told me that these were really only for display for the exhibition and they didn't have any other sizes in black with them but she was happy to sell me the mustard one if I wanted it. With its thick pull up collar and extending well below my knees, it would certainly keep me warm through the Russian winter but I still wasn't sure about the colour. However, when she showed me the price, I couldn't believe it, a winter coat for less than £10. I decided at this price, winter warmth was more important than a fashionable colour. I handed over my money and wandered back to the InterClub on a warm September afternoon with my new winter coat slung over my arm. Although both my colleagues and the InterClub staff found my choice of colour highly amusing, with taunts like here comes the yellow banana, they all agreed that it looked a good coat and was excellent value. And so it was to prove as I wore my duvet coat non-stop through the coming winter and it kept me warm through the coldest weather I have ever experienced. Indeed, I still have it and occasionally wear it on cold winter days in the UK, even if I do look like a big, tall banana.

A Tatar Concert

We really hit rock bottom (almost literally) today – there were no seats remaining in either of the toilets in the InterClub. The one in the first floor toilet had cracked irreparably a couple of weeks ago and had been removed and when I went to the other toilet this morning that one had also disappeared. The white porcelain lavatory bowl sat there gaping at me like some toothless monster. Of course, no one knew who was responsible for this disgraceful anti-social behaviour and given the parts availability for such things in Russia, I knew we would be waiting seat-less for some time. Perhaps we should have been grateful however, as at least the lavatory bowls were still in place so we didn't have to rely on the old Russian system of squatting over an open hole. Whilst this was not Friday the thirteenth, it certainly felt like it should have been as almost everything was going wrong today. It was impossible (again) to telephone outside the city, we couldn't reach Moscow or London; the lunches and dinners have been really poor the last couple of days at the InterClub; we were having visa problems again; there seemed to be a shortage of transport (no petrol) so it was difficult to attend any meetings and to cap it all a fax message from Cummins in the UK arrived saying there were problems obtaining insurance cover while we were in Russia. Tomorrow just had to be a better day.

Fortunately, things did improve, at least temporarily, as the InterClub has kindly organised tickets for us to attend a concert tonight. Despite being a relatively new city and therefore without a long cultural tradition, Chelny has a strong classical music following. It has its own purpose built concert hall and a locally based orchestra with a good reputation that performed concerts every two or three months. Tonight's concert turned out to be a mixture of well known classical music pieces together with some traditional Russian songs and several Tatar compositions. The event seemed well attended, although the Chelny concert crowd that evening was mostly women and youngsters. As people queued to check their coats and then milled around the foyer, there was a definite buzz of excitement in the air, exactly the same as any other concert hall elsewhere in the world. There were a couple of faces I recognised, including the president of KamAZ, Mr Bekh. I was a little surprised initially not to see more of the company's senior management group in attendance but then realised they were probably still working as it was a Thursday and only 7pm. On arrival, our group had been ushered into a small anteroom where we were offered fruit juice and asked to wait until the concert started. I thought nothing of this at first but then noticed a couple of dark suited young men slip into the back of the room, presumably KamAZ security people, who briefly looked us over and then left. It was obvious that this holding room was their chance to get to know our faces so that in the event of any trouble, we would be recognised. Inevitably, this being Russia, there were several long speeches to endure before the concert started but finally the music got underway. Several short pieces by Strauss and Mozart from the full orchestra took us on to the Russian traditional folk songs, performed by a tenor and a bass. The music was unfamiliar to me and had an almost Gaelic feeling to it; indeed the tenor has that lilting quality of voice that would have gone down very well in Ireland. The bass singer suited some of the later songs that sounded very Russian, mournful and full of deep feeling. I didn't care for the final Tatar compositions which were very noisy yet sombre and quite martial in places. How representative of Tatar music these were I couldn't ascertain since our escorts from the InterClub said it was also the first time they had attended a concert with Tatar classical music performed. Other genres of music could also be found in Chelny with a jazz club (more on this later) and occasional pop concerts. Indeed, Alkonost, a Russian doom-folk metal band that was later to become quite well known in Russia was formed around this time in Chelny.

Memorials and Statues

During the communist era, the design and erection of statues and monuments was probably an excellent business to be in. They were everywhere in Russia – massive blocks of concrete or stone and iron that were intentionally imposed on their surroundings – monuments to the heroes of the Revolution (mostly Lenin) or celebrating the achievements of the Russian people. Most are impressive only for their monstrous ugliness, rarely are they something to admire in their own right. Few of the Russians I spoke to had a good word now to say about these Soviet creations. Some of the more politically oriented statues had been removed with the changing political scene but many more deserved the hammer of the demolition crew as soon as time and money allowed. Most towns also had one or more seemingly obligatory memorials to the dead and the struggles and hardships during the Second World War. Chelny had several scattered around the city. In a country that suffered so much at the hands of the Nazis as well as its own leaders during this period, this was perhaps understandable. I read once that the building of these prolific war memorials became for the Soviets almost like a religious cult, designed to heighten nationalist feelings and solidarity versus a common foe (always unspecified), still encircling and menacing the country. I think there was some truth in this. Certainly, the visual impact of these memorials was usually strikingly aggressive, unlike the quiet dignity of the memorial to the unknown soldier close to the Kremlin walls in Moscow.

On September 16*th* we experienced our first snow flurries in Chelny. Blown in on a cold north-easterly wind from Siberia, they were the advance guard of the approaching long winter season. What a rapid change and shock to the system. Two weeks ago we were enjoying 25 degree temperatures, now the cold reality of a prolonged Russian winter seemed much more imminent. Whatever happened to the autumn, we must have missed it yesterday! The Russians however, seemed to welcome the onset of winter, for them it was a season to be enjoyed rather than simply endured. As it effectively lasted for six months, I suppose that this was the best attitude to take though not one I felt I could genuinely share.

Chapter Five

St Petersburg the Great

Along with several other members of our consultant team, I returned to Chelny in early October after a ten days break in England. The temperature here had been fluctuating daily but was clearly on a downward trend. It was 10 degrees today and raining, which was actually warmer than when I left. In contrast, the UK weather had been unusually pleasant for the time of year and on my final day it was 25C in London. I started to wonder what the chances of an Indian summer in Tatarstan might be and briefly remembered my ideas of enjoying some warm sunshine when I had first agreed to come to Russia. We arrived around 11pm at Chelny airport and KamAZ had once again arranged dinner for us in the InterClub and as usual we declined the offer and went straight to our hotel. We had tried on several occasions to explain that after a full day travelling (even longer for our US colleagues), dinner at this time of night was not required and would simply be wasted on us. It was a difficult situation for both sides. Food was organised and staff from the InterClub would be waiting to host us but we were tired and simply wanted to get to bed. The Russians were only trying to be hospitable and were, as we knew, only doing what they would normally do for any visitors to the factory – whether from within Russia or from overseas. Perhaps the Russians' stamina and appetite (especially when a free meal and drink is involved) were greater than ours. Anyway, this saga of our being offered and declining a late dinner continued on for many months before either realisation dawned or, as I suspect, budget cuts at the InterClub took effect.

For a couple of weeks now, I had been trying to plan a business trip to St. Petersburg, something that on the surface would seem relatively straightforward. Agree who is to go, set up the meetings, book the hotel and flights and Bob's (or Ivan's) your uncle. But I didn't allow for the internal company politics at KamAZ. The problems seemed to multiply by the hour; there continuously seemed to be a mysterious hand pulling the strings from behind the scenes. Initially, I had been told there was a weekly direct Aeroflot flight from Chelny to St Petersburg so the timing of our trip was organised on this basis. Then it transpired that the flight didn't operate at this time of year so we looked at the logical alternative of going via Moscow. Flight timings however, meant either overnight stays in Moscow or a wasted day hanging around for connections to Chelny in each direction. We finally settled on going out on a charter flight, then travelling by overnight train to Moscow and returning on the KamAZ plane to Chelny as being the easiest and most practical solution.

Next came the surprisingly complicated issue of who would accompany me on this trip from KamAZ. Interest in this three day visit to St Petersburg seemed peculiarly high and it was obvious that it wasn't solely down to the attractions of the museums and shops there or an intense desire to spend a few days with me. As I was soon to discover, trips away from the office provided an important perk for the staff in the form of travel allowances and expenses paid in cash. If your salary is low and paid irregularly or substantially in arrears, the attractions of a cash advance are obvious; so competition was strong. It took a couple of days of difficult negotiations to finally find a compromise between my choices of effective personnel from the sales department and management's desire to send their 'friends', regardless of capability.

With agreement finally reached, four of us set off on the chartered Russian plane late in the afternoon. We reached St Petersburg late in the evening, after a re-fuelling stop in Nizhny Novgorod, caused by strong north-westerly winds that slowed our progress. It was my first time in this reputedly interesting historical city and I was excited by the prospect of seeing some of the sights. We were booked into the hotel Astoria, right in the centre, close to Nevsky Prospect – the main street in St Petersburg. The rooms were comfortable and well modernised and its grand imperial style reminded me of other similar hotels I had stayed at in Geneva or Paris. The city was originally mainly designed by Italian architects and is often called the Venice of the north but I think that's unfair to both cities, each of which has a quite different character. Once we had checked in, we went out for a late evening stroll along the canals under the northern stars. After the industrial bleakness of concrete Chelny, St Petersburg felt like a magical city, full of fine buildings and beautiful vistas – at least in the centre. A wonderful sight and I was much impressed. As we walked around, I remembered how many years before when I lived near Chicago in Illinois and I had flown south on cold February day to New Orleans for the first time. We had left behind sub-zero temperatures and snow and arrived on a balmy late afternoon with people out jogging, playing tennis in the parks or just strolling enjoying the sun's warmth. I thought then how can anyone live in the northern USA with its extremes of temperature when there are such pleasant alternatives in the southern part of the country. The answers were obvious of course – jobs, family ties etc. I now had the same thoughts here in St Petersburg; how could anyone live in towns like Chelny (and there are lots of them across Russia) when there is a stunning place like this. The answer is just the same as it was in the USA, except that in Russia jobs are even more difficult to find and housing restrictions make it extremely hard to move to St Petersburg or Moscow for those who would wish to relocate.

The two main reasons for coming here were to carry out a pilot market survey with the local KamAZ dealer and to attend a major automotive exhibition at which they were participating. After the exhibition, the dealer hosted an lavish reception at the city mayor's official residence – a modern building impressively set alongside one of the main canals –

where I was told Queen Elizabeth had stayed during her visit some years before. We enjoyed the champagne and the French style canapés that were served by smartly dressed waiters; a significant step up from what would have been provided in Chelny and another welcome reminder of the quality and style of life possible in St Petersburg. The following day, I was fortunate to have some time in the morning to do some sightseeing and the dealer organised a local professional guide to show me around. We toured St Isaac's cathedral with its magnificent roof top view across the city only matched by the view from the top of the eight storey former KGB building. From here, I was told, all those who entered could see Siberia, in the sense that they knew where they would end up. My guide said that the building was actually larger underground than the eight storeys on view above ground, similar to an iceberg, which seemed appropriate given its previous chilling function. The St Peter and Paul fortress was equally as chilling, with its prison where the Tsar's political enemies were held and usually executed. Touring the cell block with pictograms of the former inmates outside each cell, was very eerie as I was the only visitor at the time. Standing in the cell block corridor, my imagination raced in the silence and I was momentarily certain that a prison guard would appear round the corner with his keys clanking and boots stamping on the stone floor.

Mafia and Hitch-hiking

I asked my guide how the tourist business in St Petersburg was doing now that Russia was more open for overseas visitors. I was surprised to learn that in fact business was not as good as ten years ago; visitor numbers were down around 50%, largely due to the fall off in eastern European tourists, especially the cruise ships. Now that the iron curtain had been withdrawn, these countries had a much wider choice of holiday venues and were obviously taking advantage of the new opportunities elsewhere in the world. However, for me, it was heartening to see streets with a wide range of shops again after the very limited facilities in Chelny.

Perhaps not unsurprisingly, given its cultural leanings, the city benefitted from a good number of bookshops and on my last day, in a moment of ambitious conviction that I would do something to improve my Russian, I purchased a large Russian – English dictionary and an excellent technical phrase book. This momentary literary extravagance was wasted however, as later in the day I left my newly acquired books behind in a restaurant and didn't realise this until I was on the train to Moscow. I don't think my progress with Russian ever recovered from this unfortunate mishap – at least that's my excuse.

St. Petersburg was founded in 1703 by Peter the Great as a window onto the West and all its new ideas. The city was one of the first in the world to be built according to a preconceived plan that encompassed the full scope of its development. Although the central part of St Petersburg is filled with impressive buildings and interesting sights, for those that venture away from the established tourist routes, the city presents a quite different aspect. Constructed at great cost, both financial and human, the city became the new capital of Tsarist Russia in 1712 and remained so until after the Communist revolution. As the capital, it not only became the focus of the empire administratively, culturally and intellectually but it also developed as a major commercial and especially in the 19*th* and early 20*th* centuries, a manufacturing centre. Although the Communists moved their capital back to Moscow, St Petersburg's port and manufacturing skill base meant that it continued to develop as an industrial city throughout the 20*th* century. Small brick factories, warehouses and later heavy engineering works were built across the city, many quite close to the centre. This industrial legacy was not only in stark contrast to the imperial splendour of the Tsarist buildings but also sadly posed a serious pollution problem in the region. I didn't know how or if this situation was related to one of the other facts mentioned to me by my guide, that the city's death rate was higher than its birth rate.

One of the other unfortunate drawbacks to St Petersburg was the notorious presence of the mafia and other criminal elements here, despite (or maybe because of) the fact that this is the home town of President Putin. For most ordinary Russians, life continued without this having any apparent direct impact but the racketeering, gangland shootings and occasional murders of prominent figures all had an adverse impact on life in the city and its reputation. Indeed, the Astoria hotel in which I was staying turned out to be a popular haunt of the mafia and soon after my visit, I remember reading of an innocent foreign businessman being killed in a shoot-out in the coffee shop. 'Heavies' with none too well concealed guns under their black leather coats could still regularly be seen in public places. Peter the Great was a great reformer and he tried to introduce many new scientific ideas as well as much needed change to the system of government and administration. Then as now, corruption was endemic, especially among officials. Peter's idea was to introduce a law that those who stole enough to buy a rope should die by one. His procurator fiscal at the time advised Peter that if implemented, there would neither be any rope left nor any officials in Russia.

It was in St Petersburg that I was first introduced by my guide to the Russian practice of waving down passing cars when you needed to go somewhere. More practical than taxis, which were then relatively scarce in Russia and of course far cheaper too, this system worked very well across the city. Naturally, the imported luxury Mercedes and BMWs didn't stop but it was usually easy to find a co-operative Lada or Volga. Quite a few car owners were effectively operating an unofficial mini taxi service, eking out whatever other earnings they might have by driving around and picking up paying 'guests'. You simply tell the driver where it is you wish to go and if it's generally in a convenient direction, you agree a price and your car whisks you off to your destination. During the first couple of days, until I realised what was going on, as we regularly drove past people waving at our car, I foolishly thought they must be friends of our driver. Later on, when working in Russia for the British government, I was advised against this marvellous means of local transport because of security fears. But it was a convenient method of travelling short distances around the city and fortunately I never experienced any problems. Anyway the British embassy staff also seemed happy enough to do it regularly.

The Winter Palace

For our last night in the city, we were joined for dinner in the hotel by the two owners of the local KamAZ dealership. As this was to be partially a business meeting, I decided it would be better to wear a suit, especially as Russians are still reasonably formal at meetings such as this. I was not prepared however, for the fact that our hosts arrived in black ties and ordered gin and tonics as we reviewed the hotel menu. Whether this was some ill-informed idea of what I as a British man would wear or simply to impress me, I never fully understood, but they were charming and good company. They were both relatively young – mid thirties I guessed – and were former university lecturers who had set up as businessmen a couple of years ago, after perestroika. As I travelled more in Russia, I found that this type of career change was not uncommon, whereas it is quite rare in my experience, to find any Western academics setting up their own sizeable business. I was curious to know how they had raised the money to set up a dealership in a major city like St Petersburg but didn't really receive a satisfactory answer. As is so often the case in Russia, you don't push too hard on the subject of money and financial sources. Anyway, they had sound, progressive business ideas, appeared to be making money and clearly enjoyed the good life.

As the next day was a Saturday, I had reserved the morning for a visit to the world famous Hermitage museum, next to the Tsars' Winter Palace. After some frustrating confusion outside as to whether the museum was actually open that day and at what time, my guide finally got me inside. To say that the Hermitage is impressive is totally inadequate; with some 2.7 million artefacts in their collection, it is simply mind blowing. My guide pointed out that if you stood in front of each item in the museum for one minute and spent eight hours each day and seven days each week doing only this, you would need to pass two years, two months and two days to complete the viewing. I didn't have time to check the arithmetic but the point was well made. Of course in reality, not all the items are on display at once – there simply isn't room to house everything. But as I wandered through room after room full of Dutch, Italian, Spanish, English and French masters, it was impossible to take it all in, there just wasn't enough time. We ended our tour in a special exhibition of impressionist paintings; there were so many it was overwhelming. I envied the inhabitants of St Petersburg who could take their time and visit the museum on a regular basis. Since that first trip, I have been fortunate to be able to return many times to St Petersburg and each time I leave, I always look forward to the next time.

Night Train to Moscow

We journeyed on to Moscow by overnight sleeper train and although I had heard all sorts of horror stories about the risks of robbery on Russian trains, I was quite looking forward to it. It would be a new experience for me and would allow me to see a little more of the country – even at night – than was possible from the air. We duly pulled out of the station on time at 11.30 pm and with a seven hour journey time (there were lots of stops and Russian trains only average around 50mph), were due to arrive in Moscow around 6.30am. As we settled into our bunks for the night, I noticed one of my companions take off his trouser belt and wind it tightly round the compartment's sliding door handles. 'Just a safety precaution' he said. I didn't feel particularly at risk but pushed my wallet a little further under my pillow, just in case. As it happened, our journey proved trouble free, although as I couldn't sleep much, I spent most of the night staring through the window into the dark night, catching occasional glimpses of the flat, moonlit Russian countryside. Images of one of my favourite films, Doctor Zhivago came drowsily to mind as we clattered on our way.

Once into the bustling Moscow station and off the train, we made our way to a buffet since I was feeling hungry and needed a coffee and some food to revive me. Having bought my black coffee and a roll, I made my way to the only empty table and was about to sit down when I felt the chair being pulled out from under me. Another man had obviously also seen this chair and on the basis that whoever held the chair was going to sit on it, he yanked it away from me, dragging it across to another table, without so much as a word. The resultant gymnastics in my attempt to avoid falling onto my backside and spilling coffee all over myself caused much amusement on the part of my two colleagues as well as the rest of the buffet. After a day of meetings in Moscow, we reluctantly caught the KamAZ plane back to Chelny late that afternoon, arriving to a bracing temperature of 2C. Once in my hotel room, I found the heating system wasn't working again – welcome home! I reached the conclusion that this was a money saving idea by management. When there were only a couple of us in the hotel, they must have thought we wouldn't mind if the heating was turned off. After strong complaints in a mixture of Russian, English and international sign language, the hotel manager eventually produced a dusty old electric heater from a basement room, which was passed over to me with a look that said 'if you must have heating, then you can clean it yourself'. Dirty it may have been but it was reasonably effective at taking the chill from my room and I held onto it until the main heating system came on in November. There were a couple of other things in the hotel that I never got fully used to. The first was the small thin towels that were provided in our shower rooms, similar in texture to linen drying up cloths in the UK and not much bigger. They proved quite inadequate at drying off a normal sized human body. The second was the rough, non-absorbent lavatory paper we were given. However, this we were ultimately able to replace with better quality paper in our periodic shipments from Moscow.

The few days I had spent in St Petersburg and Moscow once again brought home to me how limited the facilities were in Chelny, especially the shops. For a city of its size, the quantity and quality of the shops in Chelny were very poor. There was no large central shopping or commercial district of the kind one would expect to find and certainly no large department store. Indeed, there didn't really seem to be a city centre as such at all. The city's retail, administrative and social amenities had all been widely spread around the central district by the original Soviet planners with a logic that escaped me. There were a few specialist retail shops providing things such as electrical goods or women's fashion clothing but you had to know where to look as they were often hidden away off the main streets in converted apartments. So although you could find most things eventually, it wasn't easy, even for the locals. With no advertising or a Yellow Pages directory, everything depended on personal knowledge and word of mouth. Shops and businesses usually displayed external signs that indicated what they offered – food produce, shoes, fruit, café etc. and on the bigger stores these would often be illuminated neon signs. However, it was rare to see a personalised store sign such as Marks and Spencer, Ivan's grocers or Natasha's café, even when it was a privately owned. There seemed to be a reluctance to use personal names in the way we do in the West. Maybe this anonymity was a remnant from Communist times or possibly simply an attempt to confuse the tax man.

A Satellite Telephone

We were finding that it could take up to six weeks for so called air mail letters to arrive in Chelny from the UK or USA. This meant that the postal service was ineffective for regular and timely communication with our families at home or Cummins' office in the UK. Although we could telephone from the InterClub, as already described it was often impossible to obtain a line and when we did, it often went dead after a short time. Overseas calls were very expensive and understandably, KamAZ asked us to limit our calls – an unnecessary request perhaps as the Russian telephone system automatically did this anyway. So, for most communication with Cummins in Moscow and London, we ended up using faxes. Although these were transmitted by the same unreliable telephone lines, at least we could leave them with the InterClub staff to be sent while we pursued other activities. These communication problems had been recognised by Cummins and eventually a shiny new satellite telephone was shipped down from Moscow. Part of the reason for the arrival of this expensive toy were the concerns about our safety and security while in Chelny and we were told that the satellite phone would give us an independent and portable means of communication in an emergency. I had momentary visions of escaping from Chelny in an old Lada car pursued by a bunch of screaming Muslim terrorists while frantically trying to raise someone on the satellite phone. I quickly pushed these thoughts to the back of my mind. By its very nature, the unit had to be located facing the area of sky where the satellite would appear on its twice daily journey overhead. Unfortunately, we couldn't receive a signal in our own office so the phone was placed in a spare small, lockable room across the hall; not terribly convenient but it was secure and provided limited privacy for the occasional confidential calls and faxes. Because it was hard to have any privacy in the busy arena of the InterClub, we tended to make our few calls home from our hotel. Calling overseas from the hotel in the evenings was marginally better but again it was very expensive, the line was often poor and there was usually a long wait to make a call.

I was constantly surprised by how much the InterClub people seem to know about where we had been or what we had been doing, both during the week and at weekends. Evidently, we were still being carefully watched. For us foreigners, Chelny was like a small village, everyone knew our movements and the lack of any privacy in our lives became a little annoying. However, it was pointless complaining. We spent a large proportion of our time in the InterClub and maintaining good relationships with them was vital for our daily routine. The staff were not only important to us but their activities (or lack of them) were a frequent cause of amusement, frustration or outright incomprehension. Though most of them were very friendly and many of them conscientious often working very long hours, there were far too many occurrences of poor organisation, misunderstandings and simple ineptitude. It was also obvious at times that personal rivalries and petty internal squabbles were the root cause of many of the day to day problems in the InterClub.

Local Entertainment

The staff at the InterClub did their best to try to organise some kind of social event for us most weekends in the early months – trips to the dachas, the occasional music or theatre concert etc. But as the weeks went there were less organised activities and we were increasingly left to our own devices. For a city with a population of some 600,000, there was relatively little for us, or indeed the locals to do. Since we worked late during the week, the evenings weren't really a problem. A bit of reading, the occasional video, a game of cards or just sitting talking over the day's events, were usually sufficient to fill the time. As the weather steadily deteriorated and our visits to the dachas ceased, we needed to find some other forms of entertainment. The local KamAZ sponsored football team played in the Russian first division and tickets were generally available for those who wanted to brave the winter cold. I did go once but the game was lacklustre. The crowd was smaller than I expected due I assume to the combination of the team's current lowly position in the league and the lack of spare cash for tickets. The Russian football season was actually split into two with a break between November and March to avoid the worst of the winter weather. Although the KamAZ team, like others in Russia, went off overseas to play the occasional friendly match, it must have been difficult to maintain fitness and focus during such a lengthy closed season. Some of the younger, more energetic members of our team joined the aerobic classes in a local gymnasium. I suspected that this sudden and unexpected desire to attend aerobics classes was actually due more to the presence of several attractive young Russian women than a genuine interest in personal fitness levels. However, it appeared that those who attended enjoyed it and as well as improved fitness, this activity led to an interesting expansion in their Russian vocabulary though sadly with little benefit. Phrases like 'hands up' or 'knees bend' only had limited use in our day to day work environment.

In October, our team expanded further with the arrival of a Scot called Mack. We had worked together before at a UK truck company, so we knew each other well. Mack was level-headed and easy to get along with and it was good to have a friend with me in Chelny. As we moved through the month, the weather became increasingly awful – rain and sleet showers most of the time. My Sunday walk from the hotel to the market had really become quite hazardous recently. There were no proper pavements and the footpaths that did exist were very muddy and treacherous underfoot so most pedestrians walked along the road, getting a drenching from the passing cars as they carelessly sped on through filthy pools of water. The pleasant stroll to the market in warm sunny weather seemed more than just a few weeks ago. Now that I was unable to go for long walks to the river, I tended to explore different sections of the city close to the hotel or InterClub. I found a museum and local art gallery that I visited a couple of times and which, like many public places in Chelny, always had paintings by local Tatar artists on display for sale. Most of the pictures were very modern in style, crudely painted with gaudy colours and not at all to my taste. There was only one painting that I did like, a large rural scene with at its centre a run-down wooden dacha, almost American old west in style but when I asked, I was told it was not for sale. I encountered the same problem at the InterClub where there were always dozens of mostly rather amateurish pictures on show. The only one I (or any of our team) really wanted was a striking, ethereal, semi-nude portrait of a girl with sad, staring eyes. It was hung on the landing of the main staircase on the way up to our offices on the first floor so I saw it every day. But again, it was not for sale and no-one could say why. I did take a photograph of it on my last day in Chelny however, just as a reminder of those Russian eyes. Unfortunately, when I had the film developed back in the UK, I found that the camera flash had reflected too much in the glass framing the painting and so even my attempt to capture the mysterious girl's image in a photograph proved a failure.

I had also recently discovered a rather basic exercise room in the hotel basement which I now started to use a couple of times a week. The equipment, although relatively new, was limited and had been severely mistreated, leaving it in a poor state that was never rectified during my stay. However, the room did offer table tennis facilities. The table was in reasonable shape and a few battered bats and balls were available on request from reception. It was rarely used, none of the other consultants or periodic hotel guests seemed to play but occasionally I would find a couple of local youngsters down there having a game – presumably friends or family of one of the hotel employees – and I used to join them for a while. Conversation was limited but they clearly enjoyed the challenge of trying to beat a foreigner. Being in the basement without windows or air conditioning, the room did tend to suffer from a very sweaty odour, especially when in use and a couple of games were normally about as much as I could stand in there. The lingering smell of perspiration may have explained why it was rarely used by hotel guests.

Chapter Six

Market Surveys

Following my pilot market survey in St Petersburg a couple of weeks ago, it was agreed with KamAZ that we would test the methodology in a couple of nearby cities and if everything went well, to then expand this into a broader nationwide study. So this week I organised a visit to Kazan for a couple of days while my colleagues Roy and Mack travelled to Izhevsk, both groups accompanied by KamAZ marketing department personnel. Despite the worsening weather, both teams were to do the four hour journeys by car. My team duly arrived in a Volga at our hotel on time so we packed in all our gear and sat to wait for the other car to show up. After half an hour, tired of waiting, we were about to set off when Roy's car finally stuttered into the hotel car park. As it pulled up to the entrance the engine coughed and died. It was an old Lada – a bit tight for five people on this length of trip – and it didn't look as if it would make it out of Chelny, never mind all the way to Izhevsk. Worse, was the fact that the driver now explained why the engine had stopped. There was no petrol in the car when he collected it and he didn't have money to buy any. After some discussion (including a few rude remarks about the driver's mental capacity), we agreed to advance the cash to finance the petrol and he rushed off in the Volga with a large can to buy some. He returned soon after, mission accomplished and filled up Roy's car, only to find it still wouldn't start. We were now running seriously behind schedule so I insisted my group set off, anxious to reach Kazan before nightfall. As we pulled away, my parting image of Roy, Mack and team was of them trying to push start their uncooperative Lada in front of the hotel in the sleety rain. They had even more fun to come however, and we will catch up with the adventures of Roy's team later.

Our journey from Chelny to Kazan proved trouble-free; mostly along straight roads that took us through relatively flat countryside with little of any interest to see. We stopped half way at what was the closest provincial Tatarstan offered to a motorway service station; that is no motorway and little service. It was really not much more than a busy roadside halt with a couple of open air stalls selling refreshments, including dried fish. Many of the stallholders were clearly of southern origin with dark tanned skins and the men sporting large black moustaches. Standing there all day in temperatures hovering around zero was a hard way to earn money. I eventually found a stall offering hot drinks; by that I mean I was given a sachet of instant coffee pre-mixed with sugar, a dubious looking mug and hot water was added from a pan boiling on a wood-fired stove – at least it was warming and very cheap. I noticed that the sachet of coffee was packed in Singapore. What intricate trading deals brought coffee from South America or Africa via Singapore to the road side in Tatarstan? A possible visit to the toilet block was quickly over-ridden when I was shown the facilities, or lack of them. My Russian colleagues suggested that the woods behind the stalls would probably be a better alternative and this proved to be the generally preferred solution. Although this was clearly a popular and busy stopping place on the road to Kazan, there were no petrol pumps. Instead fuel was being supplied by a rusty old tanker towed behind a KamAZ truck that was parked up at one end of the roadside halt. I had already noticed the surprising absence of petrol stations in Chelny, despite the large number of vehicles in the city. In the immediate aftermath of perestroika, it seems that fuel supplies destined for the relatively few state owned petrol stations were frequently 'diverted' elsewhere and this system of roadside tankers had grown up to meet demand. I never got to the bottom of who owned these tankers and the source of their fuel but as it involved large amounts of ready cash, it seemed logical to conclude that the Russian mafia were behind it somewhere along the line.

The long drive to Kazan gave me a chance to chat to the Russians and find out more about their country and how they viewed life. One of them was of Ukrainian origin and I asked what brought his parents to Chelny. His answer was surprisingly simple – they had come in the 1970s when Chelny (or Brezhnev City as it was then known) was a new boom town with plenty of well paid jobs on offer. At that time it was populated mostly by young people and there were no long queues for buses or at the shops he said. While talking of shopping, he told me the story of the man who walked into a butcher's shop during the hard times immediately after perestroika when there was little food available.

'Do you do sliced sausage?' the man asked, to which the butcher replied 'Yes, of course, bring as many of your own as you like and we'll slice them for you!'

Another similar story was the tale of the old lady walking down the street with an empty shopping bag in each hand. She bumped into one of her old friends and after a long chat, she hesitated, not sure which way to go. Her friend asked if she was alright and the old lady said 'Well, yes but I can't remember if I'm on my way to the shops or if I've already been.'

We entered Kazan accompanied by light snow flurries and this early winter snow was clearly giving the traffic some problems as we saw several cars skid and passed by what looked to be a very serious accident. We had been booked into a small, privately owned hotel on the outskirts of the city, which we were told had good food and service plus satellite television – all proved to be correct. Only recently opened, the hotel's interior décor was a little strange to my eyes, very much in the local Tatar style. It's hard to describe but it was something I was starting to recognise as I spent more time in the region. Brown, black and beige were the dominant colours for furnishings with occasional brighter shades of purple or green, a lot of moquette fabrics and simulated leather with thick, nylon carpets in gaudy patterns plus the ubiquitous, ultra modern paintings on the walls.

The peculiarities of Tatar interior design were also evident the following day when we were taken to the restaurant at the Kazan racecourse for lunch. Externally, it was like most horse racing circuits the world over with a large grass oval track and several brick buildings. But inside the restaurant, the atmosphere and decor seemed more like a 1950s brothel (or so I was told), with red velvet and white lace everywhere. There was no racing that day and the only other restaurant clients were a few prosperous looking businessmen relaxing on red leather bench seats in separate dining booths. Young blondes in tight miniskirts, low cut tops and high heels constantly click-clacked in and out of these booths across the restaurant's wooden floor. The place oozed, no, it pulsated with sex. I found it hard to concentrate on any conversation and for once, had absolutely no recollection of what the food was like.

Kazan, capital of the Tatar people is an old city, strategically located at the northern end of the Volga and straddling trade routes to the east and south. It has a kremlin, many old buildings, some of which are gradually being restored, a pedestrianised main street with shops, popular weekly horse races in summer and an airport with international connections. It's also where Stalin's son is buried (I never discovered why here and not in Stalin's home country, Georgia) and there are strong links with Ivan the Terrible, who had three wives and sacked the city – though whether the two deeds are linked was not stated in the guide book. As we wandered around the streets in the centre we came across a bookshop, something that didn't exist in Chelny and I went in to browse. As I looked around, I noticed on display a packet of unmounted A4 sized prints of views of Kazan and on inspecting them I saw that they had been done by an Edward Turnerelli. I asked the bookshop owner if he knew anything about the artist and he explained that Turnerelli was an Englishman who had created these fine pen and ink sketches during a visit to the city in the 1830s. Of course these were only modern reprints but I purchased a set as a souvenir of my own visit to Kazan. At the time I knew nothing more about Turnerelli but later discovered that he had lived in Russia for almost twenty years, travelling extensively under the patronage of the Tsar. He eventually returned to England, where he published several books about Russia and died in 1896 in my own home town of Leamington Spa.

We had a brief look at the outside of the kremlin which is actually a large complex of many buildings and dates from the time of Ivan the Terrible in the mid 16*th* century. Unfortunately, entry into the inside of the kremlin was restricted due to President Shaimiev being in residence in his palace there. So we ambled on up the hill, eventually trying to visit an interesting-looking old Orthodox church but as we walked towards the entrance, a priest in a long black cassock with unkempt hair and shaggy beard came out and barred our way. He said quite vehemently that as our interpreter was wearing make-up and no headscarf, she could not take us inside and he waved us away with his arm. With his dishevelled look, I found it hard to take the priest seriously, since he looked to me as if he had just wandered over from the film set of Monty Python's 'The Life of Brian'. I had never experienced this problem in Moscow or St Petersburg and our interpreter was quite surprised at the priest's decision but at this rebuff, we decided not to visit the church without her in a protest of solidarity.

A Near Miss

With our survey work completed, the four hour night drive back to Chelny was broken only by a close dice with death. Russian roads at night are notoriously dangerous and to be avoided if possible; a good driver is essential and we were fortunate. A few miles out from Chelny, the driver suddenly lurched the car hard over into the middle of the road and there looming just in front of us was a large truck carrying a huge wide load with no rear or marker lights. We skidded a bit on the snowy tarmac but the driver managed to hold his course, weaving round the truck and pulling back onto our side of the road. As we passed the truck we could also see that it had only one headlight. Back safely in our hotel, I found Roy and Mack in the bar and asked how their visit had gone. The look on Roy's told me immediately that he was not a happy man and things had evidently not passed off as planned. Roy didn't want to talk about it but Mack quickly filled me in. They did eventually make it to Izhevsk in the Lada, though they also hit snow and at one point had to push the car through some drifts. We had heard before leaving that KamAZ were experiencing difficulties in booking a hotel but we were assured the one finally selected was a pleasant 'pension' style place in which they would be very comfortable. It turned out to be a sanatorium, still being used for its intended purpose but which also took in paying guests to generate extra cash to help pay the wages and running costs. Their bedrooms were very poorly furnished and came with bars over the windows – at least they would have been safe I thought quietly to myself. The overall scene was set off by the inmates wandering freely around the place, some dressed in normal clothes, others in white tunics.

Given the weather conditions, it was impracticable to go out for dinner so they decided to try their luck in the 'hotel' restaurant. Word had obviously spread that two westerners were around because the waitress appeared made up to the eyeballs, dressed in a figure hugging, cleavage revealing red dress and spent the whole evening ogling Roy and Mack.

'If she had been the right side of forty' said Mack, referring to her age not bust size, 'she might have stood some chance but she was definitely over the top in all respects'.

The food produced was adequate if not plentiful and when offered the chance of a yoghurt at the end of the meal by the busty, red waitress, Roy and the Russians accepted – after all it had been a long, hard day and they were still hungry. The yoghurts were duly produced and as they started eating, their Russian translator asked the waitress if they were locally produced. Roy was well into his extra dessert as the translator, who had now stopped eating, explained:

'The waitress says these are special yoghurts that they give to the patients each night to help them sleep – they're laced with a sedative'.

This was too much for Roy, who spat out the remnants of his sedated treat and firmly announced that he would definitely not be staying a second night in this place. They duly cancelled the second day's meetings and drove back to Chelny the following afternoon. I was tempted to speculate with Mack whether the waitress had some clandestine night time objective in providing them with these specially treated yoghurts but we will never know the answer.

It was a pity that Roy had such a bad experience on this trip, as sadly he was due to return to the USA a couple of days later, having completed his assignment. We held a send-off party for him in the hotel that was well attended by many of our Russian colleagues who, amidst much vodka and long toasts, were also highly amused to hear the details of the Izhevsk market survey. We saw Roy off from the hotel early the next morning to catch the KamAZ shuttle flight to Moscow. With his luck, I half expected him to return later in the day due to the flight having been cancelled or some similar story but he made it out OK. He was a hard working, conscientious fellow with whom I enjoyed collaborating and who had stoically endured more than his fair share of problems. I would miss him.

Colder and Colder

Snow showers again today and for the first time since I arrived, the ground was completely covered and I was told we won't see the earth again until the thaw in April. Six months of winter – what a depressing thought. Interestingly, there were still flowers for sale in the market, obviously imported, but fresh fruit and vegetables were becoming increasingly scarce. Supplies of the ubiquitous banana still got through to Chelny but the quality was often poor with many of them bruised and blackened. I did find today however, some fresh dates that I hadn't seen in the market before – they were excellent. The price of flowers, roses say at £2 each, was more than one would pay in an English market but for the locals this was really expensive, given the difference in earnings. Despite the high prices, the Russians, both men and women, seemed to place great importance on flowers and they are more like the continental Europeans in this respect. Few occasions would pass by without the expectation and giving of flowers whatever the season, though always in odd numbers. An even numbered bunch of flowers was considered bad luck in Russia and is usually only given at funerals. Despite the poor weather, I was surprised to see how packed the market was this weekend. The crush was so great around the main gates that it was almost impossible to enter or leave. I commented on this fact later in the day over a beer in the hotel with a couple of my Deloitte colleagues. They told me that on Saturday KamAZ had made a big payment of some of the back wages, which explained why so many people had been out shopping.

On November 15th the overnight temperature dropped to a low of minus 17C, our coldest yet. The good news however, was that I received two compliments today on the improvement in my Russian – maybe there's hope for me yet. Now where did I put my Russian dictionary? Given the falling temperature, some of my colleagues had been out buying that most essential piece of Russian winter equipment – a fur hat and I too have been looking in the shops for one. The choice was enormous, all sorts of furs, colours and styles to choose from but try as I might, I couldn't find one with which I felt comfortable. Although everyone wore them, each time I tried one on, I somehow felt awkward and ostentatious with it perched on top of my head, especially in my banana duvet coat and I finally decided to stay with the black furry cap I had bought in the UK on my last visit. A few days later, a new consultant called Clive arrived from the UK to join our team with a brief to concentrate on various manufacturing issues. In his late 50s, he had worked overseas before and quickly adjusted to our Chelny routine, although we were now running out of desk space in our office as well as coffee cups.

Stavropol Visit

Despite the problems encountered with our earlier market study work in St Petersburg, Kazan and Izhevsk, by mid November we had agreed with KamAZ to carry out a more extensive assessment with three teams each visiting different locations. After detailed discussions, Voronesh near Moscow, Samara in the centre plus Stavropol and Volgograd in the south were selected as our next challenges. Mack would go to Voronesh, Clive to Samara and I was down for Stavropol and Volgograd, each of us accompanied by a KamAZ translator and marketing specialist. With somewhat more meticulous pre-planning, we hoped this time that everything would go smoothly, though there was no guaranteeing the Russian winter weather. We set out from Chelny, once again using a chartered jet and after dropping off the Samara group, we set off for Stavropol, my own destination, arriving some six hours later in the early evening. We were met at the airport by Grigori, a manager from the local KamAZ dealer and taken to our hotels. He was to prove a genial and conscientious host but events during our visit were to prove a challenge for him. He explained that my two Russian KamAZ companions were booked into a separate hotel and we would drive there first. I wasn't happy about our group being split up and asked Grigori if we could all stay in the same hotel but was told this was not possible as his instructions were that junior KamAZ staff had to stay in a cheaper hotel. I thought this was unfair but once I had seen their rooms, which were of an appallingly low standard and dirty, I was also deeply embarrassed. However, the rooms had already been paid for and there was nothing I could now do about it. I was then driven to my hotel, a large Intourist establishment in the centre of town that, like some of the staff, had seen much better days. The welcome at Intourist hotel receptions was always the same – totally absent. In all my years of travelling in provincial Russia I rarely encountered a cheery smile or any kind of greeting on checking in. As with many of the shops, the concept of customer service had yet to penetrate these former Soviet strongholds of take it or leave it attitudes. Despite my confirmed reservation, this receptionist initially claimed the hotel was full – she had obviously been a prize winner at the hotel's anti-charm training school. After my host intervened, a vacant room was reluctantly found for me and I filled in the necessary forms and handed over my passport. Whilst doing this, I noticed something scuttle across the reception counter – a large cockroach. The receptionist didn't bat an eyelid; her attitude towards the cockroach was much the same as that shown to customers – she simply ignored it. She was clearly made of sterner stuff than me for when she showed me to my room on the first floor and turned on the light, several cockroaches could be seen sliding down the walls to shadier quarters. I started to complain about the presence of these unwanted squatters in my room but she then proudly pointed out a sign at the bedside that proclaimed the room had recently been disinfected. Therefore, it must be obvious, even to a stupid foreigner, that there could be no cockroaches and I was back to the take it or leave position. With no real choice and against my better judgement, I took it.

Our first day in Stavropol was largely spent in discussions with the dealer personnel. Over lunch in a local cafe, we were given a verbal introduction to Stavropol by our host Grigori. The town had a population of 350,000 and Mikhail Gorbachev was born in the area and headed the regional government for several years. The name Stavropol has a Greek ring to it and is one of a string of towns in the south of the old Tsarist Russian Empire that were given such grandiose names; others include Mariupol and Melitopol, now in neighbouring Ukraine. Stavropol is located at the northern end of the Caucasus mountains and I was told that it was the greenest, cleanest city in the whole of Russia (not the last time that I was to hear this kind of sales pitch for a Russian city). I was not surprised that the problems with cockroaches didn't receive a mention in this little speech. Grigori continued telling us the city had lots of parks and tree-lined avenues, with little heavy industry, sat on a hill so benefiting from purer air and it never snowed in Stavropol. So I was more than a little surprised to wake up the following morning to see the sky completely filled with big white flakes drifting thickly across the city centre. Despite the snow, which continued for much of the day, we carried on with our visits, slithering around the streets with the rest of the traffic that was obviously as surprised at this unexpected weather as we were. Of course, being without my heavy-duty snow boots, I was more unprepared than the locals and had to be supported by each arm like a drunk on several occasions to avoid slipping on some of the hillier streets.

The second day was spent visiting various industrial companies in the Stavropol area and in the morning, Grigori took us to visit a factory that made a wide range of trailers for KamAZ and other companies. This particular visit sticks out in my mind as being probably the most depressing factory visit I made in Russia. A long, two storey block of half empty offices fronted a sprawling complex of manufacturing and assembly workshops that were probably constructed some twenty years earlier. Inside, both the offices and the workshops were in a dreadful condition. Walls and roofs with holes open to the sky let in the snow which gathered slowly melting in pools on the floors. A few old posters and company messages pinned to occasional notice boards flapped wearily in the cold wind blowing through the buildings. Dreary, unlit corridors and dark stairwells made the place feel worse than a prison. A lot of the equipment was in a poor state of repair or simply not working with rubbish and manufacturing waste accumulating in random heaps around the machinery and storage racks. Understandably, the labour force seemed dispirited and dejected – no-one talked to us or showed any interest as we walked round. They looked a sorry lot, shuffling around in their thick coats and hats trying to keep warm. After the depressing tour, I met with the general director in his large, unheated office. As we talked about the business and general economic situation I found him to be a buffoon, totally out of his depth and felt sorry for the workers who largely depended on this man for their future. He explained to me that sales had been steadily declining for several years and this year were running at around 20% of 'normal'. But this was just temporary and he was sure they would soon be back to previous levels. I tried to discuss with him the fact that the Russian truck market was down at least 50% and unlikely to significantly recover for some years but this was brushed aside. There was no need to restructure the business or look for alternative products he told me. Demand for their trailers would soon be back to normal. I asked how the company was surviving financially in this situation but initially received little more than a blank look. After a long pause, he then said that for the moment most of their business was on a barter basis but he was waiting for a large order from KamAZ that had been pending for the last twelve months. We both knew that barter sales didn't generate any money for wages or factory maintenance and repairs so it was not a sustainable position. I also knew there was no prospect of KamAZ placing any large orders but the director's failure to understand or admit this was blinding him to the reality of the market situation facing his company. By now, I think Grigori sensed my frustration with this pointless meeting and after glancing at his watch he stood and said I think it's time we moved on to our next appointment. As we got back into our Volga and headed out of the snow covered car park, I was glad to leave this sad place behind.

During my time in Russia, I never ceased to be amazed at the working conditions in winter; at times they seemed quite Dickensian, especially in the many older buildings. It was common practice in Russia for heating systems not to be turned on until late October or November, as was the case in Stavropol. In the offices, staff would sit in the cold rooms wearing their overcoats and sometimes, even hats; I often found it difficult to conduct my meetings in these shivering conditions. Any offer of a warming cup of tea was always immediately and gratefully accepted. In the factories and workshops, although some bodily warmth could be generated through physical activity, the day to day working conditions were usually even worse. Leaking roofs would let rain and snow into the building, puddles of water were everywhere and open doors or broken windows meant the inside temperature was not much different to that outside. Men and women continued to work daily in these awful circumstances whereas in the West there would have been an immediate strike or riot. No wonder the Russians beat back the Napoleonic and Nazi invasions – they are a very hardy race.

After a couple more visits in the afternoon, we ended up in the offices (again unheated) of a small transport company. We had some useful discussions with the owners and at the conclusion of our meeting, as is often the case in Russia, they offered us a glass of vodka. Not wishing to seem impolite and thinking it would help to warm me up, I foolishly accepted this hospitable gesture. I say foolishly because this was to result in two problems, one immediately apparent, the other not arising until later. Having said yes to the drink, one of the owners stood up with a grin, walked across to a large cupboard, which he opened and revealed a cabinet full of vodka bottles of every shape and flavour imaginable. It was immediately obvious we would not be able to take our leave with just one quick drink – the full cabinet and anticipatory look on our host's face made this fact clear enough. So as thoughts of my hotel room and dinner started to fade, we settled down for a Russian drinking session, full of toasts, always good humoured but not what I really wanted to be doing at that time. Although I was pacing myself, my need to visit the lavatory became increasingly urgent and seeing no prospect of an early departure, I ventured to ask where the lavatories were located. My second problem now started to loom into view; the lavatories were in the workshops across the large, dimly lit yard.

'You'll find them easily enough, just on the left inside the workshop but mind how you go as the lights don't work' said one of my hosts.

I put on my heavy winter coat, walked out of the offices and set off across the yard, the early evening moonlight fortunately helping me avoid the worst of the snow drifts and debris lying in my path. However, after the vodka the cold night air was welcome and refreshing. I entered the workshop groping my way towards a door on the left on which I could just make out the Russian word for toilet. Those who have experienced a Russian factory toilet will have some idea of what lay in wait for me in the dark. For those that haven't had the pleasure, I'm sorry but I don't intend to go into too much detail. Sufficient to say that as I opened the door and stepped in, not only was the smell overwhelming but I also discovered that the floor was ankle deep in liquid. No doubt due to the vodka, my reactions were slower than I would have liked; as my boots connected with the floor, I realised that my feet were getting wet, probably with something very unpleasant. I immediately decided that I couldn't really face using this lavatory and beat a rapid, squelching retreat out of the workshop back across the open yard. Still desperate to relieve myself, I found an unlit corner, unzipped my coat and quickly urinated onto a pile of snow. I then trudged back to the offices, where in the light from the windows, I leant against the wall and undid my boots, emptying out the foul liquid they contained. I reluctantly put my boots back on, wiped my hands as best as I could on a paper tissue from my pocket and re-entered the offices. No one said anything as I quietly resumed my seat, hoping that any residual odour from my recent excursion was not too noticeable. Fortunately, the party came to an end soon after my return and I was able to escape back to my hotel for a much-needed shower and change of clothes. I rinsed out my boots and socks in the bath and sealed them up in a plastic bag to await my return to Chelny where I could hopefully clean them properly. For the rest of the trip I was obliged to wear a pair of casual leather shoes that I had with me.

I woke up on my last morning to even heavier snow than yesterday with a driving wind but the old streets of the city looked very picturesque in the deep drifts. I also noticed there were very few cars about but as it was early Saturday morning that didn't worry me too much. Our car duly arrived on time and we set out for the airport to catch our charter flight to Volgograd, scheduled to depart at 10.00am. Despite some difficulties with drifts on the roads out of the city, we made it safely to the airport only to find more than the usual chaos. The place where the sun always shines and it never snows was well, snowbound and cut off; the airport was closed and we were told there were no trains out either. There was talk that the snowstorm was now passing through and flights would resume later in the day so we decided to wait at the airport and see what happened. Most Russian airports are ill equipped to handle their passengers normally; long lines at check in, limited shopping or catering facilities, few seats etc. When things go wrong, they are definitely not the kind of places in which to spend time. Together with my three Russian companions, I made for the small but now extremely busy cafeteria and joined the rapidly lengthening queue for refreshments. We bought some drinks but with nowhere to sit, we perched in a corner until after an hour or so, a table became free. We wearily dumped our bags and gratefully sat down, carefully placing our meagre snacks amongst the pile of detritus assembled on the table. The time passed slowly; several rounds of coffee, packets of biscuits, nuts and juice kept us going while we exchanged the parts of our respective life histories that as yet we had not already told. At 4 o clock, a squeaky voice finally announced over the intercom that there would be no flights that day and the airport would close with immediate effect. We reviewed our limited options. We could stay another night in Stavropol, hoping the weather would clear and allow us to fly out the next morning, although the airport staff were not optimistic. We had been told that the town of Mineralnye Vody, about 90 miles to the south east, had not been affected by as much snow and their airport was open. My Russian companions said it should be possible to hire a taxi to take us there but I think they were motivated more by the dread of another night in their disgusting hotel. With nightfall approaching, I was unhappy about risking such a journey on snow covered roads. Besides, I had heard bad things about Mineralnye Vody and its airport which was reputed to be one of the worst for safety in Russia – an accolade that is actually not that easy to win. In the end, we took the safe option, dismally retracing our path through the snow back to the city and after yet further battles with our respective hotel receptions, checked in for another night. We joined up for dinner and had an awful meal in the deserted hotel restaurant, to the accompaniment of live music from an extremely loud band and I eventually retired to my room only to be greeted by my other group of Stavropol companions, those ubiquitous cockroaches.

On to Volgograd

The snow cleared sufficiently overnight to allow the airport to reopen the next day and we finally made it out of Stavropol, arriving in an icily cold but largely snow free Volgograd by mid afternoon. As our charter plane banked and turned on its final approach to the airport, I could see the whole city spread out below, embracing the banks of the mighty Volga that stretched to the horizon. Both the river and the city's buildings seemed to exist solely in varying shades of grey as if painted by an artist with only a single colour on his palette. It looked uninviting and our initial experience on the ground was soon to justify the airborne impression. Yet another large, cheerless Intourist city centre hotel awaited us but at least we were all in the same place, which would make communication easier. On arrival we found that the hotel reception was temporarily closed, a small handwritten sign explaining this was for a 'staff change over'. We duly sat down to wait and as the minutes ticked by our small group was steadily enlarged by another half dozen luckless travellers who added to the growing pile of luggage in the entrance lobby. It was almost twenty minutes before a young woman finally arrived and removed the handwritten sign, signifying reception had reopened. Any apologies from the hotel staff for the enforced wait were of course neither given nor indeed expected.

Volgograd is a large city with a couple of million inhabitants stretching along the river Volga with a long history as a river port and trading centre. It is perhaps best known by its former Soviet name of Stalingrad and the infamous battle for the city during the Second World War or the Great Patriotic Struggle as the Russians call it. To read about this epic siege leaves one stunned by the ferocity, heroism, squalor, desperation, suffering and dogged determination shown by both sides. It was perhaps the bloodiest battle in history with over a million men engaged on each side. One of the Russian sayings is 'even a single soldier in battle still counts' and this philosophy was never better illustrated than in the struggle for Stalingrad. The Soviets drew on their last reserves, throwing wave after wave of men across the river at the Germans. Many of the Russian soldiers were untrained or unarmed, simply picking up the weapons of their fallen comrades. The fighting was bitter and intense, often at very close quarters. Stalingrad was effectively flattened in the war and apparently the advice at the time from Moscow was that it would be too difficult to rebuild the city and therefore easier and cheaper to start again further along the river. But the city leaders felt differently, having survived the siege and then won a major victory at the cost of thousands of lives, they also had the determination to want to rebuild rather than relocate. The fact that they had tens of thousands of German prisoners to do the manual work would make the task easier and so after considerable argument with Moscow, they finally won a second victory.

Later the next day, I went to see the large Mamayev Kurgan memorial to the epic wartime struggle located on a hill overlooking the city, which was one of the most bitterly fought over parts of the whole battleground. The memorial site is undoubtedly impressive, built in typical Soviet massive monument style, with an immense concrete statue on the summit vaguely resembling the statue of liberty in New York I thought. When completed in 1967, the Soviets claimed it was the largest free standing structure in the world at some 82 metres tall. The thousands of Germans and other nationalities that lost their lives predictably don't receive much of a mention, rather like the British and Russian forces at the battle of Waterloo memorial in Belgium. From Kurgan hill I looked out over the wide grey river and the buildings on the west bank where the Germans had finally been encircled and cut off by the Russians, surrendering on January 31st 1943. As we climbed the long flight of steps to the memorial's summit, there were very few other visitors on that icy winter's day and the enveloping silence made the place feel especially sombre. I shivered, not from the cold but from the thought of the bitter hand to hand fighting that took place there and the sad loss of so many young lives. As we returned to our car, Misha our guide explained that both his parents had died in the struggle for the city and as a baby, he was taken in by his grandmother. Sadly, although she survived the war, she died when Misha was six and he was then brought up by his aunt and uncle. He told me how hard life was for the remaining Stalingraders in the first few years after the war with a ruined economy, food shortages and much of the city's housing flattened. However, he felt the struggle to rebuild the city was a good decision, at least for today's Russians and proudly told me a two bedroom apartment in one of the better refurbished buildings by the river would currently sell for over $100,000.

Breakfast in our hotel on the first morning was very poor. The vast, almost empty, unheated dining room had neither fruit juice nor eggs (both very unusual in Russia), only black bread and insipid coffee. So for our evening meal I suggested that we tried the city. It was too cold to walk around trying to find somewhere reasonable but while we were driving to a meeting earlier in the day I had noticed an advertisement for a Chinese restaurant not far from the hotel. As my Russian colleagues had never eaten a Chinese meal, I thought it would be fun to take them there. Despite the relatively strong links between Russia and China, it is rare to find their cuisine anywhere, even in Moscow. We eventually located the restaurant, the Chinese Dragon and once inside, found that we were the only diners, which was surprising for a city centre restaurant even on a cold night. We were offered a choice of menus, with either conventional Russian or Chinese food and chose the latter. My Russian colleagues tried to decipher into some sort of comprehensible English for me the Chinese dishes described in Russian on the menu, which was extremely difficult, as they didn't know what they were – how do you translate egg foo yong or chicken chow mien if you've never had it before? Whilst they were doing this I was at least able to read the prices in roubles and was astounded at the cost – there was nothing under $10, not even the soup, which for a Russian provincial restaurant in 1995 was extortionate. But like the stubborn Stalingraders, I was determined to at least try something Chinese and having eventually selected three modest dishes we called over the waitress. We started to indicate our choices but as each one was mentioned there was a slow shaking of the head by the Chinese waitress – they were off tonight. We doggedly tried a couple more and met with the same negative response. In desperation, we asked what Chinese dishes would be available – 'none' was the short reply. The waitress then explained that they had great difficulty in regularly obtaining any Chinese ingredients and since most of their customers preferred Russian cooking anyway, that's all they did. The Chinese menus were really only for show. Why the waitress hadn't explained this when we had first arrived is beyond my comprehension – I was left dumbfounded and disappointed though I suspect that my two colleagues were not that upset and probably welcomed the prospect of Russian food that we were then forced to order. When it arrived however, they were not so happy because it was pretty dire eating – no wonder the restaurant was empty. These Chinese didn't know how to cook Russian dishes and the locals evidently knew it. The lack of diversity and almost constant poor quality of food on offer in provincial Russian restaurants was one of the enduring disappointments of my time in the country.

We literally fared much better the next night, having done some homework and asked the locals where to find a good restaurant. We found Juliana's, a small privately run place in the ferry terminal and enjoyed one of the best meals I've had in Russia outside Moscow or St Petersburg and with a friendly welcome, professional service and reasonable prices. It was so good that we actually went back there the following day for lunch. In the morning we visited the local KamAZ dealership, housed in a dilapidated concrete building and met the director who was quite short with us and didn't seem to have a good word to say about anything. I never failed to be amazed at meetings with some of the old style Russian (Soviet) managers and today's visit proved to be no exception. Despite arriving on time for our meeting, we were left waiting in the cold entrance area for over half an hour. We were finally ushered up to the director's first floor office, a large untidy room with old net curtains just managing to cling to their plastic rails around the windows. After brief introductions over cups of steaming hot tea that his secretary had brought in, the meeting began. However, it proved difficult to make any progress as the director's hectoring, almost shouting style of talking, so typical of this generation of Russian managers, made it impossible to have a quiet, rational discussion. Each time I asked what I regarded as a quite straightforward question about the economic and business situation in the city, I received a five minute lecture that frequently totally failed to address the original point raised, leaving me wondering if my translator had somehow screwed up the words. But as this wasn't the first or last time this occurred, I knew the fault didn't lie with my translator – indeed she would sometimes look across at me with an expression on her face that said 'I know this doesn't make any sense but it really is what he said'. At the end of our meeting however, it was all smiles and friendly small talk, so there was no animosity, only a lack of understanding. Perhaps if you were a Russian of the same age and on the same wave length, it would have made perfect sense but I somehow doubt it.

Late that afternoon, as we were on our way back to the hotel from our final meeting, our driver suddenly pulled up outside a factory near the city centre. It was going home time and a steady stream of workers, mostly women, were pouring out through the factory gate. In response to the evidently puzzled look on my face, my translator said 'This is a well known chocolate factory – their chocolate is very good. We're just going in to the factory shop to buy some to take back to Chelny' and with that explanation, my two Russian colleagues jumped out of the car and disappeared through the factory gate. They returned a few minutes later, each clutching small paper bags containing several chocolate bars and with big smiles on their faces. Once back in the car, they offered me a couple of pieces of their prized chocolate. It didn't seem anything special to me but then I'm not a chocolate connoisseur. For them however, this little side trip had been carefully planned and was clearly the highlight of their visit. We said goodbye to Volgograd the next morning, the first day of December and left in a biting cold wind and snow flurries with the temperature at minus 14 degrees. The taxi we had ordered to take the three of us to the airport arrived for some strange reason with a boot full of spare tyres; what he thought we would do with our suitcases is a mystery. The three of us had to squeeze inside the car with all our luggage stacked on top of us – the driver did not receive a tip. I was not unhappy to leave Volgograd, it seemed somehow a sad, dreary place, feelings no doubt emphasised by the raw winter weather. Unemployment was high, much of the manufacturing industry in the region was depressed and many of buildings looked very run down too. None of the managers in the companies we visited were confident or optimistic about their future prospects. Volgograd felt very much to be a city that had not yet moved on from its Soviet past (indeed local political control was vested with former communists) and although I later returned, I did not change my view

A Ride in the Noddy Bus

I arrived back late at night in Chelny after a week in the UK to a temperature of minus 15C and snow. Instead of the usual car waiting to take me to the hotel, I was greeted by the 'little red noddy bus' as we affectionately called it. This ancient small bus with scratched paintwork outside and quaintly curtained windows inside was normally only used for short shuttle operations around the city centre so things must have been bad if this was the only vehicle KamAZ had to send out to the airport. Or maybe familiarity was breeding contempt? Either way, I felt quite embarrassed heading into Chelny as the only passenger in this ridiculous looking, ancient bus. However, it did its job, depositing me safely at the Dialog hotel some 45 minutes later. One of the 'essential' items that I had brought with me from the UK (and always took on trips away) was a sink plug. It was rare to find a sink with an operational plug in it in Russia unless it was one of the rare modern metal plunger types in the modern Moscow hotels. The Russians were always amused to see my plug and couldn't understand why I had it; they were quite happy to just let the water run in the sink, hot or cold and quite unconcerned about wastage. It was the same in the kitchen where dirty dishes were washed and rinsed under a constant flow of water from the tap. Much later, I was involved in a multi-national project to modernise the water company in St Petersburg and well remember one of the initial objectives was to educate the public about water wastage and the real costs of producing clean water. Since the water, like the heating for most Russian homes all came from a central supply, there was little interest in conservation or waste.

Women's Basketball and a Fashion Show

Having met the KamAZ women's basketball team a couple of months ago and given them some financial help, it was no great surprise for our group receive an invitation to watch them play their first tournament of the season early one Saturday afternoon. It seemed an interesting way of passing a few hours and we knew this time we would not have to perform. Their opposition turned out to be a women's team from Poland, who although generally taller than the Russians, couldn't match them for overall talent. During the half time interval we were treated to the most extraordinary display of what I can only describe as sexy acrobatic dancing by a couple of young girls in garish leotards. The KamAZ team proved too strong for the Poles and won relatively easily but the match was poorly attended with perhaps only a dozen spectators apart from ourselves. What I didn't know when we agreed to attend was that I would be expected to present flowers to the teams and make a speech at the conclusion of the match. Since my Russian was still at the beginner stage, one of our team who spoke the language better made a few remarks and then presented the flowers to the team captains. There was also a bouquet for me to present to the Russian team coach, the same short, plump Tatar lady that I had met a few months earlier. As I am over six feet tall, delivering the required congratulatory kiss on each cheek was not an easy task – I would have much preferred the rather attractive, tall, dark-haired KamAZ team captain.

As part of the entertainment for the visiting Polish team, a fashion show had been organised at the end of the afternoon and we were also invited to attend. Fashion shows are not normally high on my 'must do' list but I admit to being intrigued at the opportunity of seeing the output of a Tatarstan design house. Attending in the company of twenty or so young women was of course, not an influencing factor. Our couturier host was a charming lady, understandably anxious to make a good impression with so many foreigners present. The clothes were paraded by some very attractive slim models brought in from Moscow, who could have graced the catwalks anywhere in the west. Their presence was certainly much appreciated by the younger men in our consulting group. The Tatar influence in the design of the clothes was very apparent – bright, striking colours, with strange patterns and styles that looked instantly out of date and reminded me somewhat of the late 1960's / 1970's period in the west. From remarks made later, I don't think the basketball players were too impressed either, at least not with the clothes. However, it was an interesting experience and a credit to local enterprise that a fashion house should be based in Chelny.

We rounded off this international event by joining with the two teams for a dinner and 'disco' (the Russians had brought along a cassette player and a few tapes) in one of the KamAZ dachas outside the city. The usual copious quantities of Russian wine and champagne had generously been provided for us but since the KamAZ team were all in training, they were not supposed to drink any alcohol. However, the old saying – where there's a will there's a way applies equally in Russia as elsewhere. At the end of the meal, someone was needed to divert the attention of their coach, so that the girls could sneak off and enjoy a little of the remaining champagne. Who better, they reasoned, to engage the coach in a little polite conversation than the person that had earlier presented her with flowers. After an entreaty from one of the girls, I duly co-operated in this subterfuge in the full spirit of Anglo-Russian relations. My reward, if that's the right word, was to be invited to dance by the coach – much to the amusement of her team. Russian fate was however, shining on the innocent for once and as we stepped onto the dance floor, the dacha's electricity system failed, plunging the room into darkness. This had the double benefit of allowing the girls to then drink unseen and me to escape from the undesirable clutches of the coach. A torch and candles were eventually produced but the moment had passed, the coach had returned to her table and I was able to sit back down without appearing ungracious or causing an international incident.

As the weeks rolled by, the lunches and dinners served in the InterClub were becoming increasingly monotonous, basically meat, meat and more meat, usually served with potatoes. I can't recall ever having fish and rice or pasta were a rarity. Even the rather pallid green apples that were occasionally placed on the table tasted strange, we were told it's because they had been stored in coal sheds once the winter arrived. Since almost all our lunches and dinners were provided by the InterClub, this unvarying diet became extremely frustrating. We explained to the InterClub manager that we found the cook's repertoire to be fairly limited and tried to encourage her to prepare a few different dishes but without any sustained success. More out of frustration than culinary ability, we attempted to cook something ourselves a couple of times but this was frowned on as the cook was understandably not happy to see us in her kitchen. Also, it was difficult to organise the ingredients to feed everyone. To add insult to injury, a new 'cook' had recently arrived in our hotel and now our cooked breakfasts were coming out covered in greasy oil. Despite trying to explain that we preferred less fat, nothing changed and I gave up having the occasional fried egg for breakfast in order to keep my cholesterol level down. However, as a small compensation, a new waitress had also appeared at the hotel – a bright, perky young blond. She wasn't the most efficient waitress and didn't speak any English but at least she brightened up our otherwise rather dreary breakfast scene each morning.

A few nights later, a couple of us decided to try a nearby cafe for dinner as a change but the menu choice was as limited as the InterClub – greasy mystery meat with greasy undercooked 'French fries'. The cafe was virtually empty; it was always a mystery to me as to how these places made money and stayed open. We walked disconsolately back to our hotel in a cold, piercing wind. The recent snow had compacted into hard ice on the pavements and walking was extremely treacherous, especially for the drunks that were starting to emerge from the bars. A young man had been tottering along the street not far in front of us, with a half empty vodka bottle in his hand when suddenly his legs just seemed to shoot out from under him and down he went, hard onto his back. Despite this painful experience, just moments later he was back on his unsteady feet and wandered on his way as if nothing had happened. Doubtless the combination of drink and bitter cold had removed any sense of pain caused by his fall. By chance the following day, I also slipped on the icy pavement outside the InterClub and fell in exactly the same way. Without the anaesthetising benefit of any vodka, the pain and shock from the fall was quite severe for a few minutes and my backside remained bruised and sore for several days. I momentarily wondered if I should take up heavy drinking.

Yelabuga in Winter

Now that winter had fully arrived, I wanted to make a return visit to Yelabuga, the picturesque old town near Chelny that I visited back in the summer. I wanted to see how it looked in the snow and so arranged for a car to pick me up for a Sunday morning drive out there. After breakfast, I grabbed my coat, hat and gloves and stuck my head out of the hotel front door to see what the weather was like. Light snow flurries were swirling around outside in a strong, blustery wind and when I looked at the thermometer on the hotel wall nearby, the mercury was well into the red with an indicated temperature of minus 22C. I knew that once out in the open the chill factor from the strong winds would make it seriously cold, definitely not the best weather conditions for sightseeing. I hadn't expected it to be this temperature when I had booked the car a few days earlier and was seriously thinking about telephoning the KamAZ dispatcher to cancel the trip when my car pulled up at the front door. I went out to the waiting car and saw that the driver was the same one who had taken me to Yelabuga in the summer and he had brought his daughter Julia along again. She must be keen to practice her English I thought, coming out in this kind of weather. Through Julia I asked her father whether he thought it wise to drive to Yelabuga in such conditions. I didn't catch his short reply but Julia's translation was along the lines of 'There won't be any problems, the roads are fine'. So full of trust in the locals, I jumped in the car and we set off for Yelabuga. True to his word, Julia's father drove us there and back without any obvious difficulty, apart from a few slithers on a couple of really icy patches of country road.

Once we arrived, I was glad I hadn't cancelled the visit. Despite the cold, it was worth the effort, seeing again the rows of old wooden houses, their roofs now weighed down with snow as if holding them in place against the blustery wind. Smoke was dancing skywards from most of the little chimneys, carried quickly away in the breeze and the piles of wood that I saw being stacked up in the summer were now earning their keep. Walking around the main square at midday, there was hardly anyone about and only the occasional car ventured out to brave the snow-drifted roads; it was even quieter than during my summer visit. It was all so still and peaceful, in fact the whole town looked almost like a traditional English Christmas card scene. I walked back to the car and asked Julia's father to drive me over to the old Devil's Tower by the river that I had visited in the summer. He did his best but could only drive part way along the snow covered track and was forced to stop a hundred yards short of the tower. Julia and her father wisely decided to stay in the warmth of the car but I was determined to reach it and struggled off through the deep, wind-blown snowdrifts. It proved to be more difficult than I had imagined to stumble through the virgin snow, especially with the wind blowing full in my face. But once I reached the tower, I was able to stand inside, sheltered from worst of the weather and gazed down from a frosted window at the broad, ice bound river, meandering off into the distance. Despite the dramatic beauty of the scene below me however, it was far too cold to hang around for long and I beat a retreat to my warm waiting car. Once we were back at the hotel in Chelny, I invited Julia and her father in for a coffee as a small gesture of gratitude for turning out in such conditions but they declined my offer. I'm not sure whether this was out of a misplaced sense of politeness or disappointment that I had nothing stronger to provide. Anyway, despite the bitter weather, I was glad that I visited Yelabuga again.

More Visa Problems

Back in the office at the InterClub the following week there were quite a few changes taking place. Many of our Deloitte consultant colleagues were packing their bags and returning home, their assignments apparently having been terminated. Another of the staff translators had quit, having found himself a teaching job that he hoped would pay him more regularly and I was having yet another of our constant battles over visas. Having been in and out so many times now on single entry visas, one would have thought the system would work fairly smoothly. I was told however, there was no visa approval office in Chelny and they all had to go to Kazan to be stamped. I didn't entirely believe this but had no choice other than to wait and simply hope that it arrived in time for my Christmas departure, whoever had to stamp it. The only consistency for the moment was the snow. It seemed people were wearing more and more clothing as we went through the winter, becoming cabbage like with all the layers. Indeed, I found it was taking so much extra time these days just to prepare to attend an external meeting. At each departure from the warmth of the InterClub, I had to find and don my thick socks, boots, hat, scarf and gloves. On arrival, everything apart from the boots was then removed and placed in a wardrobe with the reverse procedure taking place on departure, carefully checking to make sure nothing was left behind.

Following various death threats that I issued to several InterClub staff, our new visas finally arrived and so on December 21st Mack, Henk and I were able to return home for our Christmas break. The usual Tupolev charter jet had been booked to fly us from Chelny to Moscow with a scheduled departure of 9.30am. On leaving the hotel the weather didn't look good, it was minus 15 and a snowstorm was blowing through with 40kph winds. When we arrived at the airport our plane was parked waiting on the runway, having fortunately come in the night before but we were told that it couldn't take off in the high wind so we were ushered into the small VIP suite to wait. There were six of us travelling to Moscow (a couple of the Deloitte team were hitching a ride with us), two Americans connecting with flights to the USA and four Brits going on from Moscow to London, all on late afternoon flights. As the wait became longer and the hours slipped slowly by, we all realised that we were in danger of missing our international flights. As noon came and went, with no let up in the weather, we were getting very worried and I asked if I could call Moscow to find out if we could make alternative flight arrangements. However, a quick chat with the woman in charge of the VIP suite revealed that not one of the six telephones on her desk could be connected with Moscow. This could only be done from the emergency telephone in the airport control office and we were most definitely not allowed to use it. After a nail-biting five hours, the snowstorm finally lifted and we managed to take off in the early afternoon, arriving into Moscow's Sheremetyevo domestic terminal two hours later. This gave us just thirty minutes to transfer to the international terminal, pass through customs, check in, negotiate the lengthy queues at passport control and board our London flight. Luck was with us though and somehow we made it in time onto the BA flight – the fastest ever connection yet in Moscow (though on a later occasion, I had to do it in just twenty minutes). As for the two Americans, I found out later that they unfortunately missed their flight and had no choice but to stay overnight at the airport hotel.

Chapter Seven

A Russian New Year

After two weeks back in the UK, with both my body and mind reasonably replenished during the Christmas break, the rigours and challenges of Chelny had retreated to the far corners of my mind. But this temporary state didn't last long and on January 8th 1996 I flew back to Tatarstan. As we touched down at Chelny airport, the stewardess announced a temperature of minus 23C and as I walked across to the terminal over compacted ruts of icy snow, with the biting wind tugging at my coat, I was forcibly reminded that there were still four more months of winter to look forward to. By the next morning, the temperature had dropped even further to minus 26C but the InterClub was thankfully warm if not otherwise particularly welcoming. The offices looked as if they had been totally abandoned whilst we had been away with litter lying around and unwashed cups and glasses decorating the desks. A later visit to the lavatories revealed them to be in a most appalling state – dirty, smelly and as ever no lavatory paper. Someone had evidently been using the offices while we were away but nobody had thought about cleaning up.

One of the few benefits of being in Russia at this time of year was the pleasure of celebrating Christmas and New Year all over again. The Russians still use the Orthodox calendar which is basically thirteen days behind the western Julian calendar so Christmas Eve occurs on January 7th and New Year's Eve falls on January 13th. Staff at the InterClub arranged for us all to celebrate the Russian New Year together by going out for dinner to the nearby eponymous Tatar restaurant. The food turned out to be little different from that served at the InterClub but it was arguably cooked better, although the one hour wait between the starter and delivery of the main course meant we would probably have eaten anything put before us. This long delay didn't seem to bother our InterClub staff and even when the main course finally arrived, they were slow to eat it. Almost ignoring the food, they seemed quite happy just drinking and chatting while the food grew cold on their plates. I noticed this habit time and again when eating out with Russians and assumed it was probably a reflection of the generally poor quality of food served in Russian restaurants. We emerged from the restaurant into the freezing night air to find the streets lively with people, despite the temperature. In the town square, locals were dancing – or as best as they could in the snow – to an accordion played by a bearded old man, huddled inside a large brown fur coat. Children were having immense fun playing around the large snow sculptures that had been constructed over the recent weeks. These are a wonderful Russian tradition and some of the sculptures were the size of a small house, quite beautiful and intricate in their design. We lingered for a while, enjoying the scene but quickly decided that our own celebrations would be more enjoyable if continued back in the warmth of the Dialog hotel.

Contrasting Styles

As the months rolled by, I steadily met a growing number of the extensive KamAZ office staff from a wide range of departments and functions. One of the most interesting was Kamishkov, who had previously been national sales manager but was now demoted to handling a few major accounts. His small office on the third floor of an old KamAZ building confirmed his reduced status in the organisation. I had a fascinating two hour meeting with him one morning listening to his views on the company, the sales department and what was now going wrong. He was one of those people who don't have a first name, everyone just used his surname. He was quite tall and stocky with a good head of thick white hair, a heavily pock-marked face and strong, oversized hands that a football goalkeeper would be proud of. He was an amicable, old-style salesman who had clearly wielded considerable power in the company during the former Soviet period. Now around 60 years old and close to retirement, Kamishkov was probably a formidable man to deal with in his prime. He explained to me how things worked in the good old days when demand exceeded the factory's annual production. He would personally receive all large requests for vehicles, usually by telex from the main dealers and major customers such as the military and large state construction or utility companies. He would then either travel to the KamAZ Moscow office or fly around the country meeting with those who had placed the orders and over a bottle or two of vodka, decide who received what. Trucks were simply allocated by him, largely on the basis of who he liked most which in reality meant who wined and dined him the best. The process was simple, a small so-called sales department handled a minimum amount of administration and life for Kamishkov and his buddies had obviously been very enjoyable, as now evidenced by his large paunch and alcoholic's red-veined nose. While talking, he would often bang his goalkeeping hand firmly down on his desk to emphasise a point and I wondered if he had studied at the same school as Nikita Khrushchev[1]. Like many of his generation, he found it hard to understand the post perestroika situation. The lack of sales was only temporary and there was no need for modern marketing, pricing and discounts he told me. If only he was allowed to travel again, he was sure he could bring in many large orders from his old contacts. He was quite persuasive and at times I almost believed him.

For some months, I had been regularly attending the weekly sales department meetings, held on Saturday afternoons. These were usually run by Victor Maslenikov, the general sales manager who had presumably

---

1 Khrushchev, the former Soviet leader, became infamous for banging on the table during a speech at the UN in 1960.

replaced Kamishkov. I gradually developed a growing respect for Victor: he was intelligent and seemed to have the confidence and support of the sales team. He was a tall, dark haired Tatar with a genial, oval face and a quietly confident manner, in stark contrast to his excitable boss Oleg Belenyenko. We didn't always see eye to eye on sales matters, especially regarding his sales forecasts which were unrealistically optimistic, something I found very frustrating. Up to now I had found it difficult to build a close rapport with him but at the end of this afternoon's meeting we sat and chatted for a while. I asked about his hobbies and he told me he enjoyed fishing when he was able to find the time which unfortunately seemed to be increasingly rare these days. He then asked me if I had ever been fishing and I told him about a salmon fishing trip in British Columbia I had enjoyed a few years ago. To my surprise, Victor then asked whether I would like to go fishing with him sometime, once the spring thaw arrived. Whether he truly meant it or not, I didn't really know but we both understood it represented a small breakthrough in our relations and I quickly replied that it would be a pleasure for me to go with him. It was also the one and only time any of the KamAZ managers offered to socialise with any of our group.

A Slip on the Ice and a Skiing Trip

A few days later, as we arrived at the InterClub on a bright frosty morning, my colleague Clive slipped on the ice and fell awkwardly onto his back. Mack and I helped Clive up from his spread-eagled position but it was evident that he was badly shaken, although once we had assisted him upstairs to our office he seemed to rally. I kidded him that the problem was that he hadn't been in Chelny long enough to have fully learnt the Russian shuffle. Although he carried on working normally that week, he increasingly started to complain about headaches. This was very worrying so the InterClub organised a check up for him at a local clinic but they couldn't find anything wrong. However, he never really seemed to fully recover from this incident and was clearly unhappy much of the time both at work and in the hotel in the evenings. With still no change in his manner after a couple of weeks, it was agreed that sadly he should leave our team and return home. Fortunately, as I later found out, there were no long term adverse effects and Clive soon found a new consultancy job. However, his fall was a salutary reminder to the rest of us that walking around in Chelny, even just a short distance, had to be done with great care. As the almost daily falls of snow continued, many of the side streets were rendered all but impassable. With no apparent attempts at snow clearing other than on a few main roads, the snow was steadily compacted into icy ruts leaving many streets with just two tracks down the middle from the car tyres and kept open (just) by the traffic. It was often difficult to differentiate the pavements from the road and passing in these streets was impossible leading to some interesting head to head confrontations. When two cars met, the most aggressive driver would try to force the other into reversing back up the street or pulling over onto the mound of snow to the side where they risked getting stuck. Watching these antics from our office window over a cup of coffee was a regular diversion for us.

There had been a mounting excitement during the past week among the consultant group. We had been promised a visit on Sunday to the local ski resort – the Chelny Alps as they were soon to become named by us. Although cross country skiing was possible in the countryside around Chelny, this was the only place in the region where downhill skiing was available. Of course none of us had any proper skiing clothes or equipment in Chelny so we all raided our normal winter wardrobes to find suitable coats, thick trousers, hats and gloves. The InterClub staff told us that there would be skis and boots for us to use at the resort. When we all met together early that Sunday morning outside the InterClub in our hastily assembled outfits, we looked a very disparate and comical group. The Chelny Alps proved to be not much more than a large hill some forty five minutes drive by bus from the town. It featured a single T bar, giving access to three short runs and a large wooden Alpine style building providing ski equipment plus basic café and toilet facilities. On arrival, we were directed down to a room in the basement of the building to be fitted out with boots and skis. I was almost the last person off the bus and by the time I arrived in the boot room all the large boots seemed to have been taken. I take a size eleven shoe and despite trying on several pairs they all proved to be too small and I couldn't find any boots that fitted my big feet. The man in charge of the equipment finally produced a very smart looking pair of almost new boots, saying they were the largest available. Fortunately they were a perfect fit but it was only later that I discovered that the boots I had been given were the personal property of Mr Bekh, the president of KamAZ. It was the only time that I stood in the president's shoes but it was satisfying to know they fitted very comfortably.

The weather was bright and sunny, with a temperature of only minus 15C and once equipped, our group of some fifteen consultants and interpreters enjoyed the experience and the welcome exercise. Like most leisure facilities in Chelny, this ski lodge and equipment had been built by KamAZ in its Soviet heyday. Now that there were insufficient company funds to properly support it, things were clearly starting to deteriorate and the skiing was no longer free, as in the good old days. As with so many of our visits to these types of 'social assets', we were asked by the manager if we could help find ways to raise money for urgent maintenance and new equipment. Although touched by the problems they faced, sadly there was nothing we could realistically do. We could not be the solution to so many problems, even if we were willing. In this cash-short, corruption infested, oligarchic society, the answers lay elsewhere. The pace of reform was exceedingly slow and the pain for many was great. The transition to a truly democratic, market economy still had a long way to go, especially in this part of Russia. When we returned to Chelny in the early evening, the bus dropped us off at our hotel and we were puzzled to find the interpreters also getting off the bus. We asked why they weren't staying on the bus and they explained that the driver was not allowed to take them back to their homes, even though it was late and they had given up their Sunday to look after us. This example of poor and insensitive treatment of the staff by the company was something that we came across periodically and was always hard to understand.

A Lucky Escape

By the end of January, our consultant team was ready for a few days of welcome leave back home. As usual, our small, chartered jet was waiting at Chelny airport to fly us to Moscow to catch our various international flights. But a journey that had previously passed off without major problems was this time to turn into something of a nightmare. We boarded the plane on time and took our seats whilst the bags were loaded and the plane was re-fuelled. The rear steps were still open at this point when we started to notice a definite smell of fuel in the cabin. At first, we didn't take too much notice since they were re-fuelling the aircraft after all. Then as the fumes became much stronger, the flight crew emerged from the cockpit and rushed down the rear steps and we could hear some shouting outside the plane. We knew something must be wrong but were unsure as to how serious it might be. Just as we started to wonder whether we should 'abandon ship', a piercing klaxon noise started up inside the plane. For a few seconds we sat hesitating in our seats, wondering what this meant. We turned to the Russian stewardess for explanation or guidance but the puzzled look of panic on her face made words unnecessary. An unspoken consensus rapidly emerged between us that we should get out and get out fast. However, as we bolted for the rear and tried to exit down the steps, we were confronted by the pilot coming back up. Although we didn't understand why, it was clear that he didn't want us to go down the steps but indicated we should go back into the cabin and move towards the front of the plane. He then pushed past us and opened up the forward emergency exit, motioning for us to go out this way. Even though there was a drop of several feet down onto the icy runway, it was clear we had no choice and the risk of a broken ankle would be small compared to possible incineration in the plane. As luck would have it, we all landed on the ground without problems, including the pilot.

The young co-pilot appeared, oblivious to the biting cold in his standard issue, short-sleeved white shirt. Fortunately, he spoke reasonable English and proceeded to explain to us what had happened, as he ushered us away from the plane. As we suspected, there had been a serious leak as the plane was being refuelled and the aviation fuel had formed a large pool at the rear of the plane. Had we used the rear steps as an exit, we would have ended up in the middle of this highly flammable liquid. This was why we had to jump out of the front to escape. As with many other mysteries in Russia, the reason for this extensive spillage was never fully explained. Had the fuel nozzle's automatic shut off valve malfunctioned or frozen; did the engineer fall asleep or leave the job? We never knew the answer.

This inevitably meant a long delay to our departure but even if late in leaving for Moscow, at least we were still alive for which we were very grateful. In some ways, it was quite ironic because only a few nights before, we had been discussing the poor safety record of Russian airlines. There had been several cases, well reported in the international press, of a run of crashes by Aeroflot and other Russian regional airlines. One infamous recent fatal disaster had occurred when the Russian pilot had passed the controls over to his young son who was riding in the cockpit. The other crashes seemed to be mainly due to pilot error though poor maintenance and parts shortages may well have been contributing factors. We had always felt safe flying our charter between Moscow and Chelny. Although we travelled in Russian planes with local crews, they were owned by a western company and its operating and maintenance procedures had been fully checked out. In the end however, none of this could offset the element of a human mistake that appeared to have caused the refuelling problem with our flight. On arrival at Gatwick, I found that the British Airways shuttle flight to Manchester was delayed for 45 minutes due to bad weather. I couldn't help thinking that compared to the conditions in Russia, they don't know what bad weather is. Then, once on board we had to wait a further 15 minutes on the stand because someone had forgotten to organise the tow truck to pull the aircraft onto the runway. The human element again……

A Negative Reaction

One of my urgent tasks before Christmas had been to prepare a detailed draft report on our Russian truck market survey for review by the Cummins and Deloitte senior management teams over the Christmas holiday break. The conclusions were not good and there were very few positive points. It was clear there had been a significant drop in overall demand for trucks, reflecting the decline in Russia's economic activity and the position seemed unlikely to change in the foreseeable future. Competition was growing from imported vehicles which many customers felt offered better quality and durability. We heard frequent complaints about the quality of KamAZ trucks and demand from the military, formerly one of the largest KamAZ clients, had also collapsed. In the commercial market, many of the larger users of KamAZ trucks had no cash and could only acquire new vehicles through barter deals. Negotiating these was complicated and time consuming as well as depriving KamAZ of much needed cash to finance its ongoing operations. Also very worrying were comments we picked up about new KamAZ parts frequently being offered at cheap prices through non-official outlets. Although some of these derived from barter deals where KamAZ had supplied new parts to pay off debts, it was clear that the majority were somehow coming from the factories in Chelny. This inevitably reinforced concerns that we had earlier expressed to the KamAZ board about the extent of theft and corruption within the organisation. We agreed that on my return to Chelny in January I would finalise the report, circulate copies to the KamAZ board and then seek an urgent meeting with them to discuss the survey and its findings.

Compiling the final detailed version of the survey took longer than expected, mostly due to translation issues and occupied much of my time during the month of January. But by mid February it was ready and was circulated to the board of KamAZ. A week went by and I had heard nothing so I followed up with Yuri Borisov, our main contact in KamAZ for the survey, to try to find out if he had read it and if so, when he would be ready for a meeting. The days dragged by without any response but finally after another week of chasing, I received confirmation of a meeting the following morning. When I arrived at his office the next day, I found him quite sullen and clearly not in a good mood. I noticed a copy of my report was lying on his desk and I enquired whether he had the chance to read it yet. He confirmed that yes, he had gone through it but then added in a rather off-hand manner that it wasn't very good and didn't really tell the company anything. As if to emphasise his point, he reached out and pushed the report away to one side of his desk. I was quite shocked – KamAZ and Cummins had invested a lot of time and money in this market survey which we felt raised some important issues regarding the future plans of the company. I tried to explore with Borisov why he felt this way, explaining the methodology used for the study and our own confidence in the findings, especially the forecast of a continued fall in market demand. The figures were wrong Borisov replied and at this point he pulled out from his desk drawer a short report in Russian which he waved at me. We had our own report done almost year ago by Russian consultants and their conclusions about the market are very different to yours. We think their findings more accurately reflect what is happening in our market. This was the first I had heard about another survey and said it would have been helpful if we had discussed this before conducting our own. Clearly, there was some other agenda going on behind the scenes of which I was unaware and so I asked Borisov where we went from here. KamAZ doesn't intend to do anything further with your report was the short response and with that Borisov rose to his feet signalling our meeting was now over. His abrupt, almost disdainful behaviour was odd and as I left his office I desperately tried to think what was going on. KamAZ was heading into very stormy waters but the ship's officers seemed bent on ignoring the warnings, refusing to change course.

Although I never really got to the bottom of this particular situation, I think our report had touched some raw nerves, especially the comments about bad quality and corruption. The report was not well received in KamAZ and our conclusions and recommendations were strongly contested or simply rejected by most of the management. Their inability to accept our survey was not only disappointing but meant that much of our work over the past few months trying to help the business adapt to the changed market conditions was likely to be ignored and wasted. It gave me no satisfaction to soon hear that truck production was to be cut in March and to then watch as monthly sales levels dropped in line with our predictions. This meeting turned out to mark a watershed in the relations between the KamAZ board and our consulting group as well as Cummins and Deloitte. Sadly, there would be serious future consequences for the company, its investors and employees. By the end of the month, the remnants of the Deloitte consulting team had packed their bags and left Chelny. Within twelve months, almost all the senior management team, including Bekh, had left or been replaced and the company's financial position continued to deteriorate. Much later I discovered that there had been growing disagreement at this time among the directors and with some external stakeholders, in particular the government of Tatarstan. It seemed especially ironic to me at the time because this week was the 20th anniversary of the first truck built by KamAZ – 1,459,268 was the official number of units produced so far.

Trams and Buses

One evening later that week, after an unscheduled meeting at one of the KamAZ offices, there was no car available to take me back to the InterClub. My interpreter cautiously suggested we take a tram as it was too far to walk and there was a stop just up the street. It was a cold night, minus 23C today and fortunately, we didn't have long to wait and managed to push ourselves into a packed tramcar. The heat from the crush of bodies had partially melted the frost on the tram's inside windows which were almost fully covered with condensation, making it impossible to see out clearly. How the passengers knew where they were and at which place to alight was a mystery to me. As we trundled up to each stop, the tram doors jerked open unsteadily as if unsure whether anyone would really want to step out into the bitter cold night air. As they briefly opened, giving a view onto the world outside, you had to make an instant decision. If this was your stop, you pushed through the crush of bodies and leapt out before the doors closed again and the tram moved off. Luckily, when the time came, my interpreter made the right decision and I instantly followed her lead, arriving back at the InterClub without any problems. Having survived my tram baptism, I felt confident enough to use the system on my own and over the next few months I took advantage of the tram several times to explore Chelny a little more. As we walked back to the InterClub, my translator chatted a little about the changing attitudes in Russia, especially towards the older generation. The old people in Russia suffered not only from the decline in respect but more importantly from a poverty enforced by their almost worthless state pensions and a deteriorating health system. She then told me a joke that crudely illustrated the changing social and moral attitudes in the country. On the trams and buses, as in most countries, it was traditional for young people to give up their seat to the older generation. An old lady complaining about her aching legs asked a teenager on a bus to give up his seat.

'Did you always give up your seat when you were young?' he said.

She proudly replied 'Of course, I always did when I was your age.'

His response was quick 'Then I won't because I don't intend to end up with aching legs like yours!'

The tram system in Chelny actually seemed quite efficient, linking most parts of the city and was very cheap. My only experience with local public buses was when I went off one Sunday to visit Nizhnikamsk, a nearby town. Although I had some difficulty finding the right bus stop, the outward journey was fine. I wandered round for a couple of hours but there wasn't anything of interest, just another 1970s town with lots of apartment blocks. I returned to the bus station and caught a late afternoon bus for Chelny. It was fairly full and as we got well into the journey, our rickety bus seemed to be going more and more slowly. Then, when we were perhaps about half way home, going up a hill in the middle of nowhere, the bus suddenly juddered a few times then quickly came to a complete halt with a loud clattering noise – an unmistakeable vehicular death rattle. The driver tried several times to restart the engine but without success. We had clearly broken down and the driver explained that we would have to wait for the next bus to Chelny which should pass by in an hour or so. There was nothing to do but sit and wait and ponder on why transport seemed to be such a problem in Russia. The next bus duly arrived about an hour and a half later and somehow, everyone managed to squeeze in for the final leg of our journey back to Chelny.

A Russian Burns Night

With two Scotsmen on our team of consultants, it was inevitable with February 15th approaching that a Burns night dinner should be organised, probably the first ever in Chelny. Through careful planning, we were able to ensure that between us most of the essential ingredients for a successful Burns night were imported from our leave in the UK at the end of January. Our luggage was laden with bottles of whisky and drambuie, plus haggis, oatcakes, a book of his poetry and kilts of course for the Scottish contingent. We didn't know it at the planning stage but importing a book of Burns poems was unnecessary. If Robert Burns had not been born a Scot, then he would almost certainly have been a Russian – at least by adoption. Amazingly, the love of Burns poetry is widespread across Russia and we were surprised at how many people knew of him and appreciated his work. Several of the locals that attended our dinner even brought their own Burns books, both in English and Russian. The event was to take place in the InterClub restaurant and we had been careful to ensure that they had ordered sufficient quantities of potatoes and turnips. Our two Scotsmen also made sure they were on hand in the kitchen to supervise the cooking of the haggis but what we hadn't reckoned on was a last minute request from the kitchen for us all to help out with peeling the vegetables. However, consultants are nothing if not flexible so we rolled up our sleeves and set to work. The dinner proved to be a great success and as in Scotland, brought life and humour to a cold winter's evening. Although the Russians, in company I think with several other nationalities, were unsure about the merits of haggis, tatties and neaps, they fully joined in the spirit of the evening. The Russian tradition of frequent toasts fitted the occasion well and speeches and readings were made by Scots, English, Dutch, Canadians, Americans and of course the Russians.

Unfortunately, the convivial atmosphere had all but evaporated on my arrival at the InterClub the next morning. Our Russian support team was in turmoil and looking very sullen. I eventually found out the problem lay in the fact that the translators had not been paid again and had also been told that they would now have to pay for their lunches (they normally joined us free of charge in the canteen when working). Added to this, their workloads had been increased and individual responsibilities changed. The problem of pay was endemic at KamAZ and indeed across much of Russia at the time. People went months without being paid and it was amazing how they managed to survive. Support from family and friends was vital, as was the food grown on the dacha during the summer months and preserved for winter use. Sometimes the employees would be offered company coupons instead of pay and these could then be exchanged for goods that KamAZ had bartered for the vehicles they produced. But this system was understandably very unpopular as the available bartered goods were often unwanted the staff still needed cash for everyday living. Today for example, the employees were being offered multiple bags of sugar as payment. It took some days for life in the InterClub to settle back to some semblance of normality. The shortage of cash across the whole Russian economy had become a major problem, particularly outside Moscow. Large companies like KamAZ were increasingly finding they had no money to pay wages or suppliers regularly so individuals and small businesses had no cash to support the retail or service sectors. Government was unable to collect the level of taxes due, exacerbated by a punitive tax system and inefficient, corrupt collection methods. It therefore had no money to pay its own employees and no resources to pump prime the economy. As many large companies were still very dependent on a declining number of government contracts, the vicious circle continued. So a large part of the business of trade was carried out in the burgeoning black market or survived by the complicated and inefficient system of barter and offsets. At one stage we had measured KamAZ' own sales and found that 90% was being done by barter or offset. No wonder they had cash flow problems.

Russian Women's Day

March 8th marked the celebration of women's day in Russia, which primarily dates from Soviet times. The previous day everyone at the office had been very careful to ensure that we all knew of this event. It's a nice tradition that we don't have generally in the West; the closest event being mother's day. But it isn't the same. There are parties and social gatherings and this is an opportunity for all women, not just mothers, to celebrate their achievements, independence and freedom. The Russian men take it very seriously and few would even fleetingly consider going through the day without buying flowers for the women in their life, despite the relatively high cost of blooms at this time of year. The flower sellers do a roaring trade of course and we followed suit at the office and our female support team were inundated with bouquets of flowers. I had an interesting conversation with a couple of the KamAZ managers that evening about the status of women in Russia. The Soviet Union used to make great play on the apparent emancipation of women in their society, promoting their success in the arts, sciences, sports etc. But in the USSR at the time, these men claimed, most women were emancipated only as a unit of production on the farm, in the factory or as a mother. Apparently, the Soviets tried to conduct a census in the 1960s to try to establish who was the real head of the family but it had to be withdrawn due to the level of vociferous protests from both men and women. Despite the Soviet era's propaganda portraying full equality of the sexes, my own experience from earlier visits to Russia had been quite different and I certainly saw no evidence to support the assertion that Russian women were able to achieve more or enjoyed a better lifestyle than in other countries.

It did, however, seem clear to me that in post perestroika Russia there was one way women were showing greater freedom than in the past and that was in the way they looked and dressed. The fashion and dress style of Russian women was fascinating, frequently being both exotic and erotic. All the girls wanted to be blonde in some caricature of the scenes in imported American TV soaps or magazines. The presence of so much blond hair in a mainly Slavic nation indicated the popularity of the chemist's bottle, similar really to the fashion in the west in the 1950's and early 1960's. The younger women tended to wear clothes of excessively bright colours, though black was also popular, with striking lipstick to match. However, given the drab and often dispiriting surroundings, it was perhaps not surprising that Russian women took a pride in their own personal appearance and dress style. Skirts ranged from very short, tight minis to long slinky dresses with suggestive side slits up to the hips, often worn with long, diaphanous tops with a vaguely oriental look. In the West, many of these outfits would have been considered more suited to a party or as evening wear rather than as casual street or office wear. There was no doubt that the women were making a statement to the men and society in general – we may not yet have real equality but we are attractive, desirable and really rule the roost at home. However, in complete contrast to this, Russian women seemed to provide a disproportionate amount of the labour for menial tasks such as street cleaning and roadside maintenance work. As I travelled around the city, it was clear that many of the gangs doing this type of hard work were entirely composed of women. They were also the ones who tended and weeded the parks as well as planting grass and summer flowers in the occasional roadside strip. The women clearly cared more for the environment and the extra income, small as it probably was, would have been useful to their families. It seemed strange to me however, in a country where so many men were not fully employed, that more of them were not to be seen doing this kind of manual work.

In contrast to their women, most Russian men dressed in a fashion (and I am stretching the word in this context) that seemed largely indifferent to their general appearance. Apart from jeans and leather jackets, which were extremely popular throughout all the countries of the former Soviet Union, most men's clothes were a curious mixture of colours, patterns, stripes and styles. Shirts and ties, when worn, usually clashed with the rest of the wearer's outfit rather than matching. The men often seemed a little down at heel, wearing clothes that were well worn and old fashioned. I don't know whether this was due to a lack of good dress sense or the fact that the wives took all the spare money for their own clothes.

A Decent Restaurant at Last

Someone had told us about a good restaurant they had discovered in the 'old town' of Chelny and a group of us decided to try it one Saturday night. It was called the Mill and although the internal décor and music were comparable to most other Chelny restaurants, the food was definitely better. They also had decent wine and good imported beer and we all enjoyed an excellent evening. It certainly wasn't cheap but the restaurant was full and the rest of the clientele appeared to be so-called 'new Russians'. Despite the economic problems in town, there were clearly people making good money and who enjoyed spending it. On the small dance floor in the middle of the restaurant, men were stuffing rouble notes into the bras and skirts of some of the young women. Whatever the relationships were, I didn't know but clearly everyone was having great fun and no one objected. We left the restaurant around one o' clock in the morning, in a rather inebriated state and decided to walk back to our hotel to clear our heads. It was a fine bright night and the snow crystals on the ground seemed to glisten like diamonds in the moonlight – or was this simply the effect of the alcohol?

Several of us went back to the Mill again a couple of weeks later and found the food to be just as good as the initial visit. But instead of walking back, one of our Russian colleagues said he had ordered a taxi to take us to the hotel. This was a great surprise as taxis were virtually unheard of in Chelny at the time. However, on our departure, a bright yellow Lada taxi stood waiting for us and efficiently whisked us back. This turned out to be one of a fleet of ten such taxis that we started to see around town with increasing frequency. I was never able to accurately discover who was behind this new venture and briefly thought it would bring me increased freedom. Instead of having to try to organise a KamAZ car if I wanted to go somewhere at the weekend, I would now simply be able to take a taxi. However, on exploring this newly found concept of freedom the next day in the InterClub, I was told that the taxis' licence did not allow them to travel outside the town limits. One of the Russians most favourite sayings is 'hope dies the last' but in this case my hopes had hardly had time to formulate themselves.

The Presidential Visit

Mack and I were curtly informed at breakfast this morning that we had to vacate our rooms for the night. We were told that it would shortly be election time in Tatarstan and the president was due in town on a rare visit to drum up votes and would be staying at our hotel. As we were on the top floor where the president and his entourage wished to stay, we had to move for 'security reasons'. We were allocated a pair of small single rooms on the ground floor and had to rush around madly to quickly pack all our things and clear our top floor rooms. I facetiously asked the hotel manager whether there would be a plaque over my bed the next day saying 'the president slept here'. My attempt at humour was wasted on him however and he gave me very stern look that came straight out of the Soviet era. For him, the president's visit was evidently no joking matter. The town was crawling with police for the visit, partly due no doubt to concerns about possible hostile demonstrations or threats from local separatist Tatars. Around lunchtime I saw the president's cavalcade of vehicles sweep past at high speed along one of the main avenues near the InterClub. I noted with interest that most were Mercedes or large imported four-wheel drive cars, hardly a Russian vehicle to be seen. Seemingly, the absence of any presidential support for the large domestic automotive industry was not a vote loser here.

Back in the hotel that evening, we found the bar and restaurant closed to us foreigners. The presidential party had thoughtfully brought their own cooks and waitresses but had evidently forgotten the portable restaurant, so we were forced to eat elsewhere. The hotel was invested with muscular, dark-suited security men, all wearing sunglasses and very discreet earphones. There were lots of pretty, well dressed young women wandering around also – something that was not a normal sight in down-town Chelny. After our enforced dinner elsewhere, Mack and I returned to the hotel and thought we would have a bit of fun. We went to our rooms to each get our stereo earphones and met back in the lobby wearing them stuck in one ear. We then stood next to some of the security guards pretending to communicate with each other through our earphones. Needless to say the president's guards took no notice of us, no doubt having been warned that the hotel unfortunately had some strange foreigners as guests. We enjoyed this brief interlude of insanity though, especially as it gave us time to ogle the pretty girls and wonder which of the top floor rooms they would end up in that night. On regaining our top floor rooms the following night, we were a little disappointed at not finding any of the women still in residence. Such a small 'thank you' present from the president for throwing us out of our beds would have been appreciated.

The first round of the Tatarstan presidential elections duly took place a couple of days later on a Sunday and apparently, the current president, Shaimiev, was the only candidate. This partly explained the lack of ballyhoo and general excitement in Chelny that one would normally associate with such an event. In a small gesture to democracy, the incumbent had to obtain 50% of the vote however, to be re-elected. To me that seemed to indicate that there might be an awful lot of spoilt ballot papers and abstentions to ensure the correct result. Interested in this process and with nothing much to do that Sunday, I persuaded one of the InterClub interpreters to take me with her to a polling station near to our hotel. As we walked along the street, I asked what happens if the president doesn't get the required 50% of the vote? This was obviously a silly question that only foreigners would think of asking and induced a grimace and protracted silence.

'Well I'm not exactly sure' was the eventual reply, followed by the conclusive remark 'and in any case that's never happened before'.

The voting was taking place in a local government building and the overall arrangements seemed very similar to an election in Britain. The main difference was that although each person was registered and then given a voting slip, to my great surprise they didn't have to mark it in any way. They simply confirmed their voting intention by posting the slip in a sealed box in the voting booth. Obviously, there would be no spoilt ballot papers with this simple process and at the same time, plenty of opportunity for 'stuffed' ballot boxes. The place was certainly busy with voters and I was told they have a very efficient system during the day to chase up those who haven't voted yet. I didn't dare to ask what they did to encourage the recalcitrants but I assumed there were few abstentions. Unsurprisingly, a few weeks later it was announced that president Shaimiev had been re-elected for a further term of four years. No-one in the InterClub seemed to know what percentage of the vote he actually obtained, it just didn't seem important to them.

CHAPTER EIGHT

Ice Racing & Talking Donkeys

By mid-March, the daytime temperatures would occasionally creep above zero and the ice was starting to melt. For a few days we experienced high winds but it remained sunny and we had a high of plus 2C; for once our winter temperature was actually warmer than the UK according to the evening television weather. This was officially deemed to be the start of spring in Tatarstan and it was interesting to see how people increasingly began to wear lighter clothes. The men replaced their fur hats with flat caps and started to wear black or brown leather jackets instead of their thicker winter coats. Women also began to lose some of their heavy winter layers, regaining something of their normal figure and hemlines definitely moved up. At home in the UK, these temperatures would have been regarded as definitely still winter-like but it was all relative I suppose.

Once we were into early April, spring finally arrived or so I was reliably informed by the woman on the hotel front desk. Certainly when I looked out of the window of my room that morning there was not the slightest trace of snow to be seen anywhere. Winter had been very long, effectively starting with those early snow flurries last September. As I gazed out beyond the hotel, a few birds were wandering around on what passed for a lawn last summer. I idly wonder if they were as happy to see the end of winter as I was. As if to confirm the arrival of spring, this week saw fresh tomatoes back on the menu in the InterClub, the first since last autumn.

However, as I was to find out, winter wasn't quite finished in Chelny and we had further light falls of snow at the end of the month. Indeed, by mid April, although the weather continued to slowly improve, the Kama river in Chelny remained stubbornly frozen over. But the river ice must have been thinning as the numbers of men venturing out to cut holes in the ice to catch fish were much lower over the past few days. Whenever I saw men cutting holes in the ice to fish, I was always reminded about the winter after the Bolshevik revolution. So many people were being killed and with the ground totally frozen, it was impossible to bury them all. The Reds disposed of the bodies by simply cutting holes in the ice and pushing them down into the water. It was known euphemistically as 'being transferred to the Republic of the River'. That evening over a few beers in the hotel, we got into a lively discussion on the design and engineering of the KamAZ range of vehicles, especially their small two door city car. One thing led to another and someone came up with the idea that it would be great fun if we could get hold of a couple of these mini cars and organise a day of ice racing on the frozen Kama river. We knew the location of the compound where the cars were stored after assembly and just maybe we could persuade someone there to let us borrow a couple for a day. With the beers flowing, this crazy idea rapidly gained momentum with ideas being floated about where best to get the cars onto the river and whether the concept could go national. After all, there were lots of frozen rivers in winter in Russia so the promotional possibilities for KamAZ were enormous. Our group of normally intelligent consultants then started to discuss whether it would be better to somehow attach skis to the car's wheels or simply race with the normal rubber tyres. Fortunately perhaps for KamAZ and our own safety, we eventually realised that this wonderful idea had come to us too late as the ice in Chelny was already melting. Maybe we could organise something next winter......

On top of my daily afternoon meetings with senior management, I was now also invited to attend some of their early morning meetings. Held each week day at 8am, these were designed to tackle urgent day to day problems within the company. Such daily 'crisis' meetings were quite normal in business which by improving internal communications and focus could prove very effective at achieving rapid progress. Sadly, the KamAZ meetings that I attended generally proved to be less than satisfactory and often seemed simply an exercise in criticising and humiliating junior staff. Those that attended were cowed by the intensity of the situation and usually unable or unwilling to satisfactorily answer the questions shouted at them by the directors. Rarely was any responsibility taken by senior managers for mistakes or problems and any sense of teamwork was totally absent. As I was more of an observer at these meetings rather than a direct participant, I decided after a couple of weeks that I had observed enough and subsequently only attended if there was something of real interest on the agenda. However, in contrast to these depressing meetings was a series of sessions organised by KamAZ with a group of young graduate management trainees drawn from various departments across the company. They had been tasked with coming up with new ideas to tackle some of the company's serious problems and I was asked to join their discussions as a mentor, advising on how things were done in the west as well as challenging their ideas. Over a period of about a month, I sat in on their meetings two or three times a week and found it a fascinating, if sometimes frustrating experience. It was interesting to have the chance to see such a group of generally bright young Russians in action. Whilst they occasionally had difficulties managing the dynamics of such open group sessions, many of them clearly had sensible ideas about how to move the company forwards. However, a couple of them had some very strange thoughts about business in general, politics and Russia's relationships with the west. It was odd to find that these intelligent young people had difficulty understanding the concept of a market driven economy and even stranger to find that some had little interest in what I would have called a democratic and open society. We occasionally had quite animated debates about how they felt the west was exploiting Russia and that we were only interested in grabbing its natural resources, especially oil and gas. At the end of the month, the group prepared a series of presentations for senior management on their conclusions but sadly, I never heard any feedback on how their ideas were received. I suspect that rather like our own market survey, they were quietly filed away and the door on this particular experiment firmly closed.

One of the KamAZ managers in the economics department with whom I occasionally worked was an Uzbek called Dimitri. At a guess he was in his late forties with short, dark frizzy hair that was just turning grey around his ears and a typical central Asian sallow complexion. He always seemed friendly and approachable so I asked him one day what he thought of the consultants and the work we were doing. He dropped his head a little and stared at me over his glasses for a few moments as if trying to decide how best to reply. His eventual response was to relate to me a particularly appropriate old Uzbekistan fable. It seems there was once a rich emir who met with a local folk hero. The latter was asked by the emir if he could teach a donkey to talk. The folk hero thought about it for a while and then said that yes it was possible but it would take fifty years and cost ten percent of the emir's fortune. The emir wasn't initially impressed with this response but excited by the thought that he would eventually own the world's only talking donkey, he paid up. Later, back in his village, the folk hero was asked how he was going to teach the donkey to talk. I don't know he replied but in fifty years either the emir or the donkey will be dead. In the meantime, I have the money to enjoy myself.

This little story neatly summarised what Dimitri and many other Russians thought about the help or advice they were receiving from the west. For the folk hero read foreign consultants and instead of teaching the donkey to talk, read helping the Russians to adapt to a market economy. For many, the hoped for improvements in their quality of life after perestroika still seemed a long time coming and probably would not be seen in their lifetime. Meanwhile the consultant's goose was getting very fat. Of course there was some truth in this opinion; progress was slow and by local standards, the consultants were generally well paid. However, this conveniently ignored the fact that the real fortunes were being made by Russians. Some of them by luck and entrepreneurial good judgement but many by cheating, thieving and committing outright crime against their fellow citizens. As I pointed out to Dimitri, there had also been many changes for the better over the past few years and few people genuinely wanted to give these up to go back to the Communist ways. I don't know if he fully agreed with me but the subject never came up again and at least he remained friendly and open to new ideas during our subsequent business meetings.

Easter week had now arrived in Russia which like Christmas, always comes a week or so later than in the West. The Orthodox traditions however, are much the same. For religious Russians, the season of Lent is marked by not eating meat, eggs or other animal products during the forty day period of fasting. Historically, all theatre and music performances were banned during Lent, as they were considered distractions from the Lent tradition of reflection and repentance but this practice rarely occurs now. During Easter week, the Russians bake special bread and cakes as well as preparing hand painted hard boiled eggs. On Easter Saturday an important midnight mass is held and after breakfast on Sunday, people go out to visit friends and neighbours, exchanging their painted eggs and Easter bread and cakes. Sadly, the only thing I saw of all this were a few small Easter cakes that one of the staff brought to share in the InterClub and meat remained firmly on the menu at the InterClub.

Summer Arrives at Last

I had left Chelny in a flurry of snow showers at the start of May for a two week business trip to the UK. When I returned, summer had already arrived and the temperature was up to 25C. The evidence of this warmth was immediate as we drove away from the airport terminal. We could see several young women sunbathing topless quite brazenly on the grass at the side of the building, a sight that almost made me glad to be back. This country really only seemed to have two seasons – summer and winter. There were just a few weeks in between when either the snow was just starting and before everything froze over or a brief spring melt as the temperature steadily soared. In what seemed like days, the grass shot up and trees became green with a full canopy of leaves; the change was quite dramatic in such a short period. It was almost as if some overnight party revellers had been out painting the town green. If only KamAZ and the Russian economy could have made such rapid progress.

We had been hearing rumours about a jazz club somewhere in Chelny for some months now and finally one warm Saturday night late in May, the InterClub arranged a visit for us. It turned out to be quite small, not much bigger than a large sitting room in a house with a tiny bar area. Intimate as I suppose jazz aficionados might have called it. The music and atmosphere however, were good with everyone clearly enjoying the scene and we were told the pianist and trumpeter had come in to play from Moscow. The place was full, with hardly any spare seats and although we had booked, the owner had great difficulty finding any space for our group. As far as I knew, this was the only place in a town of 600,000 people with any live music, apart from occasional performances in the concert hall and the generally poor quality amateur bands that played in a few of the restaurants. It seemed to me that this club must be a small gold mine and I later chatted to the owner about when he had started, how well he was doing and so on. To my amazement, he told me the club was only open once a month. He explained 'This is partly because people don't have enough money to come more often and partly due to the fact that people here prefer to watch television.' He added 'This is intelligent music, not for the masses.' Now I understood why it had taken so long to organise a date to visit the club. I wished the owner well for the future and as I write, would love to know whether the club survived and even eventually managed to open a little more regularly.

The Tatar People

A pair of young women in traditional Muslim dress walked past the InterClub offices today, completely cloaked in black burquas with only their eyes visible. This was the first time I had seen anyone dressed this way in Chelny, despite its considerable indigenous Muslim population and it was an incongruous sight. The population of Tatarstan is a mixture of Russians (around 40%), Tatars (50%) with other central Asian peoples making up the balance. There are some 5 million Tatars spread across Russia, with the greatest concentration in Tatarstan itself. Although they have their own language, which is Turkic with a significant admixture of Russian and Arabic words, most Tatars spoke Russian as their first language. The majority were Muslim, though not necessarily practicing, although there certainly were mosques in many of the towns in Tatarstan. The inhabitants of Chelny itself were a mixture from all over Russia, mostly drawn in a generation ago, when the city was being built and workers were needed to fill the rapidly expanding number of jobs in the KamAZ factories. This meant the ratio of Tatars to Russians was lower than elsewhere in Tatarstan, although they still represented over 30% of the population. Many of the people we worked with were Tatars or at least of Tatar origin but few seemed to be fluent in the Tatar language or particularly interested in Tatar or Muslim culture. In terms of cultural attitudes and general approach to life, the majority seemed to me to be exactly the same as the local Russians. Fridays for example, seemed to be a regular workday for everyone and I never heard any mention of Muslim religious festivals such as Ramadan or Eid. A few of the locals stood out as being more obviously Tatar with their dark hair, swarthy faces or more almond shaped eyes but these were not certain indicators of racial origin as many Russians had the same features. Knowing nothing about the Tatars before I arrived in Chelny, I wondered what they would be like to work with but they generally proved to be a warm, open and friendly group of people.

The Tatarstan Muslims appeared generally well integrated into Russian society and culture due to the fact that the region has been part of Russia since the 17th century when it was taken by Ivan the Terrible. Other areas further south with large Muslim populations such as Chechnya and Ossetia in the Caucasus, are quite different and not nearly as stable. They were only added to the Russian Empire in the latter part of the 19th century and although a large number of Russians had moved in over the years, their influence was not as strong as in Tatarstan.

Talking to the manager of the Dialog hotel one evening, I discovered the privately owned group now owned thirty new hotels in Russia. This was really hard to believe and I pressed the manager on his statement but he repeated what he had said and produced a kind of brochure which listed many of the group's hotels. Where did all the money come from to finance such rapid growth in only a couple of years? The cost to construct and equip thirty new hotels was a massive project in such a short period of time and would have stretched the resources of the biggest multinational companies. Since the Russian banks were an unlikely source, I had to conclude that the money probably originated from some form of mafia activity and was now being 'washed through' in a more legitimate business. The low level of room occupancy at the hotel (we were frequently the only guests) meant that it was hard to see how the owning and operating costs could have been fully covered. I had occasionally picked up the odd negative comment in the InterClub about the Dialog almost from the start of my time in Chelny and these now seemed to make more sense.

Summer Snow

Something seriously wrong was suddenly going on in the town. For some mysterious reason, only local Tatar beer was now available in the InterClub and shops, all other brands having totally disappeared from the shelves. After much heated discussion in the hotel one night we concluded it was presumably someone's idea of 'protecting' local industry and jobs – it smacked of collusion and corruption by a senior Tatar government minister. I predicted it couldn't last and sure enough, after a few weeks we returned to normal with both foreign and beer from elsewhere in Russia back on sale. Long may the market rule! The 12th of June turned out to be a Russian national holiday so the office was closed. Yesterday I had asked one of the Russians who worked on our team what the holiday commemorated but he couldn't remember. 'Don't worry about it' he said, 'just enjoy it'. Later investigation revealed that it was Russia's Independence Day, though for some reason that I didn't understand, not all of the schools were off. As the InterClub restaurant was closed due to the holiday, I went out that evening for something to eat in a small place near to the hotel that had recently opened. I had noticed their new neon sign 'café bar' outside earlier in the week and decided to give it a try. Newly refurbished in what I can only describe as the local version of the minimalist style, I discovered its range of food matched the décor – there wasn't much of it. The only other clients – a couple of young men – were heavily into a bottle of vodka and I decided that rather than risk the food, a couple of beers would be the safest choice. Towards the end of my second beer, I found that the local minimalist style also didn't include any provision for customer toilets. A brisk walk back to the hotel saved me any embarrassment and worked up an appetite for my dinner – a can of pasta which I cooked in the hotel kitchen, followed by a banana and chocolate bar in my room. As the KamAZ budgets tightened further and the quality and quantity of food noticeably deteriorated at the InterClub, I increasingly preferred to do my own cooking in the hotel, especially at weekends, using the supplies I brought back from the UK. The hotel's cook was quite happy for me to use their kitchen as long as I cleaned up afterwards and I think she found it a source of amusement to see a foreign man cooking his own meals. My culinary skills weren't great but at least I could eat when I wanted and I knew exactly what I was eating.

This was the time of year when the cottonwood trees all started to drop their fluffy white seeds. The streets of most towns in Russia are lined with these trees and at its peak it felt as if someone was emptying the contents of a thousand feather pillows somewhere overhead. The Russians quaintly say this is God, scratching his head over their problems. But like most

Russians, I actually found this experience quite unpleasant and wished that God had less to worry about. The seeds were easily carried in the wind and got everywhere. They stuck to your clothes and hair and the street gutters were filled with the stuff, almost as if there had been a fall of unseasonal snow. No one appeared to know the name of the Soviet planner who originally decreed that these trees should be planted everywhere but a spell in a Siberian work camp would not have been an unjust reward. What was more astounding to me was that the Russians continued to put up with these trees and it seemed odd that there was no push to remove or replace these troublesome trees. Their towns and cities would have been all the better for it. I think they secretly enjoyed the annual ritual of suffering and complaint; it was all part of the Russian psyche.

The first round of the Russian presidential elections was due to take place the coming weekend and unusually, the past few days have seen a lot of discussion in the office about politics. On the surface there appeared to be a surprisingly strong level of support for the extremist candidate Zuganov rather than Yeltsin. But on probing deeper with some of the Russians in the office, it became clear that this was all about election strategy. The consensus seemed to be that Yeltsin would get in anyway and that by voting for other candidates in the first round, he would not be in too strong a position once elected as president in the second round. Whether the theory was right or wrong, I thought such strategic voting was surprising in a country that had only recently gained the right to free elections. Interestingly, the management of KamAZ issued an unusual order this week requiring everyone to work on Saturday, the day of the election. The carrot of some of the overdue back wages being paid on the Saturday added strength to the order. It was hard to fathom what was behind this move as the need for all to work seemed unnecessary, given the situation of the company. It was more likely that this was a rather crude attempt to ensure people didn't disappear off to their dachas and fail to vote. Big business and politics were closely linked in Russia, even in remote Chelny and Bekh had probably had instructions from Moscow.

Last night, sitting in my hotel bedroom, I couldn't help wondering why 600,000 people still lived in Chelny and what they felt about their lives in this city. I could understand why people had come here originally with the lure of well paid jobs and in some cases, no doubt firm direction from the Communist Party. But why did people stay now, especially the younger generation? It certainly wasn't an easy location in which to earn money and raise a family. There was little to do in Chelny but live, work (if you were lucky) and die. Whilst I realised there were worse places in Russia, there were of course many better ones too. Although people sometimes said to me they would like to move to Kazan, Moscow or St Petersburg, I could see no strong evidence of any significant labour mobility or exodus from Chelny. I talked to some of the KamAZ employees about how static society seemed in Chelny. They told me that apart from Moscow, job prospects and living conditions were really not much better in other cities and it was difficult to find accommodation for rent if you did move. Indeed, in Moscow tight control of accommodation by the government was an intentional method of limiting the numbers of people who wanted to move to the capital. Those few who did relocate usually had to share an already cramped apartment with family or friends and if things didn't work out in Moscow, it was then hard to come back. Most of the apartments in the city were owned or controlled by KamAZ who, on your departure, would then allocate your space to someone else, making it virtually impossible to return. There seemed to be a general shortage of accommodation in most cities that had been exacerbated by the lack of new construction in recent years – apart from dachas for the wealthy. In Chelny there were several half-built new apartment complexes around the city but since perestroika the money to complete them had apparently not been available. They sat unfinished with their high-rise cranes standing idly alongside in some kind of forlorn, abandoned memorial to the former Soviet economic system. However, life in the city went on and I realised most people had come to terms with the situation in which they found themselves. But as I came to know Russia and its people better over the next few years, I increasingly realised just how many Russians desperately wanted to escape the hardships and move to the west. The lucky few, mostly those with connections and money, were already voting with their feet.

As we moved into the latter part of June, the temperature soared; it was often 30 degrees or more at 9am. In our office at the InterClub this morning I sat casually chatting over a cup of coffee to Mack about an item of news I saw on TV last night. Apparently, there had been rumours of further small radiation escapes at Chernobyl in Ukraine where the world's worst nuclear disaster had occurred some ten years before. Lydia, one of the office translators was standing nearby and had clearly heard my comments. She suddenly let out a scream and rushed out of the room in tears, leaving Mack and I wondered what on earth was wrong. A little later, another of the translators explained that Lydia came from Ukraine and had lost several relatives in the original disaster in 1986. Her son was currently working in Chernobyl as part of the ongoing clean-up team and my comments came as a complete surprise to her. It later turned out that the rumours of a new leak were untrue but my casual, unfortunate remark had instantly brought back sad memories for Lydia as well as understandable fears for her son.

As widely expected, this month the second round of the presidential elections saw Yeltsin through again, though many people expressed doubts regarding his health and fitness for the job and on the TV news he certainly didn't look the man he was four years earlier. Overall though, there seemed to be relief that he had been re-elected and that the process of reform, slow as it was in Russia would continue. In the first round of the elections, voting had been strong for the communists. Local concerns about poor job prospects and wage arrears amongst both Tatar and Russian voters no doubt played a part in this. But the fact that many local Tatars (mostly Muslims) were seeking increased autonomy or separation from Moscow also provoked fears within parts of the Russian community about security and Tatarstan remaining fully integrated with Russia. Those fears would have influenced some Russians into switching back to Yeltsin in the second round. The desire for stability and the continuity of a strong central government probably helped swing the Tatarstan vote behind Yeltsin.

The Final Days

From various telephone calls and faxes during the past few weeks, it had become clear to both Mack and I that our assignments in Chelny would be coming to an end very shortly. It seemed project funding from Cummins and the external foreign investors was fast coming to an end. Although we were not told the full picture at the time, apparently there was understandable disappointment at the slow pace of change in the company leading to disagreements between these investors, the Tatarstan government and the board of KamAZ about the future structure and ownership of the company. With the realisation that we would soon be leaving, there was a frantic, last minute scramble by some of the KamAZ managers to get time with us and life became quite hectic with our diaries becoming fuller by the day. We tried our best to accommodate as many of these requests as possible and to complete as many projects as we could. As our final departure loomed, my feelings were mixed. After more than a year of working in Chelny, it would be hard saying goodbye to my many friends in KamAZ, knowing that it was unlikely that we would see each other again. Also, it was sad knowing that although we had achieved much, there was still a lot more that could be done to help KamAZ and its employees restructure the business and adjust to the market economy. However, thoughts of a more normal life back in the UK compensated for the regrets and I inevitably now found myself planning for the future. After Chelny, I felt I was ready for anything! In my hotel room that night I reflected on the last twelve months in Chelny and both the good and bad times I'd experienced. Russia had proven to be a constant challenge, never knowing if the flights would be OK, whether my contract would be extended or if my visa would come in time. No wonder that Shakespeare's Hamlet was so well liked by the Russians – the immortal phrase 'to be or not to be' seemed constantly appropriate to life here.

Our departure was eventually set for Friday June 28th and I spent much of the final week packing up all our files and paperwork, most to be forwarded to Cummins Moscow office and the remainder left in storage boxes at the InterClub. Some of our equipment was given to KamAZ, including the fax machine and a couple of office laptop computers. The last few evenings in the hotel were busy too as I sorted through the various possessions I had accumulated during my time in Chelny, trying to decide what to cram into my already bulging suitcases and what to give away to staff at the InterClub. The last couple of days in the office were rapidly consumed in a flurry of final meetings and exchanges of contact details plus good wishes from all our friends. I went to pay a final visit to Victor, the sales manager at KamAZ. He looked quite depressed when I walked in and I jokingly asked him whether it was my imminent departure or business problems that were the cause of his low mood. 'A little of both' he replied and I was surprised that he seemed genuinely sad that I was leaving. I reminded him of our conversation earlier in the year when we had talked about going fishing together one weekend and expressed regret that sadly, time had now overtaken us. In an attempt to try to cheer him up I said that if he ever made it to the UK, he should call me and I would take him to Scotland to do some salmon fishing. As we stood to shake hands, Victor smiled and said 'Yes, that would be good... maybe one of these days. Who knows?'

I'm still waiting for that call from Victor. On my final afternoon in Chelny, I also went to see Ivan Kostin, the deputy director of KamAZ for a short private visit – i.e. without translators. I always felt that Kostin was the only one of the directors who truly seemed to grasp the enormity of the challenges facing the company and the need for real change. Although we hadn't spent a lot of time working together, I always got on well with him and felt him to be a very genuine person. Recently, it had become clear that his star was rising in the organisation and I later learnt he had taken over from Bekh as general director of KamAZ. Our respective limited capabilities in each other's language prevented any in depth conversation but he warmly thanked me for all my work while at KamAZ and I wished both him and the company well for the future.

The next morning, Mack and I were collected from the Dialog hotel for the last time and driven to the airport in bright early morning sunshine. It seemed hard to take in the fact that this was the last time we would make this journey. At the airport, luck was on our side for once and the final charter out of Chelny to Moscow went without a hitch, as did the onward flights into London and finally on up to Manchester. I couldn't stop myself from thinking that just maybe mother Russia was co-operating this time simply to be rid of us.

Postscript

Although I subsequently revisited Tatarstan, I never went back to Chelny after that summer of 1996. However, whilst doing research for this book, I came across an article written by someone who did. Adrian Blomfield, the Moscow correspondent for the UK newspaper The Daily Telegraph paid a brief visit to the city in November 2007 and this is an extract from the article he wrote:

> 'Before I began our three-hour taxi ride *(from Kazan)* to Naberezhnye Chelny, Tatarstan's second city.... I briefly flicked through the city's official English language website. Prominently featured among the section headings detailing the city's proud industrial past and hopeful present was an internal link entitled "Russian women." Following it, I discovered that the website's authors had recommended www.loversplanet.com as their favoured agency for westerners seeking Russian brides. There was, I suppose, a remarkable honesty about all of this. Yet was this not a pretty damning indictment of Naberezhnye Chelny? The website's authors were essentially admitting that a substantial number of the city's womenfolk would rather shack up with a lonely and quite possibly unpalatable westerner they had never met than endure another day here.

For a city that bore the unfortunate name of Brezhnev (*a disliked former Soviet president)* in the 1980s, perhaps this was no surprise. As we circled endless grey apartment blocks, all identical in their gargantuan soullessness, an oppressive mournfulness fell over me. No wonder the girls wanted to get out. I wanted to get out, and I had only been here an hour. Yet for Ilnur, our Tatar guide, Naberezhnye Chelny was a place of exquisite beauty. Perhaps Ilnur was suffering from the self-delusion that afflicted many of the official Soviet guides of yore, seeing magnificence where there was none. Or maybe beauty really is in the eye of the beholder. Among the endless sea of anonymous concrete, our driver finally located the address we are looking for. We stepped into a stairwell that clearly doubled as a public latrine and headed up to the pokey apartment of a Muslim man who had been jailed and tortured as part of Tatarstan's continuing crackdown on even the faintest whiff of radical Islam.'

Perhaps Blomfield was a little harsh on the Naberezhnye Chelny that I remember but evidently in the intervening ten years, not much had changed. Incidentally from my experiences, it was not just the women that wanted to leave but also many of the young men who felt the same way.

PART TWO

FROM THE BLACK SEA TO SIBERIA

1997 – 2000

CHAPTER ONE

Joining the Foreign Office

On our return to England from Tatarstan, Mack and I kept in touch with each other and met up again in September for a final dinner with a couple of the Cummins senior managers who had been most closely involved with the KamAZ project. But after that, Mack and I went our separate ways, each busy with our own lives. I was quite surprised therefore one morning several months later to receive a phone call from him telling me he had seen that the British Foreign & Commonwealth Office (FCO) was looking for a part time adviser to handle their enterprise restructuring projects throughout Russia. Mack thought I might be interested – and he was right. In a strange way, I found that I had missed Russia and here was the possibility of seeing a lot more of the country but without the problems of actually living there. As it was part time, it also seemed it would fit in well with my other business commitments and I felt I had the kind of experience the FCO was looking for.

I duly applied, was interviewed and eventually offered the position as a part time adviser to the 'Know How Fund' in Russia (then part of the Foreign & Commonwealth Office) in early 1997. I was initially required to provide 60 days on a one year contract split equally between the Know How Fund's offices in London and travel in Russia. At the time, the KHF occupied cramped offices in a rather run-down part of the Old Admiralty Buildings in Whitehall, just up from the Foreign Office and

Downing Street. I was fortunate to find myself with a spacious, if a little down at heel room on the second floor, looking out onto Whitehall and part of the Horse Guards parade ground. It was shared with another adviser but as he was also part time, it meant I often had the luxury of an office in Whitehall to myself. Working for the government and dealing with civil servants would not only be a new experience for me; it would also be quite a challenge. I would now have to quickly understand their way of working and get to grips with a wide variety of programmes in many different parts of Russia whilst operating in an unfamiliar non-commercial organisation. Delivery of all the major KHF projects was handled by a range of competitively-selected UK consultancy companies who worked with agreed Russian partners to achieve the required results. An important part of my work would be to liaise with these firms both in the UK and in Russia monitoring their performance and I spent much of my contracted time over the next couple of months in familiarisation meetings with these companies.

In May 1997, the Labour party was elected to government and things were to change significantly at the KHF over the coming months. Clare Short was appointed Secretary of State for International Development and demanded a seat in cabinet with her own department to be called the Department for International Development which was to eventually include the KHF. The acronym for this new Department – DFID – was awkward, sounding more like a Welsh county as one of my civil servant colleagues said wryly but we slowly became used to it. The new broom brought not only a new organisation but also new policies. Clare Short boldly stated that the aim of DFID was now to eliminate poverty – a worthy goal but impossibly unrealistic, both in view of the comparatively small budget we had and the fact that poverty is in many ways relative. In any society run by humans, there will always be some people who are better off than others and the latter will always see themselves as poor. I attended a meeting in Whitehall that summer with Short at which she expounded her views and how the Department would have to redirect its efforts to meet the new goal. Along with several others, I came away from this meeting with mixed feelings. Firstly, I couldn't believe that a government minister could have such naive views and secondly, I was concerned about the possible effect this would have on our work in Russia. As it turned out, there was no immediate impact on the KHF and some months later the new policy was quietly amended to *reducing* poverty rather than eliminating it – common sense prevailed.

My very first visit to Russia for the KHF was to be a two week trip in mid September 1997 taking in St Petersburg, Moscow, Nizhny Novgorod and Kazan, giving me a chance to make contact with some of the local project and British embassy staff with whom I would be working over the coming year. My outward journey to St Petersburg and then Moscow passed off without any problems – maybe travel was going to be better under the Foreign Office's auspices. An embassy car met me at the airports and my local KHF contacts ensured I was in the right place at the right time for my meetings with a variety of Russian government and foreign organisations active in the area of economic development. I was surprised to find just how many foreign aid programmes were being run in Russia. The largest donors were the USA and the European Union plus very significant activity by the World Bank and European Bank of Reconstruction & Development, mostly in the form of loans. In addition, along with the UK's KHF, more than half a dozen European countries were also running their own individual projects as well as Canada and Japan. Of course, not all this activity was related to economic development – at least not directly. There were initiatives covering health, drug miss-use, education and media as well as improving civil society. This plethora of largely uncoordinated programmes was confusing and resulted in donors competing for time and influence with Russian government ministers as well as local partners to assist in delivery. Also, measurement of the true effectiveness of all this activity, involving hundreds of millions of dollars annually, appeared rather patchy.

Part of my remit involved representing the KHF on the management board of a new consulting business they had helped set up to assist new small Russian companies to develop. The business, called the VVCC

(Volga Vyatsky Consulting Centre), was based in Nizhny Novgorod with branch offices in Kirov and Saransk but for various logistical reasons, my initial contact with them was organised during my visit to Moscow. Strangely for a British funded project, they had an American called Ken as a resident adviser who had been seconded from the Moscow office of a large international consulting firm. In his early 30s, Ken was bright, personable, spoke very reasonable Russian and made an important contribution to the development of the business. He had originally come to Russia with the US Peace Corps and had found the place so interesting that he had stayed on, subsequently marring an attractive young woman from Nizhny and was now raising a family there. In fact, with his dark hair and small goatee beard, he actually looked Russian. I spent a morning with Ken in his room at the National hotel reviewing the background to the project and current financial position before going on with him to attend a board meeting in the afternoon. The Russian managers that attended were a mixed bunch with a variety of previous experience but they all seemed keen to work with the KHF and motivated about their project. The VVCC's Russian director Boris, was an affable but relatively quiet and serious man who came across at our meeting as rather hesitant and unsure of himself. But as he had only recently been appointed, this was perhaps understandable. Once the board meeting was finished in the late afternoon, an embassy car took Ken, Boris and I to the airport where we caught an Aeroflot flight to Nizhny, arriving late evening.

This was to be the first of my many visits to the city, the fourth largest in Russia with a population of over 1.3 million. Nizhny lies to the east of Moscow and was founded in the 13*th* century. With its strategic position at the confluence of the Volga and Oka rivers, the original settlement provided an important strongpoint protecting Russia's eastern borders. The city's imposing red brick kremlin with 13 towers overlooking the Volga dates from the early 16*th* century and was soon in use repulsing the Tatar sieges in 1520 and 1536. Nizhny's excellent river communications steadily encouraged trade and growth and by the mid-19*th* century, the city was firmly established as the principle trade capital of the Russian

Empire. In the latter half of the 19th century the Nizhny Novgorod trade fair was Russia's largest and attracted millions of visitors each summer from across the Empire and around the world. At the time a popular Russian saying was '*If St. Petersburg is Russia's head, then Moscow is its heart and Nizhny Novgorod its wallet*'. In the 20th century it also became a major industrial centre and in the late 1920s Henry Ford was involved in establishing an automotive plant here called GAZ (Gorky Automotive Factory). During the Soviet era, Nizhny was a 'closed' city and no foreigners were allowed to visit. The human rights activist and Nobel Peace Prize winner Andrei Sakharov was exiled here in the 1980s so as to limit his contacts with foreigners. Despite its size, I found Nizhny's central commercial district to be relatively small for such a large city. The main focus was a couple of pedestrianised streets that held the principle retail stores, a couple of decent restaurants and cafes together with a branch of the Russian state bank which occupied a large, heavy-set stone building. With its pseudo Gothic design, it looked to me as if it had been uprooted from somewhere in southern Germany. Of more immediate interest to me was the fact that Nizhny was the base for Boris Nemtsov who at the time was one of Russia's leading economic reformers. He had recently been appointed deputy prime minister in Yeltsin's government but had previously been governor of the Nizhny Novgorod region and in this capacity had introduced an extensive market reform programme that resulted in a significant burst of economic growth for the region. His reforms had earned praise from Margaret Thatcher who as British prime minister had visited Nizhny in 1993. It was this view of Nizhny as being in the vanguard of reform that had encouraged the KHF (along with other foreign donors) to set up various projects in the region to assist and further encourage the process.

Although it was rather late by the time I was dropped off at my Nizhny hotel, my initial impressions were quite favourable. The Octyabrskaya hotel was a relatively modern and quite stylish multi-storey structure in white concrete, not like most architecturally-drab Soviet hotels. It had a pleasant location at the edge of a small park just outside the city centre on a bluff overlooking the broad Volga river with fine views. The hotel staff seemed courteous and my room although small, seemed functional with a single bed, Russian TV, desk and a working shower. Not having eaten since lunchtime, I was extremely hungry but sadly, the restaurant was closed and not unexpectedly, there was no room service. I wearily unpacked, showered and hungrily went to bed at which point my earlier favourable impressions of the hotel started to fade. The single bed was too short for me and my feet stuck out past the end of the mattress resting on the unyielding wooden frame of the bed. The situation was made worse by the large, overstuffed pillows which seemed to take up a third of the bed, pushing my head and shoulders upwards while forcing the rest of my body down towards the end of the mattress. It felt as if the bed was only five feet long, though in reality it was probably more like five and a half feet (discounting the two projecting feet of course). I tossed and turned and tried all the different positions in the bed that I could think of but was unable to get comfortable and fall asleep. I thought about getting dressed and going down to reception to ask if there was possibly a room with a larger bed. But it was late and I knew there was no way that my tired brain could come up with the Russian words to explain why I wanted to change rooms. Eventually, I decided to remove the mattress from the bed and place it on the floor and by using one of the large pillows as an extension, I was able to create a reasonably flat surface that was long enough to allow me to stretch out and finally drift off to sleep. I was to experience the same short bed problem in many other Russian hotels on my subsequent travels around the country and employed the same technique of sleeping on the floor many times. I never understood why so many of the beds in Russia were this size when there are plenty of tall people in the country. Were they all made in the same factory as the standard issue Soviet single bed? If so, who had decreed the length of these short beds? Was it some Soviet bureaucrat with a deficiency in the height department perhaps, wanting to have revenge on the taller people in this world? Or maybe it was simply a manufacturing error during one of the Soviet five year plans that no one dared to correct?

After my restless night, the morning seemed to come too soon but temporarily fortified with a breakfast of a hard-boiled egg, rye bread and some weak coffee, I was collected from the hotel and driven to the VVCC's project offices in a multi-storey office block just outside the city centre. During my time with the KHF, I was to be a regular visitor to Nizhny and eventually felt quite at home there. I enjoyed working with the local staff and made good friends with Ken our resident American adviser and Boris the VVCC director. Although the couple of city centre hotels I regularly stayed in were fairly awful, it was easy enough to walk to the shops or a couple of decent cafes and restaurants in the evenings or at weekends. For journeys further afield, there always seemed to be plenty of taxis around, mostly beat up old Volgas (made at the huge GAZ plant on the outskirts of Nizhny) and the fares were very reasonable. Later, as I got to know the city better, I visited both the local cinema and theatre. With little street crime evident in the city centre, I always felt safe wandering around, even late at night.

From Nizhny, I was taken by car to Kazan, stopping off on the way in the town of Cheboksary to visit a company making large industrial tractors and construction equipment. Cheboksary is a major river port on the Volga with a population of around 500,000 and is capital of the semi-autonomous Chuvash republic. Its economy was heavily dependent on manufacturing with several large engineering and machinery plants. The company I visited was another large, monopolistic former Soviet enterprise that had been privatised in 1993 and like many others, was experiencing severe problems in the prevailing Russian market conditions. I met with the managing director who gave me some background on the company's situation. The initial privatisation process had been typical of the time – 50% of the shares to the employees, 40% to external investors and 10% retained by the state. After privatisation, production and employment declined severely from its 1989 peak and two years ago the company hit a major financial crisis ending up in administration with the Federal Bankruptcy Agency. Typically, most of the employees (or now former employees) sold their shares at penny prices to external investors to raise money to live on and the business was now controlled by a Moscow investment company who had appointed a new president. Despite introducing new products, sales were currently running at less than 15% of the previous peak and employment had declined by almost 50% to under 10,000. Cheboksary was essentially a mono-company town; the company had been and was still the primary employer in the area and understandably, this loss of jobs had devastated the local community. Most of the social assets owned by the company had been sold off or closed, adding further misery to the town. As the director said, they were trying to pull themselves up by their own bootstraps but it was extremely hard without any real interest or support from the government and no way now of raising money for investment and much needed factory maintenance. A few of the former employees had shown initiative by trying to set up small businesses but without a thriving local economy, most had failed or remained one man outfits. I toured the manufacturing facilities and although there was some new equipment, most of what I saw was very run down and in a dilapidated condition – I found it sad and depressing and could see little hope for the company as it stood. Their market in Russia would grow but only slowly and their outdated production processes meant they could not realistically hope to seriously compete in export markets. I have spent some time describing the situation at this company because during my years in Russia I was to see this kind of problem in so many towns and cities all over the country. The rate of industrial decline and loss of employment through the 1990s was one of the most important problems facing Russia and in some of the more remote communities the future looked very bleak indeed. In a one company town, life becomes very hard when the one company goes downhill. It was a pity therefore that the government failed to do more to address the situation as well as turning a blind eye to the dubious activities of some private investors and financial institutions in acquiring large chunks of corporate assets at rock bottom prices. Quite simply the government failed the people of Russia in this respect. On my return to England, further research showed the debilitating impact of the region's economic decline on the Chuvash population. In the past ten years, the birth rate had fallen by 50% and the death rate almost doubled.

I took my leave of Cheboksary and in warm early evening sunshine, continued my journey eastwards to Kazan along the main road that roughly follows the path of the Volga. I was booked into a new hotel there that had been built since the time of my earlier visits from KamAZ. It was an impressive high rise building, the tallest in Kazan with comfortable bedrooms and good views across the city. I was told it had been built on the back of the rising oil price and resulting increase in business visitors. In fact, the next day I met a British businessman who was staying in the hotel and involved in oil trading. I was in the hotel business centre trying to send an urgent fax to the KHF in London and was having problems with the machine. While I was complaining in Russian to the receptionist that their machine didn't seem to be working properly, he walked up to ask her for some paper. I saw him later that evening in the bar and we chatted for a while about doing business in Russia. He spoke some Russian and had visited the country several times over the last couple of years. He was one of the very few British businessmen that I met in Russia outside Moscow or St Petersburg. As we parted to go to our rooms, he said to me 'I thought when I heard you complaining in the business centre that you were Russian.' I was surprised but pleased – it was worth coming back to Kazan just for this compliment. I replied that my Russian wasn't that good; it's just that I'd had lots of practice making complaints in Russia.

It felt strange to be back in Kazan wearing another hat and I half expected to bump into someone from KamAZ but of course never did. Apart from the construction of my new hotel and the ongoing refurbishment of several city centre buildings, nothing much seemed to have changed in the eighteen months since my last visit here. Throngs of people still bustled along the pedestrianised main street in daytime, the traffic around the centre was just as hectic and the potholes in the roads were just as numerous. The bleak concrete Intourist hotel that I had stayed in once before was still in business and looking... well just as bleak. One of my meetings took place in the old kremlin buildings which I now saw housed several government offices. It was interesting this time as an official visitor to be able to see inside the citadel as on my last visit I had been unable to go in. As with the Kremlin in Moscow, there are some interesting old buildings inside, including the Annunciation Cathedral which dates back to the 16*th* century and the Kazan kremlin was actually declared a world heritage site in 2000. I finished my meetings by mid-afternoon and decided to wander into the nearby city centre and explore a little. Along one road that curved down towards the kremlin I noticed several quite large brick-built mansions, probably dating from the mid-19*th* century and presumably built by the richer merchants of the day. They looked to be in a poor state at the time of my visit but I was in no doubt that in a few years they would either have been modernised or demolished to make way for the current generation of wealthy city residents. There was nothing along the main shopping streets to hold my interest but further on in one of the side roads, I found a small antique shop. A couple of framed wooden icons on display in the window caught my eye and I went inside to ask about them and how much they were. Both paintings showed an attractive group of figures, one was some eighteen inches square and the other twelve inches square. I preferred the colours and condition of the larger one but knew it was too big to fit into my hand luggage for the flight home and was concerned whether it would be safe in my suitcase. The smaller one had clearly been poorly restored in one section but would be easier to carry back to England. The owner knew little of their provenance but claimed they were probably at least 150 years old and said he rarely had such items for sale. I immediately discounted the sales pitch but since I liked them, I decided I would try to buy one anyway as a souvenir. The larger painting was priced in roubles at US$130 and the smaller one was US$80. We started to haggle and I ended up purchasing the smaller one for US$50, paying in dollar bills. The icon, which now hangs on a wall in my house and is an attractive reminder of this visit to Kazan, was one of the very few things I found to buy during my years in Russia.

CHAPTER TWO

Novosibirsk, Nizhny Novgorod, Kirov & Saransk

As I settled into my role at the KHF, I was steadily asked to provide input on a growing number of topics relating to Russian economic development. Sitting in my office in Cheshire one day in October, I received a call from one of the KHF managers in London to say a confidential fax was on its way to me. True enough, a couple of minutes later, my fax machine suddenly jolted into life and a multi-page message started printing out. I wandered over to see what it was and was startled to see that it was a copy of a letter from Boris Yeltsin to the Foreign Office regarding a new inter-government initiative for training a large cadre of Russian managers in the West. I was asked to review Yeltsin's proposals and to email my comments to the KHF by return. Somehow it seemed amazing to me that I should be dealing with correspondence from the President of Russia and briefly made me feel much more important than I really was. In fact, as it turned out, this interesting programme never got off the ground – at least in the way originally envisaged. There were too many political and logistical problems and other priorities soon replaced Yeltsin's interesting concept.

I returned to Russia in late January, flying from Manchester with Lufthansa via Frankfurt and on to Novosibirsk in western Siberia. This was to be my first visit to Siberia and I have to admit to experiencing a tingling apprehension at the prospect of visiting this intriguing part of Russia.

Before leaving, I had looked at my world atlas to check the exact location of Novosibirsk and was surprised to find my journey would hardly take me half way across Siberia. Brad Newsham[2] in his book wrote that *'from central Siberia, the rest of the world is a casual afterthought'*. Certainly once there, embraced in its vast open spaces, everywhere else felt very distant and of little importance. Russia is a vast country and for many people there, the rest of the world seems largely an irrelevance (although one could equally argue the same attitude exists at times in some the parts of the USA). Such an enormous entity has inevitably frequently generated big plans and big thoughts as well as some big books, as anyone who has tried to read up on Russian history will verify.

Like the American West, Siberia's early development was built on optimistic hope and a desire for freedom. The early settlers that came here believed that somewhere further along the track would be a better life and the opportunity to escape the controls of the aristocracy, Orthodox Church and corrupt bureaucracy in western Russia. This vast region has always had an independent spirit and indeed, was one of the last parts of the Tsarist Empire to fall under Bolshevik control. If it ever became an independent country, Siberia would be the largest in the world with almost 5 million square miles, bigger than the whole of the USA and western Europe combined. With eleven time zones, Russia in many ways is the wrong shape, both geographically and economically and Siberia is the absolute epitome of this problem. The region has been a constant obsession of Russia's rulers for 250 years. Their desire to first open up and then exploit Siberia's considerable riches of wood, metals, diamonds and more recently oil led to a massive expenditure of resources, especially human capital in their attempt to lay claim to this cold, unforgiving territory. The initial slow trickle of voluntary immigrants was increasingly supplemented by criminals, political or religious exiles plus large numbers of ordinary people who found themselves in the wrong place at the wrong time. As the flow of forced immigration from the west increased, isolated labour camps gradually grew into villages or towns and occasionally

2 Brad Newsham – All The Right Places

became cities. But cold means cost and in the Soviet period, construction and living costs were 50% higher in Siberia than in western Russia. In an interesting study[3], a comparison was made between the situation in Canada (which is similar in climate and size) and that of Siberia by using a 'temperature per capita' indicator. The authors showed that the average Russian citizen has grown colder over the past 50 years while those in Canada have become warmer. Canada's cities have expanded along its relatively warm southern border with the USA but in Siberia, government policy has continued to push its people into facing nine or ten months of winter further north and east. Many of these towns and cities were economically and socially isolated, facing a questionable future in the post Soviet era and posed a severe long term socio-economic problem.

It was a long trip to Novosibirsk on three flights, with an eight hour time change and a daytime temperature of minus 22C to cope with. Novosibirsk is a relatively old city by Siberian standards, having been founded over 100 years ago on a key river crossing as a trading and regional transport hub. It experienced major expansion after World War II with the growth of hi-tech research and mainly defence-related industries that were located here for strategic reasons by the Soviet government. Because of this, Novosibirsk was a prohibited city for foreigners until quite recently and it was clear from the close attention I received during my visit that foreign visitors were still a rarity. As I stepped outside the hotel entrance in my fur lined boots onto the compacted pavement snow, I felt that maybe I should have stayed away too. The city now has a population of around 1.5 million and surprisingly, given its remote location, is Russia's third largest city. Due to its rapid industrial growth in the 20*th* century it was known as the Chicago of Siberia and just like Chicago sits by a large lake and can get very windy. Although it has a modern appearance with row after row of high rise apartments and wide streets and boulevards, it felt rather soul-less to me as there wasn't really a proper city centre to give a heart to the place. The city has a spacious emptiness like the surrounding Siberian countryside that somehow seemed to reduce the

3 Hill & Gaddy – The Siberian Curse, 2003

impact of its one and a half million inhabitants. As the travel writer Colin Thubron[4] said in his book about Siberia, *'this city is a claustrophobe's dream'*. However, as I stood there on the street outside the hotel, I realised this openness also allowed the Arctic winds full rein and the wind chill effect meant the early morning temperature felt more like minus 40C. I pulled up the thick collar of my banana duvet coat (the one I had bought in Chelny a few years ago) to protect my face and pulled my hat firmly down against a bone-chilling wind. It wasn't the moment to stop and admire the view and I jumped gratefully into the white Volga car that had come to collect me.

My host Dimitri, was the Russian president of a regional consulting business that was the local partner in one of our projects. In his pine panelled office, we sat and discussed the local economic situation and the problems faced by businesses trying to survive and prosper. Fair haired and with steely blue eyes, he was a bright, dynamic man with interesting, progressive ideas and I enjoyed meeting him. Later, as we travelled round the city visiting a few companies and government officials, it was obvious to me that he was very well connected and commanded respect – surprisingly so for the manager of a small business. When I returned to England I learnt that he was a former apparatchik, a senior official in the Novosibirsk communist party – interesting to see how easily the Siberian leopard can change his spots. Apart from the cold weather, the only problem during my visit to Novosibirsk was the fact that Dimitri hadn't booked a hotel room for the second night of my stay, despite having been requested to do so by our embassy staff in Moscow. I'm not sure what he had expected me to do for the night – sleeping on the street was definitely out. However, he was full of apologies and eventually persuaded the hotel staff to let me stay another night. My hotel was a large, modern building in the centre; the restaurant food was forgettable but my room was delightfully warm for which I was extremely grateful.

4 Colin Thubron – In Siberia, 1999

From Novosibirsk, I flew on to Moscow for a few days for meetings and then on for a whistle stop tour to meet local staff involved in KHF projects in Kirov, Nizhny Novgorod and Saransk. In Moscow, I was fortunate to find myself staying at the Kempinski hotel for the weekend, one of the best in the city – business was slow at this time of year so the embassy had obtained a very special rate. A couple of visits to the hotel coffee shop during my stay provided a fascinating glimpse into the life of a part of Moscow society. One of the most noticeable changes since my visits to Moscow during my time with KamAZ was the arrival of the mobile or cell phone; everyone who was anyone in the city now had one. Gazing around as I lingered over a coffee, it was easy to get the impression that all Muscovites were rich; most women were very attractive blondes; everyone had a mobile telephone and all the men wore black leather jackets or coats with a few having suspicious-looking bulges. At the time, the opulent Kempinski was a favourite haunt of the Moscow mafia as they apparently felt safe there because the hotel's security was reckoned to be so good. Of course this was a distorted picture of life in Moscow which was (and still is) a city of tremendous contrasts, similar to London or New York in that great wealth jostles alongside immense poverty. But somehow Moscow seems more excessive in its opulent display and hedonistic enjoyment of wealth. Life in the multiple rows of high rise apartment blocks that lined the ring road around the city was vastly different. There, the problems of poverty, overcrowding, drugs and crime were as depressingly familiar as on any 'sink' estates in London, Paris or New York, only on a larger scale. For a fortunate few, the city is a pot of gold while for the harassed majority it is a place of almost incessant struggle. *'A Big Apple it is not. More of a Big Potato'*[5]

One thing that hadn't changed in Moscow was the chaotic traffic situation and predictably, the traffic today was intense. Traffic jams often quickly built up and it was hard to predict the amount of time needed when travelling around the city to keep appointments. Road surfaces were often poor with large jolting potholes and pavements were no better.

5 Martin Walker – Martin Walker's Russia, 1989

In heavy rain, as it was that day, the potholes rapidly filled up, making it impossible to tell whether they are an inch deep or a foot. As a result, drivers were continuously liable to suddenly swerve all over the road (and even onto the pavement) in an attempt to avoid these obstacles to their progress. Many of the wider major roads, especially in Moscow, had a special, single lane running down the centre called the 'Zil lane' where one would otherwise expect the central reservation to be. In Soviet times, these restricted lanes used to be the preserve of government vehicles (mostly black Zil cars, hence the name) rushing along at high speed with their blue lights flashing. However, now that the free market ruled in Russia, any driver in a hurry and feeling sufficiently daring or foolhardy, was able to tempt fate and try his luck in the centre lane, especially if they were driving a Mercedes or BMW. This new automotive democracy worked fine until you came up against a similarly important person travelling in the opposite direction. Then a kind of mobile Mexican stand-off occurred until one of the cars was forced back into the normal traffic lanes. On a few occasions, these confrontations became violent and an exchange of gun-shots was not unknown. The 'Zil lanes' were also a convenient temporary resting place for broken down vehicles, which were a fairly common sight and a major hazard. Driving in Moscow was definitely not for the unadventurous no matter what time of the year. Winter driving was bad due to the difficult weather conditions and summer driving could be dangerous too due to the podsnegniki or snowdrops – cars that are stored for the winter and only driven in the summer, the Russian equivalent to our Sunday drivers.

All this fun was nominally supervised by the traffic police or GAI (GosAvtoInspect) who to the casual outside observer like me, seemed ineffective at both sorting out traffic problems and dealing with crime. Most of their time seemed to be spent standing at the roadside idly watching the traffic roar, or more often, crawl by. But in fact, they were seeking their next easy victim, usually a driver of a Lada or old Volga, rarely choosing an imported BMW, Mercedes or big Japanese 4x4. As the vehicles pushed past on their journeys, each driver tried to scrupulously avoid catching the eye of the waiting policeman. Suddenly, the policeman pounced; a car was chosen and waved over on the basis of some mysterious infraction and the driver's paperwork was demanded and inspected. After a few moments it was rare for the driver to escape without some fine being imposed and a few rouble notes would usually change hands. The process reminded me of a herd of impalas being hunted by a lion in Africa. At the sight of a lion, the impalas rush around in all directions, each hoping they will not be selected as the target and once one of the herd has been caught by the lion, the survivors all then relax, knowing they are safe for the time being. The GAI are neither respected nor liked by the majority of Russians.

My schedule now took me on from Moscow to Nizhny Novgorod by train, a journey of only some 230 miles but taking almost six hours on the so-called fast train. An embassy car collected me from the Kempinski hotel, drove me to the train station and as I got out the driver pointed me in the direction of the platforms. I had been on Russian trains before but always with an interpreter or guide; this would be the first time I travelled alone and was to prove a challenge for me. I walked through the concourse to where the platforms were located and looked up at the indicator board to find the right one for my train to Nizhny Novgorod. After carefully scanning the board several times, I couldn't see any mention of my destination so I realised I would have to ask someone where to go. I mentally rehearsed the necessary phrase several times and then in my haltering Russian put the question to nearby a fellow traveller. Much to my surprise he immediately told me the number of the platform to go to. I was impressed with myself; maybe this Russian language thing wasn't so difficult after all. I stood on my platform and watched several trains arrive and depart but I was early so I waited. With about ten minutes to go before my scheduled departure, a large engine pulling a long line of carriages pulled up to the platform. On the front of the engine there was a sign that looked as if it should be the destination but it certainly didn't say Nizhny Novgorod; it looked like 'Gorki' which meant nothing to me. I had listened carefully to the occasional announcements over the tinny loudspeakers but I could detect no mention of Nizhny Novgorod. People were boarding now so maybe it was my train but then it might not be – I started to feel anxious and confused. Once again I pushed my Russian to its limit and asked a nearby woman if this was the train to Nizhny. 'Da, da' came the friendly reply and with a confirming wave of her arm she motioned me forwards onto the train. Much relieved, I grabbed my suitcase and followed her up the steps into the carriage. When I finally reached Nizhny, my Russian colleagues explained to me why the sign on the front of the train was 'Gorki'. This was the name for Nizhny under the Soviets (named after Maxim Gorki, the Soviet author) and although the city had now returned to its original name, it seems Russian Railways hadn't yet got round to changing all the destination signs. I'm sure I was neither the first nor the last to be confused by this.

A whole compartment had been reserved for me by the embassy which was apparently standard practice when someone like me was travelling alone. It neatly avoided any possible problems arising from having to spend hours sharing a compartment with any 'difficult' Russians. At the time, I felt this was over-zealous on the part of the embassy but some months later when in a train in the south, I found out they were right to be cautious. I slid the compartment door shut and settled down to doing some paperwork – I had several meetings coming up during the week and wanted to make sure I was well prepared. After two or three hours had gone by and I'd eaten the packed lunch I'd brought with me, I felt the need to go to the lavatory which as in most trains is situated at one end of the carriage. I stood up, reached for the door handle and pulled – it didn't move. Now I remembered from when I took the train from St Petersburg to Moscow a year or so ago that Russian train door handles can be difficult. Like many mechanical things in Russia, the doors and handles are strongly built, even over-engineered and there is a knack required to open them. I tried again – several times – but the door mechanism held fast as if it knew I was a foreigner. No problem I thought, there's bound to be a ticket inspector or tea lady along soon who will open the door. I sat and waited as the pressure in my bladder gradually increased. I briefly glanced at the small sliding window but even by standing on the seat it was too high to be of use in my predicament. I tried the handle again but still no luck and then I remembered I had my trusty Swiss penknife in my briefcase. I inspected the door lock; maybe, just maybe I could use the screwdriver to undo it. I carefully removed the lock cover and could see how the mechanism went behind the right hand vertical door frame. This was held in place by a series of screws which after some time I managed to take out. Now if I just take this wooden frame off, I should be able to release the lock and I would be free! I eased off the frame and then to my horror discovered that the lock was still securely held in place by a small metal fitting that could only be accessed from the corridor side of the door – totally out of my reach. Russian engineering design had defeated me; I was trapped until we reached Nizhny. It took another half an hour to put all the pieces of railway property back in their rightful place. As I stood and tightened the final screws (I had a couple of screws left over but was sure no-one would notice) my head was right against the door. I noticed there was a narrow vertical crack between the sliding wooden door and the door frame of the compartment and I could just see a short distance out into the corridor. I stood there waiting for a while and soon I could see another passenger walking down the corridor towards me. As he drew near I said loudly in Russian 'Please help me, my door won't open.'

He looked up at my door for a few seconds in puzzlement.

'Please, I can't open the door' I persisted through the crack. He looked again but this time his expression was more worried. He took a step towards the door then obviously changed his mind and walked on down the corridor out of sight. I shouted after him but my chance was gone. Maybe he couldn't understand my Russian or thought it was a candid camera type hoax. Most likely he probably thought I was crazy, a drunk or on drugs or even all three.

By now, I was absolutely desperate to relieve myself. I looked out of the crack again and remembered the tea lady in her little cabin at the end of the carriage (every long distance train has one); maybe I could attract her attention. I started kicking the door and shouting out in Russian. After a couple of minutes, the door of the adjacent compartment slid open briefly, only to firmly close again. I kicked and shouted louder and saw the tea lady's head appear, leaning out into the corridor. She had clearly heard my noise and so I continued shouting. She slowly and cautiously eased herself along the corridor until she reached my compartment. I repeated my earlier plea 'Please help me, I can't open the door.'

She looked at the door, reached out and grasped the handle, gave it a sharp yank and opened my door. Russian train tea ladies are not normally the prettiest of women but she looked so good standing there with the door open, I almost kissed her. I explained to her that I had problems with the door and that perhaps there was something wrong with the lock. She slid the door to a couple of times and had no problem opening it with the handle. I watched how she gripped the handle and flicked her wrist over to release the catch and then tried again myself and this time, albeit with difficulty, succeeded in opening the door. She looked at me as if I was a totally mad foreigner but I didn't care as I rushed off down the corridor to take care of my pressing need. The urgency of my situation ensured I largely overlooked the state of the lavatory. Russian train lavatories are best avoided if at all possible. I returned to my compartment feeling infinitely better than when I had left it and decided that I would do the remainder of the journey with the door left open. In less than an hour we were pulling into Nizhny station where Boris, the Russian director of our project office was waiting for me. During the drive to my hotel, I tried to explain to Boris in a mixture of English and Russian my experience on the train which he found highly amusing. Indeed, he laughed out loud a couple of times which was the first time I had seen this otherwise serious man show any real emotion.

After a full day of meetings in Nizhny, I went on by overnight train to Kirov for discussions with our project staff there. Many long haul trains in Russia run at night and it is rare to find one in the daytime. I was told jokingly that this was largely a left-over from Soviet times when the communists didn't want anyone to see much of what was going on in the country as they journeyed along. Kirov is some 600 miles north east of Moscow and part of the journey is on the famous Trans Siberian railway line which after Kirov heads east to Ekaterinburg and eventually to Vladivostok on the Pacific coast. Somehow, I expected this relatively short trip on the Trans Siberian line to be a special experience but both the train and the experience proved to be quite ordinary. Kirov is an old city, established as a river port and now a transport hub with some light industry. It has a population of around 450,000 but felt very provincial, run down and neglected – the only building of note is the imposing cathedral dating from 1690. My memories of this brief visit to Kirov are not very favourable. It was extremely cold and everywhere seemed to be covered in thick, compacted ice that glistened in the sunlight and shimmered in the moonlight. There were no platforms at the small Kirov railway station, the train simply pulled up in the sidings leaving me to clamber down the steps with my large suitcase onto the snow covered tracks and walk out. I was happy to see Yuri, the local VVCC office manager waiting for me in the pale, early morning light with a car and driver. After stowing my suitcase in the boot, we set out for the office, some twenty minutes drive across town. Under its thick blanket of snow and ice, the town appeared to have been sculpted from a monotone palette of shades of dirty white interspersed with dark grey coagulated concrete buildings. The car really struggled in the icy conditions, frequently slithering or skidding sideways and a couple of times I thought we were going to crash. However, we eventually pulled up more or less unscathed outside an old, decrepit looking brick building that housed the project offices. I felt shaken and quite stirred from the short journey but once inside after a much needed warming coffee, I felt ready to tackle the day's programme. I spent the morning in discussions with the three office staff who totally failed to impress, seeming rather lacklustre, inexperienced and short of any good ideas about how to develop their business. In the afternoon, several client visits had been planned in the Kirov area but in view of the weather and the state of the roads, the programme was hastily rearranged and limited to visiting a couple of nearby companies only a short drive away. I was glad of the change, not wishing to chance my luck with further extensive car journeys.

I was due to take another overnight train south to Saransk that evening so Yuri and Oleg, one of his consultants, said they would first take me for an early dinner to a restaurant a few hundred yards up the road. I was used to coping with ice-covered pavements in Russia and normally wore my thick fur-lined boots in the depth of winter. Unfortunately, to save space and weight on this multi-city trip, I had left them in England. I was however, wearing some heavy duty black shoes but I soon found myself slipping and sliding all over the place and at times I just couldn't stand up. Yuri and Oleg, who either had better footwear than me or were simply more used to the conditions, succeeded in staying upright more than me but even they had problems making meaningful progress. I ended up half suspended between them and grimly holding on to their coats so that as we slid along, there was a good chance that at least one of us would find solid ground. In this manner, looking like a trio of drunks after a long night out, we staggered down the street and eventually made it to the restaurant. I would like to be able to say that it was worth the trip (or the slips in my case) but it wasn't. Yuri told me he had chosen this particular restaurant because it was American owned and he thought I would feel more at home here but actually I had the feeling that there weren't too many alternative restaurants in Kirov to choose from. From past experience in Russia, I knew that 'American owned' usually only indicated the most tenuous of links to the USA such as my brother had been there on holiday once or my great uncle died there. I found it hard to believe that any American would stay long enough in Kirov to own a restaurant and sure enough the owner turned out to be a Kirov man who had briefly worked in the USA a few years ago. In fact, it was more of a pub than a restaurant and the few clients inside were drinking not eating. But then who am I to deny a drink or two to a man who has struggled through such awful conditions to get here. When the menu arrived I understood why the others were only drinking; the prices were at Moscow levels and the choice was very limited – basically hamburger or cheeseburger with or without chips. I went for the hamburger and added chips to my order (hang the expense) as it would be a long time until breakfast tomorrow in Saransk. After what passed for dinner, Yuri telephoned for a taxi and he joined me for another hair-raising journey to the station. The train for Saransk was waiting when we arrived, clanking and steaming in the cold evening air. I said goodbye to Yuri, hauled my suitcase towards the train, cautiously making my way around the mounds of snow and ice in the station yard and boarded. I was glad to be leaving Kirov behind as I felt quite depressed by what I had seen of the town, the dingy project offices and the uninspiring staff.

My home for the night was a narrow compartment with the usual four bunk beds, mounted in vertical pairs on either side of the walls. I lifted my large suitcase onto one of the lower bunks and tried to unpack my overnight things but there wasn't enough clearance between the upper and lower bunks to fully open my case. I tried putting it on the floor but the narrow aisle space prevented me from laying it fully flat so as to flip up the top half and access the contents. I ended up sitting on the lower bunk and balancing the suitcase on the floor in a half open 'V' shape. That was precisely the moment when the engine driver released the brake and the train suddenly juddered off along the track. I lurched forward off the bunk, falling against the suitcase and trapped my still searching hands in between the two halves. It took a few seconds before I could rebalance myself and extract my aching hands. As I loudly cursed the driver, I was glad I was on my own in the compartment. By now the train was gathering speed and we were soon out into the open countryside. I then realised that the carriage lights weren't working. The station yard had been floodlit so I hadn't noticed the problem before. I groped around in the semi-darkness, eventually sorting myself out and settled down for a few hours sleep. Several hours later as we approached Saransk, I made my way to the lavatory along the unlit corridor only to find there was no water, so no chance for a wash and shave to freshen up before arriving. My guide book stated that there were more than 100 rivers and 500 lakes in the region and that it was primarily agricultural with a gently undulating, countryside. Of course, I had been unable to see anything of this apparently rural idyll from the train in the dark. The urban development of Saransk came as a bit of a shock, suddenly thrusting up in a dark grey mass from the surrounding landscape of snow covered fields. We arrived at the station around 5am and I hauled myself and suitcase out of the carriage onto the platform and went off into the darkness in hopeful search of a taxi. The station thermometer indicated a temperature of minus 25C and with a strong wind blowing, it felt much colder. To my surprise there were a couple of taxis parked up outside the station with their engines running, plumes of smoky vapour drifting around in the wind, obviously hoping for a fare from the Kirov train. I approached the first in line and after a brief price negotiation, neither I nor the driver felt like haggling very long in the cold, we set off and arrived my hotel some fifteen minutes later. It turned out to be another old Soviet style hotel with a creaking lift, decor that hadn't been touched in many, many years and furniture to match. I knew the receptionist was probably as tired as I was since it was still the middle of a dark and cold winter's night but that didn't excuse her off-hand, unfriendly attitude. It was always the same however in this type of hotel and sadly I was becoming used to it. There was never any greeting and an absolute minimum of words were exchanged – 'passport, sign here' and 'pay now'. In truth, any idea of saying 'Welcome and enjoy your stay' or some other similar pleasantries was far from the receptionist's mind. As far as I could gather, these hotel staff, like many other Russian workers, seemed totally bored with their job. Anyway, I had a clean bed and a few hours to rest before being collected by Alex, the Saransk office manager.

Saransk is some 400 miles east of Moscow and is the capital city of Mordoviva, an independent republic within the Russian Federation. The republic has its own Mordvin language and culture, though as most of the population were now ethnic Russians, Mordvin was rarely heard on the streets. I have to admit that I had never heard of Mordoviva before this visit and to me the name seemed redolent of one of those mysterious, invented places that provide the settings for horror movies. The city sits on the banks of the Sar River, a tributary of the Volga and was founded in the 1640s as a fortified southern outpost of the Muscovy Empire. In Soviet times there had been considerable industrial development here and it was essentially a closed town for foreigners. With the industry came significant pollution, exacerbated by ineffective enforcement of controls and this was now having an adverse effect on the inhabitants of Saransk. The population was declining and during the last 20 years, the birth rate had halved and the death rate had doubled – a situation not uncommon in many Russian industrial cities. At the time of my visit, the surviving industry was mostly light engineering, chemical and consumer products, including clothing. Most of the local companies were operating well below full capacity and this situation no doubt contributed to my feeling that the city itself was also run down and not firing on all four cylinders.

I was collected by car from the hotel around 10am and spent the rest of the morning in the Saransk office with its chain-smoking manager, Alex. He didn't speak any English so he had arranged a translator for the day who was waiting in his office when I arrived. She was a stunningly attractive, dark haired young woman in her early twenties, carefully made up and wearing an outrageously sexy attire of a low cut, red and black mini dress, black stockings and very high heels. The outfit intentionally displayed her trim figure to maximum benefit and her English was extremely good. In a way, I took it as a compliment that she had clearly made such an effort with her appearance and not turned up in casual clothes as did some other translators I met. But her outfit was totally over the top and made it hard for me to concentrate on the morning's discussions with Alex.

In the afternoon, Alex and I went off to visit a couple of companies in Saransk together with our overdressed (or maybe that should be underdressed) translator, Natasha. The first, a television and electrical components manufacturer, was suffering from a drop in demand due to cheap foreign imports and had halved its labour force. They were trying to diversify into other products though with limited success. They badly needed a cash injection from a new investor to restructure the company but this was unlikely to happen in the current economic climate. The second company was a factory making men's and women's clothing, run by a very capable female director who spoke good English. She showed me some of their current range of men's suits and jackets and although the quality seemed fine and the prices were very reasonable, the styles were very old fashioned. I asked her if they had looked at exploring Western European markets such as the UK. The director explained that they had an agent in London but no business had ever come their way – perhaps not surprising given the designs. Alex then left to drive back to his office for an urgent appointment, asking me as we shook hands outside if I wouldn't mind paying the translator (he certainly knew how to keep his costs down). So Natasha took me to my hotel in a taxi and waited in reception while I went up to my room to get the US$50 she had apparently agreed with Alex as the charge for her day's work. When I came back down and gave her the cash, I noticed the hotel's female receptionist glancing disapprovingly in our direction. Natasha flashed me a smile as she took the money, standing there in what looked to be a very expensive ankle length fur coat, now unbuttoned and displaying her short black dress and long legs. She looked to me as if she could have been a classy Russian model or film star but I think the receptionist had a very different impression as the money changed hands. She certainly wasn't giving me the benefit of any doubt.

I was not looking forward to spending a second night in my Saransk hotel. Dinner in the empty restaurant was one of the worst hotel meal experiences I had in Russia. Despite being the only customer, the young waitress refused to acknowledge my presence for at least ten minutes, preferring to occupy herself by re-arranging unused table settings. Eventually, the waitress finally conceded that I could see the menu but she informed me in a very offhand manner that most things on it were off and she eventually guided me to some kind of chicken with spaghetti. When it arrived on a greasy plate it was lukewarm, overcooked and quite unappetising. It was however, a form of basic sustenance that would take me through to the morning so I ate as much as I could manage. I always found it strange that in most Russian restaurants everything on the menu was priced individually and by weight. Whilst this made it clear exactly what you would be charged and the likely size of your meal portions, it seemed unnecessarily complicated. Every slice of bread with my soup, potatoes, rice or vegetables with my main meal or butter and jam for breakfast, all had to be ordered separately and were then itemised on the final bill. I wouldn't have been surprised if sometimes there had been a charge for salt and pepper. As I slowly worked my way through the tasteless food, I realised why I was the only customer. There should have been a warning sign at the restaurant entrance saying 'Do not eat here – we don't want you'. But who knows, maybe there was a sign and I simply didn't see it. On leaving the restaurant, I passed by the small hotel bar and was amazed, given what I had just experienced in the restaurant, to see a comprehensive selection of alcoholic drinks on sale. On display were ten different brands of vodka, cans of Russian and imported beers, champagne, French and Georgian brandy and even a few bottles of wine. It seemed clear that the preference of the half a dozen customers in the bar was to obtain their calorie intake through drink rather than food. Having experienced the food, I have to admit it probably wasn't a bad choice. After my unpalatable dinner, I decided to take a short walk to see something of the centre and its night life. Sadly, there wasn't much on offer and as I wandered round I felt as if I had been surreptitiously transported back to the old communist USSR. The few cafes and shops were all firmly shut; the streets were dark and poorly lit and there were very few people around.

I was up at 6am to catch yet another train, this time to return to Moscow. It turned out that this was a long distance express train that had come up from Tashkent, operated by Uzbekistan Railways and as I boarded, I could see the passengers on the train were an interesting mixture of races and faces. There were many central Asian and oriental Mongol-looking people; some of the men had a sun-worked, deep tan colour to their skins and a few bore bushy handle-bar moustaches. The service on the train was markedly more friendly than on Russian-operated railways. Tea was brought to my compartment served in an oriental teapot and bowl accompanied by two small paper packets. One was clearly brown sugar for the tea but the other was a mystery. It had a few words printed on the outside in a language that I couldn't decipher so I opened it and examined the contents. Inside was a whitish powder and for a moment I wondered if it might be a free issue of some kind hashish or marijuana, courtesy of Uzbekistan Railways but being unsure I put it to one side until the tea lady returned a little later. When I asked her about the second packet, she explained that it was 'vitamins' – at least that was the Russian word she used. However, not being sure what Uzbekistan 'vitamins' might contain, I stayed with the tea and brown sugar. Later, I decided to try to find something for an early lunch in the dining car and set off down the train to find it. As I passed along the carriages, I found that my walk turned into an olfactory challenge. In the corridors there was a pervading odour of sweat, beer and raw fish which then changed to one of urine and stale cigarette smoke as I passed the toilets at the end of the carriage. Finally, arriving at the restaurant, there was an overpowering smell of onions, coffee and lemons. Most of the tables were already occupied by groups of men busy tucking into their food but I found a place in a corner and soon satisfied my hunger with a passable omelette, some white bread and a black coffee, without vitamins.

I arrived back in Moscow reasonably relaxed after my journey and looked around the train station for the usual embassy driver but couldn't see anyone. So I stood and waited in the main concourse for a while patiently watching the hundreds of bustling, travel weary people come and go. Moscow's main railway stations, like those in any big city have their own personalities, sights and unique odours, depending on the regions and populace that they serve. The large Kazan station as Moscow's principle gateway to the east has an atmosphere redolent of burnt coffee, dark tobacco and human sweat Once you stand still in a Russian station or airport, you risk being quickly bombarded by a bunch of scruffy men offering a taxi service to the city centre; they are persistent and can prove very annoying. Even though you say no to the first one, another from the encircling group will then approach you asking the same question – taxi? If you try walking away to a different spot, a part of the hunting pack breaks off and follows you. I had long ago worked out a routine for when this happened to me, as it did today. My response to the question was to hesitantly say 'da' and then as the hopeful taxi driver's face brightened at the thought of a lucrative fare, I would look around and say 'tooda' (over there) and point to the waiting line of official taxis outside the station as if I thought he had been asking where to find the taxis. My little joke was perhaps a bit cruel but each time I was only ever asked by one driver, the others quickly realising then that I was no novice, left me alone. After fifteen minutes or so, I finally saw the familiar face of one of the embassy drivers approaching me. He took my suitcase and led me through the crowds to his waiting car, apologising for his lateness as we walked, explaining that the Moscow traffic had been bad. The rest of my stay in the city was uneventful and on Saturday I returned to the UK, courtesy of British Airways, safely but very tired.

Chapter Three

Moscow, St Petersburg, Sochi & Kazan

During 1988, my KHF workload expanded considerably with new projects in St Petersburg and Poland and I was asked to increase my contracted number of days from 60 to 90 and then eventually to 120. In mid April, I was back in Moscow, arriving at Sheremetyevo late in the afternoon. I searched the crowded arrivals hall but there didn't seem to be anyone to meet me. I waited outside the terminal in the slushy snow for a while to see if an embassy car pulled up and then with nothing happening, called Anna, my contact in the KHF Moscow office. She told me that there had been some communication problems and there was no car available so I would have to take a taxi to my hotel in the centre. Airport taxis around the world are always expensive but in Moscow they were extortionate, partly because there really wasn't any reliable alternative transport into the city. Even after negotiations with the driver, I ended paying almost as much for a forty minute ride to the hotel in a creaky old Volga as many Russians would earn in a week. Although sometimes one of the KHF staff from London or Moscow accompanied me on parts of my trips, I was increasingly travelling alone now. This was less of a worry for me as I knew most of the local project staff and how to find my way around and occasional problems like the lack of a car were just minor irritants. Before the current new British embassy was built, the KHF occupied the first two floors in a separate, older office building a mile of so north of the embassy. Although the facilities were limited and it was inconvenient at times to be separated from the embassy, there was a good team spirit and the staff generally seemed to get on well together. The KHF group was small, half a dozen British DFID or Foreign Office employees supplemented by a similar number of local hires handling administrative support, translation and security. Occasionally, there might also be one or two visiting advisers like me around trying to find a spare desk to work at. Lunch was usually a snack purchased from one of the nearby kiosks along the broad main street although sometimes we walked to a large, very popular MacDonalds about ten minutes away. After work, a group of us would sometimes get together at the 'English pub' that was conveniently situated across the road. The food was mediocre but the staff were friendly, there was a good selection of beers and it was usually quiet enough for us to find a table. Otherwise, at the end of the working day, we all normally went our separate ways unless there was something important happening such as an embassy function or a meeting in the hotel with an incoming British official.

Since perestroika, the Russian economy had seen a protracted struggle between the government and business. Most of the time, the government's attitude had been one of maximising short term revenues through imposing high taxes rather than promoting successful enterprises and thereby expanding the tax base and overall wealth of the country. At every turn, business owners, particularly the small and medium sized ones dodged and turned to try to avoid the frequently changing tax burden. One manager said to me it's been a little bit like a pair of boxers circling each other in the ring for round after round. Each one has been trying to land a knockout blow but now exhausted, they were both resting on the canvass. But sadly, some of the companies were now out for the count. A visit by the local tax inspector was probably the most feared event in a Russian businessman's life. No-one could be certain they were safe (including foreigners), no matter how well their company was run. In a country full of corruption, bribery and poor governance, it was hard for any business to operate without transgressing at least one of the ever-changing regulations. If caught, penal fines were the good news; many managers also found themselves in jail. The difficulties with the tax police applied equally to foreign companies trying to operate in Russia. During this Moscow trip I heard of a German company that was in the process of investing 8 million Deutschmarks in a project only to find the tax authorities claiming a 13 million Deutschmarks payment because the Germans had not complied with all the necessary laws. Of course, this risk equally concerned those enterprises we were involved with at the KHF but fortunately during my time with them, no-one was fined or arrested. The situation was in stark contrast with that of the UK at the time. Although in the UK, the government also did its utmost to maximise tax revenues while business did its best to avoid or reduce them, the rules of this particular game were known and set fully in a legal context. This largely removed the arbitrary or capricious nature of business life that existed in Russia which was proving so damaging to growth and economic development.

From Moscow I took an early evening flight up to St Petersburg for two days of meetings with the St Petersburg Vodocanal (the municipal water company). I was fortunate to fly in a Boeing 737 with Transaero, just about the only Russian airline at that time to operate a modern aircraft fleet and to provide a decent level of service. Although their ticket prices were a bit more expensive, their flights were always busy. The negative comments I make elsewhere in this book about Russian airline travel did not apply in this case. Check in was efficient, I was allocated a seat, the flight left and arrived on schedule and the plane was clean and comfortable. Even my luggage arrived safely on the carousel at St Petersburg's Pulkovo airport. I was booked as usual into the Nevsky Palace hotel, a centrally located modern hotel on Nevsky Prospect, the city's ultra long main street. Although the rooms were quite compact, there were two things I really appreciated in this hotel; the business centre was efficient (for sending faxes, photocopying etc.) and the breakfasts. As with all quality hotels in Moscow and St Petersburg, the breakfasts served here were buffet-style with a vast choice of western and Russian food but what I particularly enjoyed was the view. The first floor restaurant had large plate glass windows overlooking Nevsky Prospect and as I consumed my morning calories I always found it fascinating to watch the morning rush hour in the busy street below. Observing a big city gradually coming to life in the morning like this was always an absorbing experience. Even though in reality I was also a part of the rush hour, up in the restaurant with its triple glazed windows I felt detached from the hurly-burly below. It seemed as if I was watching a film version of one of Lowry's matchstick men paintings on a large screen. In the thirty minutes it usually took to eat my breakfast, thousands of people passed by, each one an individual with their own life and unique story to tell. Our different worlds had momentarily met, briefly intertwining before unravelling and allowing us to go our separate ways.

In early June of 1998, I was scheduled to visit Sochi on the Black Sea to attend an important two day meeting being held by the UK-based managers of one of our projects with all of their senior Russian colleagues. It was good to visit Russia for just a few days for a change and this would be my first visit to the Black Sea so I was keen to see it. There was some concern in London about me visiting Sochi as it is just a few miles from the border with Abkhazia, a disputed part of Georgia where there had recently been armed conflict. However, at the time all was quiet and thankfully remained so during my trip. Sochi is primarily a resort city and was popular during both the Tsarist and Soviet periods. A little run down at the time of my visit, it was actually quite large with a population of more than 300,000 and claimed to be the longest city in Europe, spreading out along the Black Sea coast for some 90 miles – at least that's what it said in some visitor information I was given. I was left wondering if Sochi was the longest in Europe, which city was the longest in the world? Who is it that thinks up all these things and then does all the calculations? It was Lenin who first opened up Sochi for the masses in the 1920s and a panoply of government bodies, the armed forces, unions and factories constructed sanatoria and holiday accommodation for their workers. Visits here were much prized and generally only offered as a reward for special achievements at work. There were some attractive neo-classical buildings sprinkled along the coast as well as in the city itself, mostly dating from Stalin's era when Sochi became very popular with the communist elite. Stalin built his favourite dacha here which is now a museum and Khruschev and Brezhnev also holidayed here. With the demise of communism, Sochi lost some of its appeal but it still had a delightful, faded glory atmosphere similar to some British seaside resorts – a Russian Eastbourne or Llandudno perhaps. Gardens and open spaces with palm trees, cypress, magnolias and a variety of flowers give the centre a pleasant, exotic feel, quite unusual in Russia. Along the sea front the lack of more recent investment showed in the rather down-at-heel buildings and infrastructure. But I liked the town's laid back, decadent feel and enjoyed walking around watching the Russians on holiday, swimming in the sea, sunbathing on the pebbled beaches, sitting in the cafes or like me just ambling around.

I flew into the small Sochi-Adler airport from Moscow, arriving in the early evening and met up with the rest of our group at the hotel in Sochi. Attending the meeting were two UK project managers John and Mike (both Russian speakers), eight Russians from as many different cities across the country plus a translator and John's wife who was accompanying him on this trip. We were all booked into the Primorskaya hotel which was well located on the sea front within easy walking distance of most places of interest. Built in the 1930s the hotel had clearly seen much better days (and possibly better guests) but my large first floor room was adequately comfortable with a south facing balcony, giving a fine view out across the Black Sea. After a quick shower, I joined the rest of our party and we strolled a short distance along the sea front promenade and found a restaurant where we could eat outside in the warm summer air. The service was friendly, the food very edible and accompanied by several bottles of Georgian wine and brandy, it all made for a very enjoyable evening – we could almost have been somewhere on the Mediterranean Sea. I made a mental note to try to remember some of the evening's frequent Russian toasts for use on the next similar occasion, although in fact it seemed as if almost anything can be the subject of a toast at a good Russian meal.

The following day was taken up with a full agenda of discussions and meetings reviewing the future organisation and direction of our project. At times, matters became quite heated and stressful as there was some disagreement among the Russians about how best to proceed. Achieving full consensus required some delicate negotiation but by the end of the day a way forward was agreed and while not everyone was still smiling, they were at least still talking to each other. With the formal business of the day concluded, we all returned to our rooms to prepare for a group dinner which was to be held in the hotel. As I was taking a long, relaxing shower, I vaguely became aware of Russian singing drifting in from the bathroom next door. At first, I didn't really pay it any attention but as it went on, I realised it was the same couple of songs repeated over and over again. As I towelled off, I also recognised the voices – it was John and his wife, evidently enjoying a bath together next door. Somewhat puzzled as to why they were singing in Russian but not wishing to eavesdrop further on their musical bathing, I dressed quickly and went down to the bar for a drink. A little later when I went into the restaurant to join our group for dinner, things started to become clearer. John and his wife were there dressed up in Cossack style outfits and presented themselves as our cabaret for the night. As well as making speeches and toasts during the meal, their Russian songs proved a rousing finale with everyone merrily joining in. I just wished that I had a video camera with me.

The latter part of July saw me back in Moscow and then Nizhny with another short visit to Kazan. I was in Moscow this time for meetings to explore several new project proposals that had been sent to the KHF offices in London. The first was with the State Committee for Small Enterprises in their central Moscow offices which turned out to be a fairly inconclusive session. During my years with the KHF, I met many government officials at national, regional and local level. I invariably felt that the discussions with government ministers and officials in Moscow were frustrating and ineffectual. Although we would discuss the evident social and economic problems facing Russia, I rarely heard anything specific about real action that was being taken to improve matters. It always seemed hard to get to the heart of the matter and obtain clear personal or departmental views, commitment and support. Of course, for many officials, working life under the new perestroika rules was as uncertain as it was for the people they governed. Only a very few felt that they had the power and authority to take decisions on their own; everything had to be reviewed and referred elsewhere. Reaching a firm decision usually required multiple meetings. Yes, the officials would be happy to support us if we were bringing money and know-how into the country but their anodyne responses seemed to belie any genuine interest or desire to change things. Perhaps this was partly due to the government's greater interest in big business – after all that's where the money and votes were but I think the Russian's deep-seated distrust of foreigners was also a factor. In some ways they didn't want our assistance and felt awkward about it. In addition, working through translators didn't help; it took away the spontaneity of discussion and it was too easy to miss subtle nuances of language and inference. A further handicap we had in the KHF was that we were not the biggest players in the donor field. Compared with the World Bank, USAID and EU money, our fund was much smaller and therefore our potential impact and size of projects were less which probably contributed to the lower levels of official interest. Of course, none of the foreign aid programmes in Russia could change this vast country by themselves. In many ways our role at the KHF was mainly to provide advice and where possible to run pilot projects that would demonstrate new ways of doing things. The hope was that by building on these initial schemes and scaling up, the Russians would have the necessary tools and skills to effect significant change. We could really only assist with understanding the cure but not insist on the Russians taking the medicine.

The only exception to the above comments about government officials was Irina Hakamada, a member of the Russian Duma (parliament) and for a time the minister for small business. I was involved in a couple of meetings with her and her officials – one in Moscow earlier in the year, the other when she later visited London. She seemed to have an understanding of the problems faced by small businesses in Russia and a genuine desire to improve the situation. Sadly however, this view was not shared within the government overall and many of the anticipated actions were never implemented. Her department was only allocated a small budget and she therefore had little influence or power. Hakamada was later to run against President Putin in the 2004 election and of all the candidates she was his most outspoken critic. My meetings with regional governors or local mayors usually proved to be more open and constructive, due in part to the fact that the KHF activities were mostly at this level and the benefits therefore more obvious.

I went on to a much more positive meeting with the IFC (International Finance Corporation) to discuss assisting to expand their leasing programme in Russia. Leasing was relatively unknown at the time in the country and it had some worthwhile potential benefits for smaller businesses. Russian banks were generally not the kind of commercial operation found in the west and did little to provide loans or finance to private businesses. Several were known to be fronts for mafia money and although different figures were quoted in the media, it seemed at least 50% were in this category. Federal government controls in the banking sector appeared very lax. We agreed to help the IFC with their project and over the next twelve months it proved moderately successful. The other proposal for review involved visiting the headquarters of the Russian co-operative movement. The KHF had already funded a very small training project for the movement the previous year and the Russians were now proposing a major expansion for some their branches across the country. The co-operative movement in Russia dates back to the late 1920s. Unlike the UK, where the movement had originated and was primarily an urban organisation for industrial workers, the Russian version's members were predominately peasants in rural areas and villages. Although it grew significantly so that at its peak around 20% of the population were members, the movement started to decline in the 1970s, mirroring the co-operative situation in many other countries. I met with the director Yevgeny, a rather overweight man in his 40s with dark hair that seemed glued in small tufts around his balding pate. He was dressed rather formally in a three piece suit which was unusual, given the mid-summer heat and he certainly didn't look very comfortable in it. He was a little portly and spent much of our meeting tugging at the bottom of his waistcoat trying to keep it pulled down over his stomach. However, he was genial enough, easy to talk to and clearly anxious that the meeting went well. Yevgeny explained that he was looking for assistance to finance a training programme in modern management techniques for the organisation's branches. We discussed the subject in detail and while it was evident that the movement's structure and management could be improved, it eventually became clear that his main interest centred on what he termed corporate governance. The real issue for Yevgeny was developing tighter control over the organisation by his Moscow centre. Reflecting in a way the general political situation in Russia, the co-operative movement had splintered in recent years with some branches effectively declaring autonomy and the chairman didn't like this at all. In many ways, it would have been appropriate for the KHF to work with the co-operative movement in Russia as it clearly had the potential to reach out to the poorer sections of the community. However, our underlying role was to support the process of democracy, enterprise and economic development and Yevgeny's ideas sounded too retrograde for me. I felt I might be wasting my time trying to explain all this to him and so took the easy way out by saying I would take his proposal back to London for review and we would let him know our decision in due course. We never did any further work with his organisation.

Somewhat disappointed with my Moscow visit, I took an evening flight to Kazan to participate in a project training session there the following day. It was hot and humid – typical weather for July and by 10am our non air-conditioned meeting room was already unbearably stifling and by noon I was drooping and dripping sweat. Our lunch break couldn't come soon enough for me. The Russian participants however, coped much better than I with the conditions and held their concentration admirably right through the day. After a quick, early evening meal with the group in a nearby cafe, I left for the station to catch the overnight sleeper train to Nizhny. As usual, the embassy had booked a whole compartment for me in what the Russians refer to as 'soft class', presumably a little more comfortable than what I assume was the alternative 'hard class'. Clean white sheets and a blanket were neatly folded and laid out on each of the four bunks and soon after boarding I was provided with a refreshing cup of lemon tea by my provodnitsa, the compartment tea lady. I selected one of the lower bunks for the night ahead, unpacked my toilet bag and wandered down the corridor to the lavatory at the far end of the carriage. I noticed most of my fellow travellers had already changed into tracksuits, the generally preferred form of dress on Russian overnight trains. All carriages on Russian trains are non smoking but it is allowed in the small enclosed spaces that connect one carriage to another. In winter, smokers needed to very dedicated, confined as they were to these unheated areas of the train. For the first hour of the journey, we travelled through a heavy electrical storm with fantastic flashes of lightening rolling constantly across the sky, revealing thunderous dark clouds and the cultivated fields below. After the storm had passed, the air became much fresher and I tried to settle down for the night but occasional station halts, accompanied by periodic announcements over the train's loudspeaker system kept disturbing me. I looked around my compartment but there didn't seem to be any way to switch off this annoying noise. Eventually however, the insistent mechanical lulling of the train's motion eased me into a few hours sleep in my bunk and I arrived reasonably fresh in the early morning in Nizhny. As we slowly pulled into the station, I looked out at the thin grey dawn light that was inexorably forcing its way into the centre of the city. Structures that a few minutes ago had been dark and indistinct were now taking on recognisable shapes as the slumbering world of Nizhny regained a sharpened focus. Outside on the platform it still felt quite cool but there was a hint of the day's warmth to come in the watery sun's silky rays.

After a full day of meetings in NIzhny, I wandered into the centre in the early evening to find somewhere to eat. I knew there were a couple of decent restaurants along the pedestrianised main street and I had a reasonable dinner in one of them, sitting outside under a canopy on the terrace. I always found it interesting to check out the brand names on the canopies of Russian cafes and restaurants to see who was currently winning the cola or beer promotional wars. Looking along the street today, it seemed pretty even between Coca Cola and Pepsi. In the beer stakes, the clear winner today was Baltika, brewed in St Petersburg and the biggest selling beer in Russia at the time. Over the next couple of days I had a variety of useful meetings in and around Nizhny and the whole trip passed off without incident. I flew back to Manchester from Nizhny airport via Frankfurt on Lufthansa or 'Luftgansa' as it is pronounced in Russia (there is no 'h' in Russian). I was glad to be back on time as my eldest son was getting married that weekend in London and I wanted to unpack and sort a few things out at home before driving down there for the wedding.

CHAPTER FOUR

Ekaterinburg & Kemerovo

In mid September I returned to Russia for a few days of meetings in Moscow and then went on to Ekaterinburg in the Urals region. My arrival in Russia coincided with one of those occasional political crises that punctuated Yeltsin's time as president. The country was only just starting to come round after the hammer blow of the financial crisis in August when the Russian stock, bond, and currency markets all collapsed. This was a result of investor fears that the government would devalue the rouble and default on its internal debt (which in fact is what happened). Annual interest rates on government bonds briefly rose to 200 percent and the stock market fell 65 percent. Inflation reached 84 percent and many banks were forced to close as a result of the crisis and millions of people lost their life savings, resulting in considerable social disquiet. Faced with economic turmoil and waning health, Yeltsin tried to bolster his position by firing his existing prime minister and attempting to replace him with Viktor Chernomyrdin, a former prime minister. But this move was blocked by the Duma, Russia's parliament and Yeltsin was forced to select a compromise candidate, Yevgeny Primakov who was approved by the Duma just a few days before my visit. Although he lasted less than a year as prime minister, Primakov successfully pushed through some much needed domestic reforms and was relatively popular in Russia. However, at the time of my arrival, the mood of the Russians I talked to in Moscow was one of considerable anxiety. Indeed a week after my departure on

October 7, a nationwide strike and demonstrations were held in many cities with around 100,000 people taking to the streets in Moscow plus some 6000 in Ekaterinburg and military units were placed on a state of alert. With this backdrop, it was no surprise to find currency exchange rates all over the place during my visit with a 25 percent variation between different Moscow banks in the US$ / rouble rate and in Ekaterinburg I was charged US$100 as commission to change just US$700.

I flew out to Ekaterinburg from Moscow's Domodedovo airport which was the flyer's equivalent of Kazan railway station. It was a large, bustling airport mostly serving a wide variety of destinations in the south and east of Russia as well as a few foreign locations. Although work had recently started on an extensive modernisation programme, the terminals were rather run down and crowded, with only basic facilities that were quite inadequate to handle the volume of passengers passing through. Although I had built up quite a lot of experience flying in Russia during my time at KamAZ, most of my travel within Russia had been on private charter flights. This had sheltered me to a large extent from the worst of the rigours of domestic flying. However, my frequent and extensive journeys for the KHF within Russia now exposed me fully to the problems involved with internal flights. Of course travel in any foreign country can be stressful but in Russia there are extra problems right from buying your ticket and checking in through to collecting your luggage and leaving the airport.

Inside the Domodedovo departure building, there was a marked shortage of seating so family groups jostled with weary businessmen, young couples and the occasional tourist trying to find somewhere to sit while waiting for their flight to be called. Many simply ended up sitting on the floor or pacing up and down, adding to a general feeling of anxiety and frustration. Itinerant traders or perekupshchiki as they are called in Russia were constantly checking and adjusting their assorted bulging bags, flimsily held together with string and plastic. These people, both men and women, are professional shoppers who shuttle around the former Soviet Union buying goods that they felt could be sold for a small profit in their home towns. With nowhere to sit, customers around the tiny bar or cafe stood trying to drink while balancing a plate of food in the other hand and at the same time keeping one foot on their luggage. The first real hurdle was yet to come – the check-in process. Although the airport had small electronic indicator boards showing the check-in desk and departure gate for each flight, they were unreliable and slow and not to be depended on. Periodic distorted flight announcements erupted out across the departure hall, apparently in both Russian and English though mostly unintelligible to me. These announcements caused brief staccatos of movement among the waiting passengers as they first absorbed the information and then reacted to the loudspeaker's instructions. A headlong charge through the crowded hall would then ensue as each passenger desperately tried to be one of the first at the nominated check-in desk further inside the building. As most flights were open seating, this rush initially seemed inappropriate and unnecessary to me but there were sound reasons behind it. The check in process was almost always excruciatingly slow and with usually only a single desk open and fifty to one hundred passengers plus bags to process, the area soon descended into chaos. As if to add insult to injury, check-in was time limited with normally only ten or fifteen minutes before the desk closed or was switched to another flight. The lucky first passenger at the desk would start to check in with three or four people hovering and jostling at his shoulder, vying to be next. Behind them, the remaining passengers would spread out in a desultory approximation of a line. In the general melee, there was always a lot of arguing, shouting and sometimes children crying – indeed, I even felt like crying in desperation at times. Occasionally, men would try to force themselves forward from the rear of the queue, clambering over the luggage and claiming they had priority. Those further forward would try to repulse the invader, usually successfully and the pushy queue jumper would skulk off to the back of the line again. Once through this test of patience and endurance, we passengers then made our way to the designated holding pens (sorry, departure lounges) where if you were quick, you might find a seat. Otherwise, you just had to stand around the gate area waiting for the chaos to resume. If you were fortunate enough to find a seat, you couldn't even think about going to the toilets as your place would be occupied by another tired passenger when you returned. The absence of any seat allocation system on the flight made Russian passengers skittish so the slightest movement by an airport official immediately precipitated a hopeful surge forward. Then a sudden crackly announcement would indicate a last minute gate change and those who heard or understood the message would rush off to another area. As I rarely understood these, I used to identify a fellow passenger at check-in and then stick like glue to him until I boarded the flight. But I was clearly not the only one to fail to take in the revised instructions and there were always flight dispatchers running up and down trying to find their missing passengers.

This was to be my first visit to Ekaterinburg which had a population of close to 1.3 million and lies some 1000 miles east of Moscow. It sits to the east of the Ural mountains (which are actually no more than large hills) and the city is therefore technically in Asia. As I sat on the plane from Moscow thinking about my destination, I realised that I knew three things about the city. First I was aware that it was the home of Boris Yeltsin and his original political power base from which he moved on to become the first president of the Russian Federation. During the 1991 attempted overthrow of the government, Yeltsin chose Ekaterinburg (or Sverdlovsk as it was known at the time) as a reserve capital of the Federation should Moscow become too dangerous for the Russian government and a replacement cabinet was based in the city until the crisis passed. The second fact that I remembered was the infamous U-2 incident when an American spy plane, piloted by Gary Powers was shot down in the area by the Soviets in 1960. Powers was captured and after a show trial, found guilty of spying and imprisoned. However, he only served a year before being exchanged for a high-ranking KGB spy, who had been arrested in the United States several years earlier. The third and most infamous thing I knew about Ekaterinburg was that it was the city where the last Russian Tsar and most of his immediate family were executed by the Bolsheviks. After some important but hesitant reforms by the Tsars in the latter part of the 19th century, the pace and direction of progress seemed to stall. Dissent and revolution were in the air and the Tsarist regime was under constant threat. The disastrous results for Russia of its participation in the First World War provided the catalyst for dramatic change and opened the door for the Bolsheviks. After the arrest of the Tsar and his family in St Petersburg in 1917, they were initially moved by the Bolsheviks to Tobolsk in Siberia. But Siberia came under the control of various strong anti-Bolshevik forces and as they pushed westwards intent on reaching Moscow, the royal family was moved again to Ekaterinburg which was held by the Bolsheviks. However, the anti-Bolshevik forces continued to gain ground and were now threatening Ekaterinburg. During this time there were negotiations between the British government and the Bolsheviks with a view to allowing the Tsar to come to England but these ended in failure. The decision was taken to eliminate the Tsar and his family and they were shot, clubbed and bayoneted to death in July 1918. Their remains were taken away by truck to a nearby forest where the naked bodies were first dumped down an old flooded mine, then a day later recovered so as to be removed to a more remote location. The corpses were then burned and finally piled into a shallow grave covered in acid to destroy the flesh in an attempt to prevent identification. The anti-Bolshevik forces took Ekaterinburg only a week later and although they found the mine, they failed to locate the Tsar's grave. However, in 1991, the remains of the Tsar and his family were discovered and they were given a state funeral in St Petersburg in July 1998, just a year before my visit. Anyone with even a cursory knowledge of the early 20*th* century history of Russia and the Romanovs would conclude that this autocratic and increasingly marginalised Tsarist regime was doomed to failure. This is the eventual fate of any system that fails to govern its people effectively, as the Soviets subsequently discovered. But the brutal, almost demonic slaying of the Tsar, his family and servants in July 1918 revealed the ruthlessness of the Bolsheviks. Their increasing disregard for due legal process and the lives of their citizens was to haunt Russia for the rest of the century. Ekaterinburg was cruelly renamed Sverdlovsk by the Soviets in 1924 after Yakov Sverdlov, a senior Bolshevik party leader who had ordered the killing of the Tsar and his family. Incredibly, a statue of Sverdlov still survived in the centre of the city at the time of my visit.

Ekaterinburg has some fine 19th century buildings in the centre, mostly constructed in the neo-classical style in white and beige stucco. The city is also culturally well endowed with theatres, an opera, concert hall, museums and cinemas. I was booked in to the Atrium Palace hotel – an impressive brick and glass building that had only recently opened. As predicted by its name, the hotel featured an extremely large, pyramid-shaped glass atrium covering an equally large reception and bar area. The rooms were comfortable and well equipped and clearly the hotel was designed to provide Ekaterinburg with a level of luxury comparable to the best in Moscow. However, this objective was somewhat negated by the front of house staff whose training had not yet achieved the level of service efficiency expected in this class of hotel. Although willing enough, the young staff clearly lacked experience and didn't have the capability to actually sort out problems, appearing at times to be scared to really do anything. I don't know who carried out their training but it was as if they momentarily expected to suffer the same fate as the last Tsar if they did anything wrong and this gave the hotel a rather strange atmosphere. The reason I was staying in Ekaterinburg's finest was because the British consulate had a small group already based there organising a British Russian trade exhibition and so it was convenient to have us all in one place. The British consulate had only been established a few months before my visit and the exhibition was part of their drive to generate more trade between the UK and this region of Russia. The following day, I visited the consulate which was located in a rather small and undistinguished two storey red brick building in the suburbs, next door to the USA consulate in Gogol Street. However, the two armed security guards manning the entrance were neither small nor undistinguished. Dressed in the usual paramilitary black uniforms, they were both tall, well built young men and very conscientious about checking anyone who entered the building. I met with Steve, the British consul, who was quite unlike the traditional image of a British embassy official. I instantly liked him; he was a lively, down to earth man in his 30s who was very open and easy to chat to and very supportive of the DFID's work in Ekaterinburg. He seemed to me to be an excellent choice to get the Union Jack flying in this part of the world.

The main focus of my visit to Ekaterinburg was to conduct a progress review of a joint project with the regional government designed to accelerate the development of SMEs (small and medium enterprises). This three year project was being managed locally by a resident British consultant, Graham, who was on loan from a Scottish university where he was a senior lecturer in enterprise development. Graham took me to visit the deputy governor whose office was on the top floor of the tall, white multi-storey government building that dominated the city skyline. On the edge of a small park, close to the river, the view out from his office over the city and surrounding Siberian countryside was spectacular. I asked the deputy governor how he managed to concentrate on his work with such a fine view. He smiled and replied that like any other view, you soon get used to it. He was very complimentary about the project results so far and seemed genuinely supportive of our work. I was generally impressed by the people I met in Ekaterinburg, they seemed more progressive, with a 'can do' attitude, compared to many of those I met in other large provincial cities like Nizhny, Novosibirsk or Kazan. Perhaps it was no coincidence that the city produced a man like Boris Yeltsin, Russia's first democratically elected president.

During the two days that I was in Ekaterinburg with Graham we got to know each other fairly well, exchanging our respective experiences of living and working in Russia. I was interested to explore why he had taken on this three year assignment. It seemed to me that his was a lonely life with few other expats in the city and a long way from his family and academic roots. Also he was not a Russian speaker, though he was taking lessons, so I supposed it was not easy to socialise with the locals or benefit from Ekaterinburg's cultural scene. Graham told me that he quite enjoyed the life in the city, regularly attended excellent music concerts (language was not a problem in this case) and was using the experience to develop his university courses for when he returned to Scotland. He managed to get home at least twice a year and the long cold winter didn't bother him. Overall, he seemed quite happy and relaxed. When I worked at KamAZ in Naberezhnye Chelny, I was able to get home every four to six weeks and benefited from the companionship of a team of British and US consultants. Although Ekaterinburg was a much larger and more interesting city than Chelny, I would have found it very difficult to live like he did for three years. My mind went back to a visit I had made many years before to Khartoum in the Sudan where I had met the English manager of an Arab-owned trading company. His drab office was in a small, insignificant building tucked away in a side street close to the city centre. He was the only Englishman employed in the business and he had been working there for over 20 years, returning home just once a year. He was short with thinning black hair, a deep suntan and a prominent nose; he could almost have passed for an Arab. His office was quite small with no air conditioning and sparsely furnished, containing little in the way of the kind of mementos that people usually accumulate after such a long time. Originally from London, he was single and in his late 50s and talked earnestly to me about his hope of soon retiring back to England. There was little for him to do in Khartoum other than work and so he was saving most of his salary to buy a house when he returned home. As I left his office, I wondered why he had stuck with this job so long in such a remote place and couldn't help feeling a little sorry for him. From later correspondence, I discovered he was still there a couple of years later but never found out when or if he eventually made it back to England.

By mid Friday afternoon, with no more appointments for the day, I decided to do what many first time visitors to the city do – visit the dividing line between Europe and Asia. I set out with Graham and our driver, heading west out of Ekaterinburg for Pervuralsk, a town with a population of 170,000 sitting right at the southern tip of the Urals. We drove for around an hour along wide, straight roads lined with fir and birch trees with their leaves just on the turn in the late September sunlight. Suddenly our driver slowed, clearly looking for something and after a few hundred yards he eased gently off the road onto the grass verge. There a few yards in from the road a granite obelisk marked the geographical end of Europe and the start of Asia. It really wasn't much to see – I had expected something more dramatic, knowing the Russian's penchant for large symbolic statues and monuments. I briefly stood in front of the column with one foot either side of this artificial continental divide and then turned eastwards and surveyed the undulating, forested land of Siberia as it stretched out unendingly before me in mile after mile. My thoughts turned to the thousands, no millions of criminals, political prisoners and innocent victims of Stalin's pogroms that had been forced to make this heartbreaking journey and wondered how they felt on reaching this point in their march into exile. As with Britain's colonisation of Australia, the drive to populate Siberia in the 19*th* and 20*th* centuries by successive Tsarist and communist governments led to the creation of a wide variety of minor offences for which the punishment was exile into hard labour in Siberia. For me, it was easy to step back and return to Europe but for them several more months of miserable trudging onwards lay ahead before eventually reaching their allotted camps or gulags. For those that survived the cold, starvation and hardship of this forced migration, often in chains and branded, a brutal, usually short life of hard labour awaited them. As the Russian poet Anna Akhmatova said, it was a period when 'only the dead could smile, happy in their peace'[6]. As I walked back to the car, these sad reflections seemed to make the previously warm autumn sunshine suddenly feel cold.

I was always puzzled during my travels in Russia by the fact that no-one ever seemed to talk about the civil war that took place after the Bolshevik uprising in 1917. I found the intricate history of the traumatic events surrounding the bitter struggle between the Reds and the White Russians very interesting. It effectively went on until 1921 and involved interventions by troops from Britain, the USA, Japan, France and several other European nations. Siberia almost seceded from Russia at this time.

6 The Complete Poems of Anna Akhmatova – 1990

In the USA, their much earlier civil war is still a regular topic in books, TV or films and is a distinct and defining part of their culture. In Russia, other than the immediate events relating to the Bolshevik revolution, the topic of the civil war didn't seem to be discussed. It was almost as if the Communist regime had erased all memory of this period when half the country was in revolt against the Bolsheviks. Any references in Russia to historic armed struggles always seemed confined to the 1917 revolution itself or the Second World War.

At the weekend, I travelled back to the UK and then drove down to south Wales to rendezvous with a group of Russians from Kemerovo in Siberia who were on a KHF organised visit to the UK. We had several projects running in the Kemerovo region and I was scheduled to go out on a visit there shortly so this was an ideal chance for me to meet some of the Russians that I would soon be working with. They were a mixed group of around a dozen men and women, led by Irina the Russian director of one of our Kemerovo projects. They were in the UK to look at urban regeneration and small business start-up programmes and were travelling around in a hired bus for a week visiting south Wales, Birmingham and London. Apart from Irina who had visited the UK several times before, it was the group's first visit to the UK. During my time working for the KHF, I was involved in several inward visits to the UK by Russian groups, visiting different parts of the country. Invariably, I found the Russian visitors very polite and well behaved on these trips, quite unlike some of the foreign groups with which I had been involved in my previous business career. Rarely was anyone late for buses or meals and I can't ever recall any serious problems from drinking or other nefarious night time activities. Indeed, if anything they were sometimes too quiet, perhaps a little overawed on what was for many of them their first visit overseas. Their impressions of the UK were mixed but generally favourable – most comments focussed on the density of traffic on our motorways, the quality and speed of our intercity trains and the number and range of shops and restaurants. Occasionally however, their reactions could be surprising. I remember having lunch with one group of Russians in a fine old country pub in the

Thames valley overlooking the river. It was a beautiful, warm sunny day and we sat at a table outside taking in the atmosphere. People stretched out relaxing on the grass, the occasional motor boat slowly chugging by, a couple of swans drifting along as the Thames meandered on its way to London – it was one of those all too rare, idyllic English summer days. I leaned across the table and asked the interpreter what were the group's initial impressions of England, expecting a comment about the charm and beauty of the scene around us or the quaintness of our pubs. Instead she replied 'We all think there are so many old people here in England, where are all the young people?' I was initially completely taken by surprise at this response but when I thought about it, compared to Russia, she was right. The high unemployment rate among young people in Russia meant that they are much more visible during the day than in Britain where most of our young people are at work. Also the longer life expectancy in Britain naturally results in a higher percentage of older people and with higher disposable incomes than Russian pensioners, they tend to be out and about enjoying themselves more. It was an interesting and perceptive comment.

In mid October, I was back in Russia for my first visit to Kemerovo, taking an overnight 'red-eye' flight from Moscow with one of the Siberian based airlines. The Russian aircraft looked as if it had been flying on this route since the time of Stalin. Everything vibrated or rattled, the interior paintwork was scuffed and the smell in the toilet was overpowering. The seats were all well worn and very flimsy, more like folding deck chairs and with minimum room between the rows. As I am over six feet tall, the lack of legroom meant an uncomfortable, sleepless flight for me. The situation was made worse by the fact that most of the Russians seemed to have innumerable packages, parcels and boxes stuffed into the small overhead racks, squeezed in around their feet or jutting out into the aisles. They seemed to operate on the principle that any empty cabin space must be filled and any apparently full space must be crammed full. The Kemerovo flight left at midnight, taking four hours but with the time change flying east, it was actually 8am when we arrived in Kemerovo. In the small baggage hall I collected my familiar large Samsonite suitcase and started to walk out through the exit when a female airport employee stopped me, demanding to see my baggage check from the flight. I couldn't remember where I had put it. I searched every pocket in my coat and jacket, looked in my briefcase and re-checked my pockets but all I could come up with was my ticket. I must have lost the tiny piece of paper somewhere in Moscow airport or on the flight. Since I was now the only passenger left in the baggage hall, there wasn't any doubt about who owned the suitcase parked alongside me. To confirm this fact, I showed the woman the name on the address tag on my suitcase which obviously matched the name on my ticket. But the woman checking the baggage was like a dog with a bone and wouldn't let go. Now, I'm all for good airport security but by this time, after a sleepless night I was extremely tired and felt very annoyed with her officiousness. In desperation, I told her I didn't need the suitcase and would leave it at the airport in her good care and collect it in a few days when I returned to Moscow. This confused her for a few moments and she hesitated, probably because she was still mentally translating my awful Russian. But then her officious lights flashed on again and she told me that was not possible, definitely 'Niet'. I tried to work out in my weary brain how to say in Russian that 'If I can't take the suitcase with me and if I can't leave it at the airport, what was I supposed to do?' Fortunately, before I could construct anything remotely intelligible, one of the Russians meeting me came to the rescue, telling the baggage inspector quite forcibly that this was no way to treat important foreign visitors, it was obviously my suitcase and that she would vouch for me. At that my antagonist finally relented and reluctantly waived me through the exit.

We joined the rest of the welcoming party waiting outside and after some quick introductions, I was taken to my hotel in Kemerovo. Once there, my hosts produced a brown paper bag – it was a welcome pack containing an orange, a chocolate bar plus a large bottle of mineral water. It was a thoughtful gift; my hosts had done this trip many times and knew what it was like to arrive feeling tired and hungry. It was now around 9.30 and

I was told I had a couple of hours to rest before being picked up in a car to go to the office. After my first couple of visits to Russia with the KHF, I had decided to revert to my habit when working in Chelny of bringing a few basic food supplies with me from the UK. So I quickly unpacked a box of cereal and some milk which, together with the contents of my brown bag, provided a quick breakfast. After an all too short snooze, it was time to go back down to reception. Our hotel, called the Kuzbass, was another unwelcoming, weary, grey concrete building, with an indeterminate style of decor and well worn furniture that had seen better days – rather like the staff I thought. It was hard to understand or explain the behaviour of the mainly female staff whose job it was to provide a service to the public, whether in hotels, restaurants, banks, shops or on public transport and airlines. It rarely made any difference whether they were old or young, in a big city or a small village, the surly, disinterested attitude was the norm. With their uncaring, off-hand manner, it was as if any customer was a transitory intrusion, to be ignored and then dispensed with in the shortest time possible. Yet I knew that when taken out of their immediate working environment, many of these people had a wonderful sense of humour and could be personable and charming. Of course part of the explanation was the generally poor management in the public sector and poor pay. Also, in the case of the older women, their behaviour was probably simply a reflection of the years of bad service they had experienced during the Soviet era – the system had become self-perpetuating and the young were now taking their cue from their seniors. However, in all the years that I spent working in Russia, I never saw any real change and I suspect there was a deep-seated cultural dimension at work; one of suspicion towards strangers and foreigners. Trust and pleasantness could only be earned with time and familiarity. The only exceptions I came across were the relatively few private or foreign owned businesses where presumably some form of training had taken place and there was more individual motivation. I made a mental to note to explore the business potential of getting one of our projects to set up a charm school.

Kemerovo is some 2200 miles east of Moscow which is almost 50% further than the distance from London to Moscow. Sadly, I never succeeded in visiting Vladivostok on Russia's wild and remote Pacific coast, a further 2000 miles to the east but here in Kemerovo I felt as if I was already at the farthest end of Russia. Close to half a million people live here in a large industrial sprawl full of smokestack factories that spread out across the surrounding rolling hills. It is primarily a coal mining region, the centre of the extensive Kuzbass coal seams, some of the world's largest. Prolonged strikes here in 1990 largely caused by unpaid wages, seriously threatened Mikhail Gorbachev's government for a time. Most of its heavy industry was old and run down and as a result unemployment was high with few job opportunities outside the mines. The region was still quite 'red' and a large statue of Lenin, with arm outstretched in the direction of Moscow, still dominated Kemerovo's main square outside the government offices. Perhaps taking their cue from Lenin's arm, many of the young people I spoke to talked of wanting to move west to Omsk, Ekaterinburg or even Moscow to find a better life but without savings it was difficult. Unless they had a relative in these places, finding a job and somewhere to stay would have been almost impossible. Some made it however, contributing to a fall in the city's population of some 30,000 in the past ten years. On a brighter note, Kemerovo is one of the few places in Russia where bandy hockey is keenly played. This peculiar form of ice hockey is more akin to traditional field hockey and is played with a similar ball and sticks and two teams of eleven players each on a football sized pitch. Unsurprisingly, with daytime outside temperatures of minus 20C, it's not a great spectator sport and I was glad that no-one invited me to watch a game.

Due to the poor economic situation and high levels of deprivation in the region, several foreign agencies were active here. The KHF had two large projects running, each managed by a resident British consultant with half a dozen British expats in the area involved with the various projects on short term contracts. It surprised me to find this relatively large group of foreigners in such a far-flung location. It was a difficult assignment – a remote location, long Siberian winters, short hot summers, difficult to communicate with the rest of the world, not much to do with a general air of poverty and depression in the run down towns. As well as meeting with city and oblast officials during my visit, I also had discussions with the managers of several local businesses, including a brewery and soft drinks company, a dairy products firm and a plastics manufacturer. All were critical of the lack of assistance from city and regional government who seemed only interested in big business, where the major payoffs (literally) for local politicians sadly lay. They also criticised the use of imported cars by officials and coincidentally, I later saw both the governor's Mercedes and the mayor's Volvo speeding across the city so there was clearly good reason for their dissatisfaction.

My visit to Kemerovo reintroduced me something that was common in many Russian hotels that didn't require any mastery of the Russian language – at least not if you were sensible. No matter what time of the day or night you arrived at your hotel, the telephone would mysteriously ring, often within seconds of walking into the room. You're not expecting any calls, it's three in the morning and all you want to do is get some sleep. It can't be a call from home because it takes hours to get an international call and you've asked for any messages when you checked in. So you stare briefly at the miracle of a working telephone and then wearily pick up the receiver. You don't need to speak Russian to understand the reason for the call – the language is international – do you want a girl for the night? Saying no or simply hanging up usually proved to be totally ineffective responses, often resulting in a repeat call either from the same source or from another more persistent one. They knew you were in there and they wouldn't take no for an answer. I eventually found that the only way to stop the calls was to unplug the telephone from the wall socket. This had the minor disadvantage of friends or colleagues not being able to reach you but this was far outweighed by the benefit of an undisturbed night's rest. I never really got to the bottom of how the local pimps knew so precisely when you were in your room. There must have been some link up with hotel staff but this was always vehemently denied when I raised the subject with hotel management. Interestingly and unusually for the normally enterprising Russians, they didn't seem to differentiate between men and women. Much later when I was travelling with female KHF colleagues, it turned out they also received the same calls offering women but never men. Fair treatment of the sexes still has a long way to go in Russia. During the drive to the airport the next day, light rain fell in a relentless cold mist and although it wasn't quite cold enough to snow, I could clearly feel the approaching chill of the Siberian winter touching my face. As I left Kemerovo and the Kuzbass behind after my first visit, I couldn't help feeling rather depressed and concerned for the region's future.

Chapter Five

Samara, Togliatti and Djerzhinsk

Over the summer of 1998, the KHF staff had been discussing the possibilities of starting some projects in a completely new area of Russia and after reviewing various alternatives, the Samara region was selected. This was for a variety of reasons. The city itself is large with a broad range of economic activity, including manufacturing, agriculture and a small but growing service sector plus the vast manufacturing complex of Lada cars in Togliatti was also nearby. In addition, although Samara at the time still had a strong communist influence, the local government authorities seemed open to reform and change and already had some limited experience with other foreign agency programmes. The fact it was the home of Rodnik vodka (my favourite) as well as Zhiguli beer was entirely coincidental. I was asked to go out to Samara to join a small KHF group to look at the potential there.

I arrived in Samara in the early evening of November 15*th* along with three other colleagues from the KHF – one from our Moscow office and two from London. As we stood waiting for our luggage in the airport, we could see that the weather outside was awful – driving rain and sleet – but at least it wasn't snowing here yet. The town dates from the 14*th* century and its position on the Volga south of Kazan soon made it an important trading centre which provided the base for its later development as a major manufacturing town. During World War II, Samara was selected as the capital of the USSR in the event that Moscow fell to the advancing German army and in October 1941 the Soviet government and foreign diplomatic missions were evacuated here. They remained in Samara until June 1943 when everyone returned to Moscow. The town has a few interesting older buildings as well as some fine modern ones but its best known site is the dugout built for Stalin during the war which was pointed out to us as we drove around the city the following day. Our driver explained that there are conflicting stories locally as to whether it was ever actually used. Stalin claimed he stayed in Moscow throughout the worst of the war so never used his bunker but some in Samara claim that he did indeed spend a few weeks there at the height of the German advance. The 20th century Russian writer Tolstoy definitely lived in Samara and there is a museum dedicated to him. Perhaps the finest aspects of the town were its extensive river views and embankments but the unwelcoming Samara weather gave us no opportunity to really appreciate them.

For the next three days we split into two teams and met with a variety of local government officials, NGOs (non-governmental organisations), universities and other academic institutions plus a range of businesses and consulting companies. As part of our programme we had arranged to visit the massive Lada car plant in nearby Togliatti. We well understood that the KHF was too small to provide assistance to such a large company but we wanted to explore how they worked with small suppliers and what opportunities might exist to develop a local automotive supply chain network. Clusters of smaller suppliers grouped close to a large 'mother' company worked well in Europe and the USA, increasing local employment as well as reducing shipment times and costs. I went with David, one of my London-based KHF colleagues and had useful but rather inconclusive meetings with a group of senior managers. We were then taken round parts of the immense factory complex which was better equipped than many I had seen in Russia. Afterwards, our tour guide offered us lunch in one of their office canteens and as we had been on the go since early that morning without a break, we gladly accepted. The large, busy dining room was pleasant enough with clean, white tablecloths and waitress service, although the menu choice was fairly limited, mostly the ubiquitous Russian soup, meat and potatoes. Both David and I elected to go with a plain omelette as being something quick and simple and our meals duly arrived a few minutes later. As we jointly took our first mouthfuls of the omelettes, we simultaneously immediately screwed up our faces in disgust and spat the food back out onto the plate. The taste was absolutely awful; it was clear that the omelette had been cooked in some very old oil that must have been in service in the kitchen for many months. Our host stared at us trying to decide if this double act of spitting out the first mouthful of food was some strange British mealtime custom and should just be ignored or whether there was something more seriously wrong with us. After gulping down a whole glass of water to try to wash away the taste, I explained to our host that sadly, the omelettes didn't taste very good. We were offered a replacement dish but we both felt so sick that the thought of any further food, at least in this restaurant was anathema to us. I'm sure the story of what had happened in the restaurant was relayed to senior management and I wasn't surprised when we didn't hear anything further from Lada.

Strangely, despite its size and importance, I didn't have a single pleasant meal in Samara and the apparent scarcity of decent restaurants in such a large city was a surprise. As elsewhere in Russia, there were clearly people who had money to spend on eating out but generally the choice and quality, as well as the service on offer were very limited. Although things were slowly changing, at least in the bigger cities, it was a shame there wasn't a greater diversity in Russian restaurants. Of course in the better Moscow and St Petersburg hotels and restaurants, there was a wide choice of good quality food on offer and in many other cities the increasing number of hamburger and pizza parlours catered for those seeking fast food. On those occasions when I did come across a better restaurant in a provincial town, the prices charged were usually at or close to Moscow levels i.e. very expensive. There rarely seemed to be a happy medium; at its best the food was plain and hearty but at its frequent worst, it was awful. Right across this vast country, I found the food served was mostly the same, generally fairly bland and often stodgy or greasy, with little regional diversity – shashlik perhaps in Rostov, good fresh fish in St Petersburg and some local variations on the pelmeni (Russian dumplings) theme. Russia's relative isolation and distrust of foreigners during the Soviet era probably contributed to this lack of interest in other cuisines. Undoubtedly, the difficult economic times after perestroika reduced the numbers who could afford to eat out as well as the availability and supply of quality ingredients, as my own earlier shopping experiences in Naberezhnye Chelny had shown. Also, with few significant foreign or immigrant communities surviving outside of Moscow, there had been little external influence on the national cuisine, unlike the Italians say in the USA or the Indians and Chinese throughout the UK.

From Samara, I travelled on to Nizhny by train for a scheduled meeting in the nearby town of Djerzhinsk with the deputy mayor. The afternoon journey to Nizhny passed uneventfully. As I gazed out of the compartment window sipping my usual lemon tea, the miles of snow-coved Russian steppe rolled on and on, broken only by the occasional village with quaint wooden houses. The fields and forests merged into a single, sun-glazed, mesmerising white mantle and I soon felt my eyelids drooping, drifting off into a sound, peaceful doze. When I woke up a little later, it seemed that the train hadn't moved at all, the scenery was just the same until we reached the outskirts of Nizhny. The following morning, I set out with the Nizhny office interpreter Irina and Sasha the driver in a black Volga car, heading for Djerzhinsk. Once out of Nizhny, our forty five minute journey took us along fairly quiet snow covered roads which were deeply rutted from the traffic. In places, there was only a single pair of deep ruts so that only one car could travel this part of the road. If another vehicle approached from the opposite direction, Sasha would pull violently at the steering wheel to yank the car out over the ruts onto the compacted snow alongside and then gently eased us back down again once the other vehicle had passed. Djerzhinsk was named after Felix Djerzhinsky, one of the early Communist leaders who ran the ruthless Cheka, the Bolshevik secret police and there are half a dozen towns in Russia and Ukraine named in his dubious honour. Oleg Deripaska, at one time rumoured to be the richest man in Russia, was born here. Djerzhinsk is a very polluted town, mainly dependent on the heavy chemical industry and as we approached the town a thin brownish haze hung low on the skyline. Even with the car windows closed, a slight acidity in the air was steadily apparent. We were soon into the town centre and our driver pulled up in a small square, devoid of people or activity, opposite the entrance to the town hall, just before 10am. It was an old building that had seen better days, seeming to huddle on one side of the square as if sheltering from the worst of the snow and wind. Inside however, it was spotlessly clean and long, wide corridors with highly polished wooden floors echoed to the sound of our footsteps as we were ushered along to an office on the first floor. I had been due to meet with the mayor but was greeted by the deputy mayor who explained that the mayor had gone to Nizhny to attend a conference with Russia's deputy prime minister. The deputy mayor, a small man with rimless glasses wearing a somewhat ill-fitting suit, sat behind a large desk in an over-sized room (I idly wondered if this was in fact the mayor's office) but he was friendly enough and seemed happy to talk to me. Over the traditional cup of black sugared tea, we chatted about the economic and social situation in Djerzhinsk. I was particularly interested in the problems relating to social assets and youth unemployment in the town and explained that the KHF was considering setting up some new projects in these areas in the Nizhny Novgorod region. I did my best to stay away from any direct discussion about the chemical industry as I had been warned in London that this was a sensitive topic due to strong links with the armaments sector. However, it became increasingly clear during our discussions that everything in the town revolved around the production of chemicals and so any project work here would soon become involved in this business. As the deputy mayor and I shook hands and said our farewells, I had already concluded that sadly, we would be unable to do anything to assist Djerzhinsk.

Returning to Nizhny that afternoon, I discussed the results of my Djerzhinsk visit with the VVCC director and then went back to my hotel. As it wasn't yet dark, I decided to stretch my legs for a while and took a stroll into the city centre. I wandered along the bluff overlooking the river, past the kremlin's long red brick walls and on across the broad square past the old woman selling flowers from a street stall. It was all fairly quiet, the local rush hour not having yet got underway. I headed along the main street, looking casually into the shops when I almost got the shock of my life. Standing outside one of the buildings was a large, rather ragged brown bear and my close interest in the shops had almost led to me bumping into it. Fortunately for me the animal was chained and in the charge of a scruffy, bearded man who was obviously begging. I felt more sorry for the bear than the man but tossed some coins into his cap nevertheless. After this scare, I needed a coffee and ducked into a nearby cafe for a while to recover and then slowly ambled back towards my hotel. As I crossed the nearby park, a sad-looking mongrel dog with only three legs hobbled up to me, its nose twitching fervently around my legs. It then tried awkwardly to squat on one of my feet and urinated. I rapidly pulled my foot away in disgust but not before some of the dog's urine had covered my shoe. This was proving to be an uncomfortable day as far as Russian animals were concerned but fortunately, I was leaving early the next morning and avoided any further problematic encounters.

On my way back to the UK via Moscow's Sheremetyevo airport, I ran into an unexpected problem with my visa. Having finally worked my way up the long queue for passport control, I wearily approached the desk and handed over my passport. The woman in the little cubicle flipped though it as usual and then to my surprise slid down off her seat, closed her hatch, stepped outside and asked me to stand aside and wait. 'Problem' she said. A little puzzled, I did as I was asked and watched her stroll off and go through a door to the security centre. To say there was a near riot at that moment in the queue behind me is a slight exaggeration but there were many loud mutterings and very annoyed looks from my fellow passengers. Anyone who has run the gauntlet of Moscow airport's long queues will know what it feels like to suddenly find oneself behind a 'problem' passenger. Fortunately I had arrived in good time for my flight so did not yet have any concerns about the imposed delay. As I stood and waited, it was fascinating to watch the decision making process going on behind me. With only one other passport cubicle open, the temporary closure of mine presaged a long, frustrating wait for the twenty or thirty passengers in my line who had to decide whether to stand and wait where they were or to join the end of the alternative line. It ended up roughly in a 50/50 split although some changed their minds a couple of times, darting back and forth between the two queues. After some five minutes, my passport lady reappeared accompanied by a more senior officer who beckoned for me to come over to him. He held my passport open and pointing menacingly to my visa, told me that it had expired. I stared at the date, surely he was wrong, the visa had been issued just two weeks before by the Russian embassy in London. But sadly, he was right; the expiry date on my visa was two days ago. It seems the embassy, for some unknown reason, had not given me the visa dates requested and never having had such a problem before, I hadn't thought to check. Why was I still here in Russia without a valid visa I was asked. I was tempted to answer a silly question with a similar response but recognising that this was a potentially serious situation I instead produced my Russian DFID business card and explained that I worked for the British government. If there was a problem, he should call the embassy I said. The officer hesitated and then said he would have to check with superiors and I was ushered into a small office and instructed to wait. He returned some ten minutes later and informed me that I would have to pay a fine of US$25 for unlawfully presenting an invalid visa at passport control plus a further US$90 to extend my visa to today's date. It could have been worse and luckily I had enough dollars left in my wallet so I paid up. The only good news was that I didn't have to rejoin the passport queue and so I was able to catch my flight to London without any further difficulty.

Most of us in the KHF had periodically experienced problems with visas, usually due to the Russian embassy in London failing to issue our entry visas in time for our trips. Each time this happened, we had to postpone our visit until the visa came through which caused all sorts of difficulties when meetings with senior government officials were involved. When this problem happened to me again in early March the following year on a trip to St Petersburg, our Russian project partners faxed me to say that it was possible to purchase a visa on arrival at St Petersburg airport and they would set it up for me. I knew British Airways would not let me board their flight to St Petersburg in London without a visa so I changed my reservations and flew via Helsinki with Finnair. I was sceptical about whether this plan would really work but followed their instructions and found that by paying US$120 I could indeed obtain a valid visa. This was an expensive method of entry into Russia and the combination of these visa problems finally convinced the DFID that I needed an annual multi-entry visa which was eventually granted a couple of months later in early 1999.

I flew in from Helsinki early in the morning and although there wasn't a lot of snow on the ground, St Petersburg felt cold, with a damp, penetrating wind blowing in from the Gulf of Finland. Lisa, the KHF co-ordinator at the consulate met me and spent the next couple of days driving me expertly around the city for our various meetings. As we were weaving in and out of the traffic, Lisa asked me if I knew how to tell the difference between Russian and British car drivers. It's simple she told me, British drivers look forwards and upwards – to check the traffic situation and road signs. Russian drivers look forwards and down – to check for potholes, drunks lying in the road and other obstacles to their progress. This was just a casual joke but in fact St Petersburg was reputed to have the worst roads of any major Russian city and drivers needed their full concentration to avoid all the potholes. I was wearing my thick padded coat that I had bought a couple of years ago when living in Chelny and as we travelled around from one meeting to the next, I was finding my mobility severely restricted. With my thermal coat plus several layers underneath, I was 50% wider than normal and found I kept bumping into things, I was forced to squeeze sideways through doorways and getting in and out of cars became an art. Each morning it seemed to take forever to dress, carefully remembering to put on each layer in the proper order. On the last evening before returning to England, I was invited to attend a social event at the consulate – essentially drinks and a few canapés primarily for the British business community in St Petersburg and I was surprised to see the diversity of British activities in the region. Sadly, however, despite the evident enthusiasm of this group, the volume of British trade and investment in Russia was a long way behind that of the USA, Japan, Germany and France.

Although we had failed a few months before at Lada in Togliatti to develop the concept of building links between large companies and smaller suppliers, I returned to Ekaterinburg in early March 1999 to explore the idea again in a different location. I visited several large manufacturing companies in the region and almost without exception, they obtained their supplies of raw materials and semi-finished components from anywhere but the local area. As an example, one company I visited had around 3000 suppliers, the closest of which was 500 miles distant and any quality critical items were sourced from Europe. The situation I found here was typical of what was happening throughout the country. The Soviet government's decision during and after World War II to strategically locate much of their industry in the central and eastern parts of the country, often in mono-company towns meant they were all separated from their respective markets. Raw materials and manufactured components were being shipped thousands of miles across Russia to be made into finished goods which in turn were then transported again over great distances to where they were needed. This system had never worked terribly well in the Soviet command economy when the true costs of production were never calculated and delays or product shortages for the consumer were largely ignored. Now that the costs and inefficiencies were becoming increasingly apparent, companies were starting to reconsider their supply linkages but changing the process in such a large country was not going to be an overnight job.

Although during my time at KamAZ, I was able to talk freely to the various people that I met, I always had the feeling that they were holding back. It wasn't like the previous Soviet times when most Russians would only repeat accepted politically correct opinions and no-one would dare to openly talk about the real problems facing the country or their own daily lives. But in Chelny there always seemed to be some hidden barrier or limit beyond which people would not go, even among the senior managers. It was probably due to a long-inculcated reluctance to critically discuss the country or company with a foreigner along with a fear that in a tight-knit city like Chelny, word of such a discussion could get out and affect their career prospects. Travelling around Russia now some two or three years later, I found a much greater willingness to open up and talk about the realities of life in modern Russia. Almost regardless of the type of person I spoke to – young, old, educated or not – there was no longer the same hesitancy. One of the most interesting examples of this willingness to discuss realities occurred towards the end of this trip to Ekaterinburg. I was taken to a small manufacturing and supply company on the outskirts of the city to meet the owner called Oleg. It turned out to be a very worthwhile visit and the more I listened to Oleg, the more I liked him. In his early forties, slightly overweight and balding, he spoke quite passable English, certainly much better than my Russian. Often at the end of a sentence, he would look at me with a slight smile using it as a kind of question mark to see if I had understood what he had been saying. We talked in some detail about his business and the problems he had been experiencing over the past few years, especially in trying to deal with the chaotic changes since perestroika. He explained it had been very difficult to keep the business afloat and make any money. He was very critical of official bureaucracy and corruption, the fall in the value of the rouble and had clearly experienced some problems with organised crime, though he wouldn't expand much on this. I gained the impression that it was some form of attempted extortion. He then said 'We ordinary Russians have seen so many changes, we have been in red and now we are in black.' He leaned forward, looking at me intensely and added 'This is not change for better, this is not progress.'

I struggled to catch his meaning, thinking at first that he was referring to the profitability of his company, earlier they had been losing money

– in the red – and now were making money – in the black. Thinking this to be positive, I asked Oleg why this was a problem. He wearily shook his head at me and replied 'For many years under communists, the Reds, we struggle, always controlled and no freedom. Now no controls, we have theft and corruption everywhere, only good business is black market. This is not real progress.' Then the penny (or kopek) dropped and I understood what he was trying to tell me. Although the colours on the doors had changed, life for most ordinary Russians was still full of challenges and difficulties. I now asked how things could change for the better and whether he saw any end in sight.

'Not in my life,' he said, shaking his head. 'It will be two, three generations to have positive changes and true democracy like in West.' He went on to talk about the Russian oligarchs, their 'get rich quick' attitude, the political corruption and how the country and people had been cheated. Oleg cited the example of Boris Berezovsky whose early business career involved obtaining Avtovaz cars direct from the factory at less than cost price and then selling them on for a fat profit. He was able to do this Oleg claimed by bribing the Avtovaz senior managers while the factory workers went unpaid for months on end. He went on to take over Aeroflot and other large Russian enterprises using his political connections with Yeltsin. Whilst the example of Berezovsky is one of the more infamous, there were, as I knew full well, many others. At the time I felt much the same way and now as I write this some ten years later, I still hold the same opinion. I came away from this meeting with Oleg feeling depressed by the situation in Russia but at the same time glad that we had been able to have such an open and detailed conversation. In the Soviet era this would never have been possible so this was an indication of progress, albeit very small.

CHAPTER SIX

Krasnodar, Rostov, Sochi & Kemerovo

During the summer of 1999 I spent quite some time in the south of Russia, first visiting Krasnodar and then later, Rostov and Sochi. Krasnodar sits some 200 miles inland from the Black Sea and was known as the Red City both because 'krasno' in Russian means red and due to its reputation as still having strong communist leanings. The centre of Krasnodar sustained heavy damage during the fighting in World War II but was rebuilt and renovated after the war and now has a population of around 600,000. I was met at the airport by Olga, a manager from a local company we were considering working with, plus Andrei a local male interpreter who had been hired for my visit. Andrei proved to be a lively and talkative young man who spoke English with a strong American accent. The three of us piled into Andrei's battered old blue Zhiguli[7] which was based on the obsolete Fiat 124 design and headed out of the airport car park into town while Andrei gave me a running commentary on the sights of Krasnodar and local politics, interspersed with his life history. There really wasn't too much to see but as we drove along with the car windows wound down, the balmy mid afternoon air felt good and with the Black Sea just over the horizon, it was briefly almost like

7 A beer of the same name brewed in Samara was the most popular Russian beer in Soviet times (possibly because it was the only one available) and it was imported into the UK for a while although I don't recall seeing it on sale anywhere.

arriving here for a holiday. I was booked into the Hotel Platan, a relatively modern building in Postovaya Street, not far from the centre of town and Olga and Andrei came in with me for a coffee to discuss the agenda for the next couple of days. We sat and chatted for a while; they were an interesting pair, both from Krasnodar and in many ways typical of young provincial Russians. Andrei was wearing jeans and an eye-wateringly bright patterned shirt, with sunglasses perched up in his dark, wavy hair. I asked him about his American accent and he explained that he had an Aunt on the west coast of the USA and had been lucky enough to visit her recently for a couple of months. He had picked up not only the local accent but many of the American words and phrases popular with the young at the time. He proudly informed me that his jeans were genuine American ones, purchased while he was at his Aunt's. This was just a fill-in job he told me, helping the occasional foreign tourist or businessman, until he found something better but he was vague on what this might be and I had the feeling that there weren't many alternative opportunities on offer in Krasnodar. Olga was the quiet one of the pair, not that Andrei gave her much opportunity to speak. In her early thirties I guessed, she had studied economics at university in Moscow and then returned to her home town to find work. She had found it difficult to obtain a decent position and worked in a variety of low paid part time jobs until joining her current company a year ago. She was divorced with a young child and still lived with her parents. On the surface both Olga and Andrei were positive about living in Krasnodar and its future but the following day both asked about conditions in the UK and were very interested in whether it would be possible to get a job there. Sadly, there was nothing I could do to help them and it seemed a shame that like so many others, these two ambitious, intelligent young people wanted to leave Russia.

From the little information that I was able to glean about wages and living conditions during my time in Russia, it was no surprise that so many wanted to try their luck in the West. Salaries for skilled workers such as medical staff, teachers or managers in the provinces were only one tenth of European levels and payment of wages was often erratic.

Even when adjusted for the lower living costs in Russia, the potential attractions of a job in the West were obvious. Similarly, the quality of accommodation (or lack of it), especially for the young, was a serious issue. I had already seen in Chelny how some of the KamAZ staff lived. Their cramped, barrack-like apartments in run-down buildings, often with shared bedrooms and communal kitchens and bathrooms seemed more akin to student accommodation in the UK. According to one study, average living space per person in Russia was only around one third of that in the USA[8].

By the time Olga and Andrei headed off in the old blue Zhiguli it was still only late afternoon, so I decided to go out for a walk to explore. I soon reached Krasnaya Street (which means red or beautiful street), the heart of Krasnodar but after a brief look, I turned round and walked back beyond the hotel to a nearby residential district. This area of old buildings, mostly single story cottages, was laid out in a grid pattern so I could wander around easily without getting lost. Many of the houses were late 19*th* or early 20*th* century, lying partially hidden in small gardens behind crumbling, faded brick perimeter walls fronting the pavement. Some of the walls were pock marked with holes and I wondered if this was war-time damage or simply day to day wear and tear. Gnarled old trees pushed up irregularly from the pavements, their lower branches brushing against the occasional passing car and fading yellow sunflowers added a splash of colour to many of the gardens. An old man in a red checked shirt sitting on a porch, enjoying the late afternoon sunshine, nodded to me as I walked by and a few steps further on, a woman was bent down, weeding her patch of garden. She paused in her work and as she stiffly stretched back up, she glanced at me and we exchanged smiles. It was unusual to encounter such small signs of open friendliness – I had grown used to the pervading brusqueness of most Russians in public places. For me, this district was a glimpse of pre-Bolshevik revolution Russia with an intimacy and gentleness that was a far cry from the more modern, utilitarian Soviet concrete apartment blocks that squatted

8 Russia, Belarus & Ukraine – Insight Guides

awkwardly not far away. Over the next two days I met some good people with progressive ideas on tackling youth unemployment, widening opportunities for women and developing small businesses. But it was clear there was a distinct lack of support or money from local government to achieve real progress, due largely to the blinkered attitudes of both the regional governor and Krasnodar mayor. Their view it seemed, was that there were fewer votes to be had from this diverse group compared with the few big local companies where more money could be made. With little official interest or assistance, the process of change here would be slow and it was not the time for the KHF to set up a project.

In the latter part of June I headed south from Moscow once more, first visiting Rostov and then travelling on to Sochi again. Colleagues in Moscow said I would find Rostov an interesting place to visit but I was rather disappointed. Although it felt quite different and southern in a similar way that Marseilles is different from Paris, there didn't seem much to see or do. I already knew well that in most Russian towns the places of interest are in fact mostly of little interest. Indeed, the subject of tourism and the hope of generating income from visitors was a regular topic of conversation with the city officials I met across Russia. Most of them had falsely placed ideas about the potential for mass tourism in their region and absolutely no concept of the kind of infrastructure investment needed to attract tourists in significant numbers to their particular far-flung part of the country. A few places did have some possibilities, particularly with hunting, shooting or fishing activities in the vast, open spaces in the north and east of the country. But such sports do not generate large numbers of jobs or money for the local community. Also, the natural landscape of Russia unfortunately fails to offer much in the way of tourist attractions, unlike the USA with the Grand Canyon, Yosemite or California and Florida. As already mentioned, international visitor numbers to Russia had fallen considerably and now that the Russians could travel more easily overseas, they did.

My hotel in Rostov was an old building close to the centre that boasted a recently modernised wing at the rear which is where I was allocated a room. It was not my style of decor, overly fussy with dark, heavy furniture but it was clean, modern and everything worked, including a plug in the bath. Although my Russian KHF colleague was less fortunate, being given a room in the unimproved part of the hotel, it was equally as clean and spacious. However when we came to check out a couple of days later, I discovered that my room was 1330 roubles per night and his was only 340 roubles. This enormous price disparity could not have been solely due to the difference between old and new rooms. It was obvious to me that the differential pricing system between Russians and foreigners that I had first experienced in Chelny was still in operation in Rostov, at least in this hotel. Founded in the mid 18*th* century as a Russian trading post, Rostov sits on the north bank of the river Don, not far from the Sea of Azov which opens into the Black Sea. It lies in the lands of the Don Cossacks and is known as the gateway to the Caucasus. Due to its strategic importance and local oil and coal resources, it was bitterly fought over in World War II and much of the city was reduced to rubble. It has since recovered and expanded and is now the region's industrial and cultural centre with a population of well over one million. On a more lurid note, Russia's most prolific serial killer Andrei Chukatillo, was tried and executed in Rostov in 1994. He was found guilty of brutally murdering over 50 people in the region, most of them girls in their early teens. Driving around central Rostov to attend various meetings, I was unimpressed by its generally rundown appearance and potholed streets, especially in the old port area. Due to the destruction in the war, there were relatively few older buildings to give character to the city, although there were some attractive, tree-lined avenues leading down towards the river. Despite the fact that Rostov was a bustling city and port, it seemed to me there was still plenty of reconstruction and renovation left to do. However, despite its shortcomings, I found the people I met in Rostov to be friendly and welcoming, without exception – amazingly, even the hotel receptionist.

The following day I left Rostov to travel south to Sochi by train – a journey of some six hours. Although a long train ride, I was looking forward to it and arriving in Sochi again for a few days by the sea. Also, I hoped it would be interesting as the latter part of the journey would be along the subtropical coastal strip between the Black Sea and the narrow finger of the Caucasus mountains that reaches north from Georgia into this part of southern Russia. As I wasn't sure until the morning of my departure exactly which train I would take, my rail ticket was booked by one of the girls in the local project office and not by the embassy in Moscow. When I boarded the train, I found my compartment easily enough but discovered that it already had an occupant. I checked my ticket and then realised that the girl in the office had only reserved a single seat for me not a whole compartment as usual. Well this shouldn't be a problem I thought, the man sitting opposite me looked harmless enough and it would make a change to have a bit of company. I stowed my suitcase, settled down into my seat and pulled out some paperwork from my briefcase to study on the train. I glanced at my companion, who was probably around forty years old with thin dark hair and a lightly pockmarked face. His well tanned skin seemed tightly drawn across his high cheekbones, almost as if he'd had a facelift that hadn't quite worked. He was relatively well dressed, wearing a dark brown jacket and blue striped tie. He was engrossed in a book but nodded to me and we said hello to each other and then both of us returned to our respective reading.

After an hour or so, our provodnitsa came by with glasses of hot lemon tea and with this interruption we slipped into a conversation as we drank. My companion introduced himself; his name was Yevgeny he said in Russian, from Voronesh originally but now living in Rostov. He asked me where I was from and where I was going and expressed surprise to find an Englishman on his way to Sochi – he hadn't met anyone from Britain before. Clearly intrigued, Yevgeny explained he was an economist lecturing at Rostov university and wanted to know what I did for a job and what I was doing in Russia. I told him that I had also studied economics at university and briefly explained my background. Our conversation moved on to our families; we were both married, I had three sons he had a daughter and we continued genially in this vein for a while. Up to this point, I had been happy enough to chat but having now finished my tea I wanted to get back to my reading and made to end the conversation by picking up some papers. But my companion wanted more and asked what I thought of Russia. Somewhere in the back of my mind I knew I should avoid giving a reply but out of politeness I hesitatingly said a few words about hard working people, difficult social and economic times but at least there was freedom and hope for the future. Thinking perhaps that my reticence was due to my limited Russian (which certainly was a factor), Yegeny suddenly switched to broken English stating that my impressions of his country were wrong. The current problems were all due to the mistakes of Gorbachev and now Yeltsin and while he was in power there was no true freedom or hope for a better future. Life had been much better under the old communist system and the economy much stronger he continued. He was becoming quite animated now and I felt as if I might be one of his university students as he pushed on with the theme of his morning lecture. The current leaders are all bandits, they've sold out to the West, you only want our oil and resources – that's why you are here he said, stabbing his finger at me. This reminded me of the weird discussions I had had with some of the management trainees at KamAZ some three years earlier. I started to say something but wasn't sure whether to reply in Russian or English and my delay allowed Yevgeny to pursue his theme. Our country is falling apart he said as he loosened his tie and unbuttoned his shirt collar. Look at the regions, some of the governors are out of control and we've lost Latvia, Ukraine and Belarus but they will be back, we're all the same people. At last, he paused for breath and I quickly replied that whilst I accepted that there were serious issues of control in some regions, places like Latvia and Ukraine had their own identity and culture and wanted to be independent. I started to ask whether his rationale also applied to Poland as large parts of it had also once been in the Russian empire. But he ignored my comment and continuing in Russian, he said forcibly we need a strong government to run this country and a true leader who understands our needs and we must remove the power of the oligarchs who get rich while the rest of us become poorer. His diatribe then moved on to modern Russian youth who were polluted by the West, low wages and pensions, the undue influence of foreign banks, state of the armed forces and lack of investment in universities.

Now I enjoy a good debate about politics or economics and had some sympathy for some of Yevgeny's views but he was becoming far too serious and I had shut down mentally. He clearly wasn't interested in my opinions or capable of any quiet rational argument. Of course, I had met other Russians with similar nationalist views but had never been stuck on a long train journey with them. Although he never became violent or overtly threatening (he was smaller than me anyway), there was a certain menace in his voice and demeanour that worried me. I didn't know where this would lead and I certainly didn't want any kind of incident on the train – we still had at least a couple more hours before we would reach Sochi. I had to get out of this situation and thought about moving compartments but in the end decided to simply excuse myself by saying I needed to go to the lavatory. I took my time and on the way back stood in the corridor for a while to gaze out of the train window. The scenery was changing; rolling arable farmland was giving way to forested hillsides with occasional villas perched among the trees painted in white or shades of ochre. When I returned to the compartment, I found Yevgeny once more firmly engrossed in his book and he said nothing as I sat down. Indeed, the rest of the journey passed without further comment between us until we arrived at Sochi and he said goodbye and wished me good luck. I don't know if he felt he had overstepped the mark with a foreigner or simply run out of things to say but I was glad to be left in peace. After this confrontation, I now understood the embassy's policy of always booking a compartment and vowed to follow the system in future.

In July 1999, I returned to Moscow for a couple of days of meetings and then flew on to Kemerovo with three KHF colleagues. On arrival at Domodedovo airport, we were surprised but very pleased to find that we had been booked into business class for the outward flight, apparently because economy was full. This meant that we could use the first class check-in, avoiding the worst of the airport hassle and then enjoy the large executive lounge on the first floor while waiting for our flight. Instead of the crushed, hurly burly downstairs, we enjoyed the unexpected luxury of executive peace and quiet with rows of empty seats plus the choice of free soft drinks and snacks. The young lady in charge of the lounge was all sweetness and light, so totally different from the normal airport service that I almost forgot I was still in Russia. There are only eight seats in business class on these Kemerovo flights and when we boarded we found that six of them were already occupied by a group of Russians, four men and two women. Two of the men were very smartly dressed, presumably businessmen, the other two from their bulky size and demeanour must have been their minders and the two giggling young women were presumably the girlfriends of the businessmen. As we three stood in the aisle unsure what to do, the stewardess approached and tried to direct two of us into economy class. She explained that this was an important group of Kemerovo businessmen and that they needed all of the six business class seats they were occupying, even though two of the Russians were actually booked in economy class. The Russians said nothing; there were no apologies for the confusion and no polite requests to exchange seats. Their wishes had obviously already been made clear to the stewardess and it was now her job to make us comply. We naturally protested, showing our boarding cards with allocated seat numbers in business class and having been fortunate enough to have been upgraded to business class, we were not about to forgo the benefit. Seeing our obduracy, the stewardess had a few words with the Russian suits who after a grimace and a final disdaining glance at us, nodded to the two minders who rose and retreated into economy class. The giggling girls moved alongside their respective expensive suits and we were finally able to sit down. It must have been hard for the two businessmen to decide whether to forgo male protection or female companionship but I wasn't surprised to see the women win out. For the rest of the flight no words were exchanged between our two groups and even the stewardess was frosty with us (she probably had to give back the bribe she had received earlier). It was a small victory for consumer rights in Russia but a good example of the way that some of the newly rich Russians could behave. However, their lack of civility towards other passengers was again illustrated when we arrived at Kemerovo. Once our plane had touched down, both men immediately switched on their cell phones and started talking, despite the standard, earlier instruction to refrain from doing do until inside the terminal building. This is something that regularly happened on Russian flights and no one seemed to bother. However, what really surprised me was the fact that the two businessmen had also lit cigarettes while they chatted away on their cell phones. The stewardess at the front of our section saw what was happening but after a brief glance in their direction, she decided to avoid any further trouble and retreated into the galley. This selfish disdain for the wellbeing of other passengers was symptomatic of the attitudes of many in Russia. They could be charming when they wanted but so often in public they behaved like uneducated morons. We found out the next day that the two businessmen were owners of some of the larger coal mines near Kemerovo, definitely men of influence in the region but not big enough to displace the VIP team from the KHF.

After several meetings with project staff and local government officials during the day, Irina the local project director invited us to dinner that evening. She organised a car to collect us from our hotel and we were driven to a restaurant a short distance out of town. It was the first time I had visited this place which although quite new, had been built to look like an old hunting lodge. Inside it was all dark wood, apart from a massive stone fireplace and chimney, with heavy wooden tables and large, solid chairs. It reminded me of a similar Bavarian-style restaurant I used to visit occasionally when living in Illinois in the USA, all very false and somewhat pretentious. However, starched white tablecloths and napkins with silver tableware and cut glass goblets immediately said this was an expensive restaurant, which explained why I hadn't been there before. Although the menu was mostly game so therefore not to my taste, it was well cooked and presented plus we were able to enjoy a decent bottle of wine with the food. Irina was of course part of the elite of Kemerovo and actually knew our two bumptious businessmen from the Moscow flight. She was a tall, very good looking woman with shoulder-length blonde hair in her mid forties; educated and cultured, she spoke excellent English and was well travelled. I asked her over dinner why she stayed in a place like Kemerovo since a woman of her calibre could presumably find equally interesting work in Moscow say or St Petersburg. Her reply was interesting. She explained that this was her home town, her husband had a good job (a doctor I think) and she felt she was making a useful contribution to improving the lives of local people through her business. Whilst all of this was true, it still seemed strange to me that a woman with her capabilities hadn't chosen to relocate to somewhere less depressing with wider career and cultural opportunities. This strange lack of labour mobility was something I came across regularly in Russia and whilst I admired her desire to help her home town, I couldn't stop feeling she would have been better off, as well as more useful, elsewhere.

One of the objectives of our visit was to look at a few of the smaller towns in the area and see what could be done to integrate them into our Kemerovo project activities. So the next day I visited Yurga and Berezovsky which are similar sized towns, each with a population around 85000 and an hour or so by car from Kemerovo. The economies of both are heavily dependent on the surrounding coal mines and like most mining towns the world over they are drab places in which to live. We had a meeting arranged with the mayor of Yurga for 10.30 in the morning and having arrived early, we drove around for a while to get the feel of the town. Low rise apartment blocks, mostly in a poor state of repair surrounded the small down-at-heel town centre where a few Soviet era shops struggled with a couple of pavement kiosks to attract the few shoppers with any cash to spend. A cafe-bar over-decorated with flashing lights advertised Pepsi and Baltika beer but there were few takers inside for either drink. The small town hall overlooked a wide patch of would-be lawn with two spindly trees throwing thin shadows over a broken, half collapsed blue concrete bench. Most activity in the town seemed to be centred on the couple of garage repair shops where men with their bodies bent under the bonnets of their ageing Ladas, were straining to keep them running for a few more weeks. These men resembled some half-eaten meal that the cars had not yet fully managed to swallow. It struck me that if the British are a nation of shopkeepers, then Russian is a country of amateur car mechanics, always fixing their problematic vehicles.

After our morning meeting with the mayor, he kindly invited us for lunch and led us outside onto the street where his assistant was waiting in a car parked just in front of our Volga. The mayor jumped in alongside his assistant, motioning for us to follow in our car. I assumed we were going some distance but the mayor's car simply pulled away from the town hall, drove down the main street a distance of no more than fifty yards and then stopped outside a nondescript cafe cum restaurant on the other side of the road. I was undecided as to whether the mayor thought this distance was too great to ask us foreigners to walk or if the mayor himself was perhaps incapacitated in some way that I hadn't yet noticed. However, neither thought turned out to be correct – at least not in the way I was thinking – the mayor was simply planning ahead. We walked inside and were shown into a small private dining room clearly laid out for our group. A waitress soon appeared and informed our group that today's menu was borsht and pelmeni (beetroot soup and Russian dumplings, similar to ravioli). I am not a fan of pelmeni but the mayor recommended them telling us these ones were large and very tasty so in the absence of any other choice, I went with the flow. A few moments later and not entirely unexpected, the waitress brought in a couple of ice cold bottles of Siberian vodka and placed then on our table. With all my time in Russia I had grown used to the drinking of vodka at mealtimes (as well as on many other occasions) and was quite happy to drink a glass with the usual toast or two. Neither I nor my KHF colleagues however, were prepared for the lunchtime drinking session that our host had planned. With a quick flick of the wrist, the mayor's assistant opened the first bottle of vodka and immediately poured out large measures into each of our glasses and then the first toast of the meal was proposed by the mayor. As the soup and bread arrived, the remnants of the first vodka bottle were shared out and our glasses topped up from the newly opened second bottle. I didn't protest, I thought I could let the vodka sit until the end of our lunch but then in a lull in the conversation, the mayor was on his feet again with another toast. I raised my glass in response to the toast and took a small sip: it would have been impolite not to have done so. The mayor must have noticed that I didn't finish off the second glass and asked me what I thought of the local vodka and whether I had a preferred brand. In an attempt to show that I knew something about Russia's most important product, I foolishly, foolishly replied that the Siberian vodka was fine but my favourite was a brand called Rodnik which I had first come across in Samara. It didn't really taste any better than other vodkas to me; I had picked it out simply because of its similarity with my first name. The mayor immediately latched onto this fact and called in the waitress to ask if they had any Rodnik. She went off and reappeared after a few minutes brandishing to my dismay a couple of bottles of my Samara vodka. Our barman, sorry mayor's assistant, soon had the first bottle open and waving it in my direction with a proud smile gestured for me to empty my glass before starting on the 'good stuff'.

It would have been churlish to refuse and so I accepted my third generous glass of vodka and rose to toast the good health of the people of Yurga. My colleagues were still only on their second glass and were smirking at my predicament. The pelmeni now arrived and fully justified the mayor's earlier description – they were double the size of the ones normally served in Russia. There were four in my dish, floating (or more accurately, sinking) in a thin soup like gravy. Despite my reticence, I took a bite from the first one; they were after all much needed calories to offset the mounting effects of the vodka. I instantly disliked the taste which to me seemed greasy and slightly rancid and I started to feel slightly nauseous. I could see that my KHF colleagues were having a similar reaction but the mayor, his assistant and our driver were tucking in, washing down their pelmeni with yet more vodka. The mayor motioned to his assistant to pour another round of Rodnik for us and then looked around the table asking what we thought of this local speciality. How does one answer such a question? I summoned up my best diplomatic language and haltingly replied with banal words like 'interesting', 'different' and 'is this your favourite dish'? The mayor laughed and stuffed another large Russian dumpling into his mouth as droplets of gravy dribbled onto his chin. I forced myself to take a few more bites aided by a couple of slices of bread. By carefully nibbling at each of my pelmeni, I managed to make it look as if I had done reasonable justice to the meal. The worst was not over however, as our genial barman now rose to make his own toast and tried to top up our glasses again. I held my hand over my glass and attempted to explain that we had a long drive ahead with important meetings in Berezovsky. But the mayor replied that we had to empty the bottle – 'it's a tradition in Russia that once a bottle has been opened between friends, it has to be finished' he said. The inference in that statement was clear and in consideration of maintaining good Anglo-Russian relationships, I reluctantly accepted the refill and raised my glass in the final toast. We finally emerged from the restaurant into the bright early afternoon sunlight and staggered off to our respective cars. Now I understood why the wily mayor, who had drunk twice as much vodka as me, had arranged for all of us to be driven the short distance to the restaurant. I don't think any of us could have walked in a straight line back to the town hall. I have no idea whether this was a regular mayoral lunchtime routine or was organised just because of our visit. What I did know was that the car journey to Berezovsky was not a pleasant one; I simultaneously felt hungry, hot, sick and drunk. Fortunately, as we arrived in Berezovsky, we found a cafe and after a couple of sweet black coffees, I recovered sufficiently to tackle the rest of the day's meetings.

I have tried in this book to stay away from the details of my project work in Russia as the day to day events are fairly uninteresting to those not involved. However, the situation in Yurga and Berezovsky was so symptomatic of the economic and social problems facing much of post-perestroika provincial Russia at the time that I feel it is worth looking at them more closely. What follows are simply extracts from the notes I took during my meetings with the two town mayors and subsequently the regional deputy governor –

'More than 80% of the population is dependent on the coal mining sector but employment is falling along with production.
Locally produced coal is becoming less competitive in central and western Russia due to rapidly rising production and transport costs.
Agriculture is small scale and has declined relatively in importance over the past 30 years.
The service sector is extremely small, providing few jobs.
The official unemployment rate is 12% but the actual rate is more like 30%.
The local population is declining, not due to migration but because the death rate is higher than the birth rate.
Although large quantities of coal are shipped out of the region by rail each month, very little comes back to the local community in taxes or wages which are often unpaid for months.
Local government has very little money to fund retraining programmes or tackle youth unemployment though there are several youth training schools and a college in Kemerovo.
The budget for maintenance and repair of public buildings is very limited.
Subsidence from old mine workings is a big problem in the area, especially for older buildings and neither local councils nor the private sector (which now owns half the houses) has the money to repair them.
There is a significant and growing drug problem in the area, especially among the young.
The towns do have a small budget to assist new start-up businesses in the private sector – usually interest-free loans.
There has been a limited amount of Federal funding for new projects in the service sector but otherwise it is very difficult to attract external inward investment.

Additional background problems –
Demotivated population
Corruption and mafia influence

Nepotism in all areas
Lack of cash in economy
Ineffective and corrupt banking system
Penal and inefficient tax system
Ineffective legal system & process of law
Struggle between central government and the regions'

Further meetings the following day in the nearby town of Anzhero Sudzhensk only confirmed the bleak picture already obtained. Although many towns in countries around the world have had to face structural decline in important local industries as well as corruption and ineffective government, it was rare to find so many negative elements coming together across large parts of the country. The scale of the problems in Russia made it difficult to formulate realistic, funded, sustainable plans that would resuscitate the economic and social heart of towns like Yurga and Berezovsky. The political and strategic decisions that led to the formation of these mono-company towns no longer made good economic sense. Increasing transport and energy costs meant it was hard to compete in many of the markets they were designed to serve and lack of investment also resulted in their products often being outdated or of poor quality. The semi-derelict dinosaur factories and mines that permeated the urban and rural landscape in so many towns across Russia simply emphasised the social and economic challenges ahead. In the longer term, it was hard not to conclude that in some cases the most likely outcome would be a gradual, remorseless decline of such places, a fate similar to many former mining towns in other parts of the world. It was hard to conceive of these towns re-inventing themselves as major tourist destinations or centres of hi-tech industries. Because the problem is endemic across much of Russia, resulting in few alternative employment opportunities, the population of these towns has largely stayed put. As a result, the most noticeable adjustment so far to the harsh social and economic problems has been a falling birth rate and reduced average life span and not mass migration. But Russia is a surprising country and with their indomitable spirit, ever hoping for a better tomorrow, the Russians may yet surprise us by finding solutions that foreigners like me could not conceive. As in other countries, most Russians simply dreamt of a peaceful life, with a decent job and a future for their children. I remembered what one Russian once said to me 'For the current generation, communism has simply been the slowest way to capitalism. We have survived the Communist hell but have not yet fully arrived in the capitalist heaven.'

On the last day of December 1999, President Yeltsin surprised Russia and the rest of the world by announcing on television his resignation that very day. Yeltsin said that Prime Minister Putin had already taken over as acting president and that elections would be held in March 2000. The former president acknowledged there were errors committed during his rule and asked the Russian people to forgive these, adding that the country needed to enter the new century with new political leaders. Yeltsin admitted that he had not delivered the hopes and dreams of ordinary Russians by stating 'I want to beg forgiveness for your dreams that never came true and I would like to beg forgiveness for not having justified your hopes.' Although Yeltsin had opened the door of democracy for Russia during his first term, his failing health, errors of judgement and links with powerful oligarchs limited his reform programme in his second term. He left office as a deeply unpopular president. The hopes and dreams of the Russian people would now rest on the shoulders of a new president. Putin was duly confirmed as president in the elections of March 26*th* 2000, winning outright in the first round and inaugurated in May. Although there were international concerns about this ex-KGB man who was little known, even within Russia, he swept to power on a wave of strong support. Many of the Russians I spoke to at this time were not enthusiastic about him and had concerns about his rapid rise to power but they felt he was by far the best of the presidential candidates. Putin matched Russia's perennial need for a strong man to lead the country, to control the regions and the oligarchs as well as the potential to push political and economic reform back on the right tracks. In time, he certainly delivered in terms of control but at the expense of a decline in human rights and any political plurality.

CHAPTER SEVEN

Kemerovo and Moscow

I was now becoming a frequent visitor to Kemerovo and on this trip in the spring of 2000 I felt fortunate to have been booked into a newly opened hotel that proved to be an excellent alternative to the unaccoladed, no-stars place that I had stayed in originally. This was a small, privately owned hotel in a renovated old pink and white stuccoed building close to the centre. It had less than a dozen bedrooms but they were bright and cosy and the staff were efficient. There was no bar or restaurant however, so I always had to go out somewhere to find an evening meal. I usually joined the resident British consultants for dinner and there were two restaurants that we tended to use, depending on our mood. One near the town centre, close to the riverside walk, was somewhat old fashioned but the food was fine and we could usually buy a bottle of wine or decent beer there. It was an easy walk from the hotel so this was the one we initially used most but we later avoided it when they brought in the inevitable loud rock band. It was a strange decision because in their relatively small dining room it was impossible to hear yourself think when the band was playing. As an economist, it also seemed questionable from a financial viewpoint as they had to remove several tables to make room for the band which inevitably meant less customers for dinner.

The other place we used was an Irish bar, prominently located on a hill some way out from the centre and so less convenient as we had to take a taxi to reach it. However, it was always a lively and noisy place, with two large open plan bar and restaurant areas, mainly frequented by the relatively few Kemerovians with money to spend. Irish bars were becoming quite popular in Russia and were to be found in many larger towns and cities though it always seemed incongruous to me to find Guinness beer sold so widely. The bar was modern and purpose built and the rumour amongst the expats that the owners were connected to the local mafia, was probably correct. This particular evening, a Friday, a large group of us had decided to head out there after work to enjoy a beer and something to eat. When we arrived the place was packed, unusually so even for a Friday night but we learnt that some of the coal mines had just paid out some back wages. We eventually found a corner to squeeze into and ordered our drinks and some food from the limited menu – hamburger and chips or chicken wings and chips. Service by the scantily clad young waitresses was always slow even at the best of times so we knew it would probably be half an hour before the food arrived. Time passed but no food came and so another round of drinks was ordered. After more than an hour, our waitress finally started to bring us plates of food which were gradually passed around the table until everyone had their meal except for me. I pointed this out to the young waitress who checked her order list, agreed she was short of one meal and headed off back to the kitchen. My order of hamburger and chips eventually arrived some twenty minutes later but with no apology from the waitress. When I started to eat I found the hamburger was cold and hardly cooked. The chips were fine so I quickly ate them as everyone else had long since finished eating and were ready to leave.

As we divided up the bill for the food and drinks between us, I said I didn't want to pay for my meal because of what had happened. The rest of the group understood my reaction but thought there was no way the bar would accept this. So I collected in the cash and volunteered to give it to the waitress and tell her why I wasn't paying. I left the group to order a couple of taxis while I went off in search of our waitress. I eventually cornered her by the cash till, gave her our money and explained why I was not going to pay for my food. The look on her face was priceless – a mixture of shock, disbelief and fear. She tried to reason with me saying it just wasn't possible to do that in this bar and I had to pay. But I was totally resolute and said she should call the manager so that I could explain my views to him. She rushed off almost in tears and a few moments later the manager appeared – a tall, heavily built man dressed all in black who I'd never seen before in the bar. He started arguing with me, grimly repeating the message that I had to pay in full and was soon joined by another even larger bald-headed man who looked like their security guard. As I countered with my complaints about the poor service and food, I could see out of the corner of my eye that my colleagues were retreating out of the front door. The worried looks on their faces told me they sensed trouble and they were doubtless heading for the taxis waiting outside. The confrontation with the manager continued with each of us standing toe to toe, refusing to back down as the noise of the bar swirled around us. He then told me that if I didn't pay, the waitress would have to make up the shortfall herself. Whether this was true or not, his statement indicated to me that he was now starting to accept that I might not pay. I seized the moment and looking him firmly in the eye said that I wasn't paying and it was up to the management to sort out the problem. With that I turned and headed out of the front door, instantly expecting to hear a shout or even to be grabbed from behind by the bar's security guard. Much to my amazement, nothing happened, no-one followed me and I made it through the door out into the car park where the cold night air hit me full in the face. I fully admit that I was a little scared and felt weak at the knees but I was alive and in one piece after having stood up to the local mafia. There was only one problem now, I didn't have a taxi waiting for me and I absolutely couldn't go back inside to telephone for one. So I took off down the hill leaving the Irish bar's flashing neon lights behind and headed into town on foot. I reached the hotel around half an hour later and found a couple of my colleagues sitting in the otherwise empty bar having a beer. They looked up at me and seemed surprised to see me standing there unharmed. 'Did you really not pay your share of the bill?' one of them asked. 'We're glad you are OK although we thought you'd end up in jail or worse – you know the bar's owned by the local mafia' he continued.

'What happened then?' interjected the other.

'Well, I didn't pay and after arguing about it, the manager let me leave' I replied. I left them staring after me as I wandered off to bed and soon fell sound asleep.

Over the next few months of summer 2000 I made return visits to Moscow, St Petersburg, Rostov and Kemerovo, attending a variety of government and project meetings. In almost five years of periodically visiting St Petersburg, I was surprised at how little it seemed to change. Of course there was continuing refurbishment of some of the older buildings in the centre and the occasional new construction project could be seen around the city. However, in contrast, Moscow was developing much faster with significantly greater spending on infrastructure, retail and office developments as well as new hotels. It remained the financial, business and intellectual driving force in Russia, attracting a disproportionate slice of the nation's capital and resources. For a foreigner, St Petersburg was a more pleasant city to visit but for business, there was really only one place to be. As I travelled around visiting the various places described in this book, I frequently had difficulty when talking to locals in differentiating between *towns* and *cities* in the way we do in the west. The Russians use the same word in their language for both a city and a town. The British have traditionally used the presence of a cathedral to denote a city, regardless of size or population but this system doesn't work in Russia as so few of their towns have a cathedral, most of those that did exist having been destroyed in Soviet times. So in this book I have tried to reserve the word *city* for the largest towns where I feel it was appropriate. However, it was very confusing at times and I recognise that I may not always have been consistent.

In general, I enjoyed the summer months in Russia – they were certainly much more pleasant than the winter. Although it could be extremely hot and uncomfortable travelling around and sitting in offices without air-conditioning, the warm evenings were usually very pleasant. In July, I was back in Kemerovo with some KHF colleagues for a visit that extended over the weekend and Brian, one of the resident British consultants, arranged an office summer picnic on the Saturday afternoon. There were ten of us in total and we all squeezed into a battered, beige Russian minibus and trundled out of the city into the vast Siberian countryside. One of the girls from the office who had evidently selected our destination sat up front to give the driver directions and after half an hour or so, we pulled off the road into a large field and parked. It was a beautiful afternoon, hot but dry and the warm air was still and so quiet; our chattering voices were the only sounds to be heard. There was no-one else to be seen, no other cars, no buildings, no electric pylons and no animals apart from a few birds. We laid out our picnic on blankets placed over the long grass in the field which gently sloped away to a small river lined with trees some fifty yards distant. The picnic was a leisurely affair; people snacked, drank beer and talked or simply stretched out to relax quietly in the sunshine. A couple of the women wore large hats to protect them from the strong sun and as I looked around it seemed to me like a scene from a Chekhov story. After lunch a few of us wandered down to the river bank. In the water, glistening rivulets bronzed by the sun's rays reflected the shimmering light back into our faces as they gently eddied by. It was a peaceful scene and fortunately even most of the mosquitoes seemed to have taken the afternoon off. Perhaps noticing my reflective mood, one of the Russians leant towards me and said 'These are the kind of days people in Siberia live for – they almost make the six months of winter worthwhile'. At that moment, I couldn't have agreed more and I was glad to leave Kemerovo with such pleasant memories for a change.

In late October I headed back to Kemerovo to conduct a detailed appraisal of one of the KHF projects that was now drawing to a close. This project monitoring was an important part of my job, not only to check that we had delivered the outcomes originally laid out and to learn lessons for the future but also to carefully audit spending. In a country where bribery and corruption were endemic, it was vital to ensure the UK tax payer's money had been used correctly and not siphoned off.

In my time with the KHF, none of my projects ever showed any sign of misappropriation of funds or resources but I was aware of a KHF project in another sector where large amounts of money had gone missing and other foreign donor programmes suffered similar occasional problems. Sadly, I was booked into the dreary Kuzbass hotel again as it was the only place with rooms available – I didn't need to wonder why. In the evening, I went out for something to eat and on returning to the hotel, I noticed the sounds of music and laughter coming from the small ground floor bar. Intrigued, I walked across the reception hall and glanced into the bar. A group of around a dozen Russian men and women were clearly having a celebration – a birthday party as I later found out. They were rushing around the room excitedly, presumably playing some kind of party game, accompanied by pop music from a portable CD player in the corner. I nodded a smile at them as a kind of apology for trespassing on their private party and moved to leave when a couple of them shouted and motioned for me to join them. I wasn't sure what to do. I didn't know any of them and whilst they weren't totally drunk, they were certainly well on the way. I hesitated but they beckoned again so I decided to join them – why not enjoy some fun on my last night in Kemerovo. The game they had been playing finished but another was quickly organised and then it became clearer why they wanted me to join them. There were six women and only five men so they wanted another man to even up the numbers. We played several different games, most of which I didn't fully understand but I did my best to follow their lead. The final game involved the man passing a toothpick held in his front teeth to his partner and after each successful pass, the toothpick was shortened. Of course, as the toothpick became shorter, the transfer from man to woman inevitably involved a certain amount of physical intimacy and oral dexterity. Everyone effectively ended up kissing their partner which was presumably the real object of the game. I admit that I was lucky to have an attractive partner called Irina, a lively woman in her late 20s I guessed, with long dark hair and a trim figure, who happily entered into the spirit of the game. We didn't win but it certainly was fun trying. After the excitement of passing the toothpick, things settled down and the group sat and chatted over a few bottles of beer. They were interested to know what had brought me to Kemerovo and what I thought of the place. I explained in my broken Russian my work for the KHF and tried to be non-committal in my comments; it was easiest to say that I didn't yet know Kemerovo well. Around midnight, the party broke up and the Russians staggered off into the night to find their cars and drive home – safely I hoped. The hotel now seemed awfully quiet without them but as I wandered up to my room I felt glad that I had the chance to join their celebrations. It was good to see a group of young Russians enjoying themselves and having fun in a town like Kemerovo.

At the end of the week, I left the cold, sleety Siberian weather behind and flew back to Moscow for the weekend, staying this time in the Marriott Tverskaya hotel in the city centre. On Saturday evening, I decided to have dinner in the hotel and as I was sitting at my table close to the entrance of the restaurant, a small, smartly dressed group of two men, a woman and two young children walked in, clearly looking for a table. After a few words with one of the waiters, he led one of the men together with the woman and children to a table in the far corner where they proceeded to order a meal. The other man stayed behind and seated himself at a vacant table almost opposite me. Soon after, the waiter brought him a cafetiere of black coffee but nothing else. A little strange I thought but maybe the single man wasn't hungry or simply wanted to sit apart to enjoy a cigarette. As he sipped his coffee, his eyes constantly flickered around the room, across to the family, over to the entrance and then back around the restaurant, almost as if he was looking for someone. As I casually looked closer at him, I noticed a slight bulge under his suit jacket and the dark shape of something slightly poking out past his lapel. Then the penny dropped, he had a gun and was presumably the minder for the family he had originally arrived with. I immediately felt nervous but wasn't sure how to react. Should I complain (Moscow hotels were normally very strict about guns in public areas) or should I feel more secure, knowing that in the event of trouble this man would deal with it. As it turned out, I hadn't been the only one to notice the gun and a few moments later, one of the hotel managers came up and clearly asked him to leave. The minder rose and after an exchange of nods with his boss across the room, he walked out of the restaurant to presumably wait for the family in a less public place. This was neither the first nor the last time that I would be close to mafia types with guns in Russia and although it made me a little apprehensive, I am grateful that I never experienced a single problem.

Sunday's late autumnal weather was definitely cool but soft rays of sunshine poked thinly through the light grey clouds making it a pleasant day for wandering around. After enjoying the excellent buffet breakfast of the Tverskaya, I left the hotel and walked down to the bank of the Moskva River cutting along past the Kremlin and then continued south soon arriving at the imposing new cathedral of Christ the Saviour with its golden domes shimmering in the pale autumn sunlight. This cathedral is actually a reconstruction of the one originally built on this site by Nicholas I which was completed in 1860. In 1931 Stalin approved the demolition of this first cathedral in order to liberate the prominent riverside site for a massive Palace of the Soviets that was to be topped by monument to Lenin. The building was dynamited, quickly reducing it to rubble which took more than a year to remove. For a long time the site remained nothing more than a large hole as a lack of money, flooding problems from the nearby river and then World War II delayed construction of the Soviet Palace. Eventually under Khrushchev, the hole was made into the world's largest open air swimming pool, greatly enjoyed by Muscovites each summer. Then with the arrival of glasnost, the Orthodox Church in 1990 obtained permission from the government to rebuild the cathedral which was eventually consecrated in 2000, just before my visit. It is claimed that over one million people in Moscow donated money for the reconstruction project. Although there were heated debates about the design and construction work, there is no doubting that it is a magnificent building and is the tallest Orthodox Church in the world.

I have always found it hard to understand the resurgence of religion in Russia after the fall of communism. Despite having been suppressed for three generations, the 1990s seemed to bring about a dramatic re-awakening of the nation's religious psyche and the Orthodox Church suddenly blossomed, once more becoming an important factor on the national stage as well as in the daily lives of many ordinary Russians, especially amongst women. It was as if the demise of communism had left a space in people's lives that Orthodox religion had now re-emerged to occupy. Hessell Tiltman[9], a British travel writer prophetically wrote in 1934 that the Communists –

'may shoot every Christian in Russia and men and women there will still nurse the image of God in their hearts. Long after the last anti-God poster has faded, the last lesson in Atheism been given and the Soviet leaders are no more, the love of God will be found in Russian hearts.'

An extensive programme of new church building and refurbishment had taken place across the country, though as with so many things in Russia, it's hard to know the source of all the funding. Yet from my experience, the Orthodox Church seemed to have little impact or involvement locally in dealing with issues like social deprivation, drugs, poverty or unemployment. In all the meetings I had in Russia during my time with the KHF, neither the church nor its ministers were ever mentioned or included as one of the potential organisations to work with on social change or reform. Indeed, the few priests that I did come across struck me as being a rather rag-tag bunch, quite unfriendly and unwelcoming. This situation was in complete contrast to that in most other parts of the world where the local church always became actively involved in trying to deal with social problems. From what I saw and heard, the Russian Orthodox Church also seemed quite xenophobic as well as strenuously trying to obstruct the spread of other religions in Russia. Although this xenophobia was partly a reflection of the general prevailing view in the country, it sat oddly alongside the teachings of Christ. Religious and cultural tolerance still had a long way to go in Russia and I was frequently amazed at the negative attitudes of some of the well-educated young Russians I met, especially towards black or brown skinned people.

9 H Hessell Tiltman – Peasant Europe, London 1934

A little further on from the cathedral, on the other side of the river I reached the strange and very controversial monument to Peter the Great. I had heard a lot about this statue but this was the first time I had actually seen it. The massive sculpture is 315 feet high is one of the world's tallest statues, so tall in fact that it has an aircraft warning light on its top. Designed by Zurab Tsereteli, the official version is that the monument was commissioned by Yuri Luzhkov the mayor of Moscow in 1998 to mark the 300*th* anniversary of the founding of the Russian navy by Peter the Great. However, the alternative popular story was that Tsereteli originally made the sculpture in 1992 to commemorate the 500*th* anniversary of Christopher Columbus' original voyage of discovery. At that time it was called the 'Birth of the New World' and the sculptor tried to sell it to the USA but the US government rejected it. After that it was offered to various Latin American countries without success and so Tsereteli replaced the head, selling it instead to the Russian government as a statue of Peter the Great. Whatever the truth, it is hard to describe this unusual structure and it really should be seen to be believed. Sitting in the river, it has the appearance of a small greenish-blue sailing ship sitting on a stylised plume of water, made from bronze and jutting out from the plume are the bows of a number of smaller ships, each sporting a gold-detailed flag. Standing proudly on the deck of the ship amongst the rigging is the reputed Peter, wearing what looks like a toga and brandishing a golden scroll – he seems totally unhappy to have arrived in Moscow. I understand that mayor Luzhkov subsequently commissioned Tsereteli to do work on the nearby cathedral of Christ the Saviour and I just hope this project was less controversial.

During all my time in Russia, I never once felt seriously threatened by any violence or criminal activity. Of course I was careful when travelling alone (which was a lot of the time) and I took precautions but I have felt more uneasy in many other places such as London, Chicago or Paris. There were problems in Russia, particularly in Moscow with muggings and theft as well as occasionally on inter-city sleeper trains – the Moscow to St Petersburg having a particularly bad reputation at one time. I was warned to use a belt to secure the catch on the compartment door when sleeping and although I never had a problem, I know people whose wallets and passports were stolen. However, I regularly encountered some of the various street scams that were prevalent in Moscow, the most popular variant being for someone to approach you in the street claiming that you had just dropped some money behind you. They would hold out a couple of rouble notes and say quite insistently that it was yours. I always replied firmly that it wasn't and kept on walking along the street so I'm not sure what happened if you foolishly stopped to see if the money was indeed yours. Presumably if you took out your wallet to check it, they would grab it and run or if you simply took the notes and pocketed them, I suspect there was an accomplice at hand who would rush over and claim that you had just stolen the money and threaten to call the police unless you handed over even more money. This afternoon however, as I was returning to my hotel from a pleasant walk around the centre a very puzzling incident occurred. I was on a wide, busy street only some ten yards from the hotel's main entrance when a man a few feet in front of me suddenly stopped, bent down and picked something up from the street. He turned back to me and held out a wallet saying that it had just been dropped by one of the men walking further up the street. Now I was sure that before he bent down, there was nothing on the pavement in front of me and felt certain that he had produced the wallet from his sleeve. So I was feeling very cautious when, as he stood next to me, he flipped open the wallet and showed me it was full of money, mostly 100 rouble and fifty dollar notes. He handed me the wallet, looked me in the eye and winked saying the man has gone, let's share out the money between us. I refused saying why don't you run after him and give it back. My would-be conspirator replied that he wasn't sure who had dropped it so it was our good luck and we should take half each. I asked him to look in the wallet and see if there was a business card or other identification but there was none. I then countered by suggesting we should take the wallet into the hotel reception and hand it in, the owner might return and ask for it there. At this, the man just shrugged his shoulders, said I was crazy and pocketing the wallet, stalked off leaving me standing in the street. I went on into the hotel and over a coffee tried to work out what was going on. It had to be a scam, of that I was sure. A wallet without any form of identification was highly suspicious but what was planned? I could easily have taken half the money from the wallet and simply stepped in to the hotel leaving the man with the other half and the wallet. I don't think he would have known I was just yards away from my hotel. If he had tried to follow me, the hotel security man might not have let him in and even if he did, what was he hoping to do then? Would he have chased me into the hotel lobby and make a scene claiming that I had stolen money from him. That would be difficult unless the money was somehow marked and even then what would be gained? It was all very odd – another of those Russian mysteries. I asked about this latest scam in the embassy the next day but no-one had come across it and they were just as puzzled as I was.

As well as my regular visits to Russia, I was also travelling periodically to Poland for the KHF and I found it interesting to compare the two former Soviet countries. Ten to fifteen years earlier, Poland was a significantly poorer country than Russia with severe economic problems and desperate food shortages but with the resurgence of Polish independence after 1989 it had changed greatly. Although suffering many of the same problems as post perestroika Russia, high unemployment, low wages, old factories and inefficient agriculture, Poland's economy had grown tremendously. It also had a more transparent tax system, a more efficient and reliable banking system, less corruption and hardly any mafia type problems. Human rights, civil liberties and press freedom were also noticeably better entrenched in Poland. Warsaw didn't have the buzz and glitz factor of Moscow but in general I felt it was a more civilised city, gentler and easier to be in. Outside of Warsaw there was undoubtedly high unemployment and poverty, especially in rural areas where the horse and cart were still in regular use on the roads. But progress was in the air and things were changing fast for the better. Although there was some government corruption and nepotism, it was no worse than in some other European countries I could think of. Poland also seemed to have a greater sense of direction, no doubt partly due to the government's objective of joining the EU which was achieved in 2004. The same focus spurred on economic and social development in other former communist countries such as Hungary, Czechoslovakia and the Baltic States. I always felt that Russia would also have benefited from some similar political focus to provide a post communist direction to the country. In some ways Russia's situation resembled that of Great Britain after the loss of its empire. It was not the power it once was and needed to find a new role on the world stage. It took decades for Britain to adjust to its loss of Empire status; Russia had only had a few years to adapt. This vast country having had such a troublesome past was experiencing an uneasy present with an uncertain future. *'Rightly famous for their endurance, the punch-drunk Russian people have a whole new challenge to face.'* [10]

Foreigners over the centuries have always found it hard to truly understand Russia, its culture and its social outlook. The proximity to Europe of the capital Moscow (and its predecessor St Petersburg) with its dominance of Russian political and economic life, inevitably developed an impression that Russia is linked strongly to western European culture. And in many superficial ways it is. But this ignored the vast hinterlands to the east and south of Moscow and the wide variety of people that live there, both of which have had a unique psychological and cultural influence on the country. The real Russia is neither the west nor the east, lying uneasily somewhere between, different and separate in so many ways. It is difficult to define and describe but it definitely is neither Europe nor Asia. All countries like to think they are different but in the case of Russia, almost everyone really believed it and as a result expected the country to follow its own distinct path in the world. This theme was a frequent topic of conversation with the Russians I met across the country but no one was ever able to fully define what that path might be and where it might lead. Although Russia has many large cities, the rural population and agriculture are still very important. Despite the Soviet state's objective ever since the Bolshevik revolution of turning Russia into an industrialised

10 Martin Walker's Russia – Martin Walker, 1989

nation, it was not until around 1960 that the urban population eventually became the majority. Even at the end of the 20th century close to 30% of Russians were still living in rural villages and settlements with some 20% directly engaged in agriculture – a very different ratio to the USA or western Europe. For seventy years, everything was controlled by the Soviet state then suddenly overnight that disappeared with perestroika and a huge unfilled vacuum was left. Some Russians have argued that the 1917 Bolshevik revolution was not a real revolution as it simply replaced one form of tyranny under the Tsars with another that was even worse. Now the population was faced with trying to adjust to a completely different system that not only required thinking and acting differently but also for the first time allowed some choice. Clearly the position in Russia was not a fully democratic open society as we would recognise it in the West but rather a hybrid, something that was still evolving. The basics of democracy, the rule of law and a market economy were present but not yet fully implemented or developed. Criminality and corruption (often state sponsored or condoned) were far too dominant and influential. If the definition of a civilised society is the freedom to do what you want, when you want, where and with whom you want, within the reasonable laws of society, then Russia's period of adjustment is bound to continue for some time yet.

Towards the end of 2000 it was becoming clear that new political winds were blowing through Whitehall and on down to the DFID's offices in Victoria Street which would result in a much reduced focus on Eastern Europe and the former Soviet Union countries. Several of the larger KHF projects I was involved with had either recently ended or were due to finish in the next few months and there didn't seem to be the appetite to develop similar new economic development work. This was due partly to an increasing frustration (and disappointment) with political developments in Russia under President Putin and partly to the arrival of new personnel in DFID with different ideas about what we should be doing. As far as Russia was concerned, greater emphasis was now to be placed on human rights issues and health improvement programmes. Towards the end of the year it became clear that the broad role I had been carrying out at DFID for more than three years was effectively over and the Know How Fund and I parted company. Although I would continue managing a DFID led international donor project in St Petersburg for another year as well as working for the DFID in Poland until late 2002, sadly, my Russian experience was drawing to a close.

Brad Newsham[11] wrote *'Stay in Russia a week – write a book. Stay there a month, write an article. Stay a year and write nothing.'*

In other words, new and fascinating impressions come fast in Russia but the longer you stay, the more you realise how little you really know or understand about the country and its people. Certainly at the end of my first year in Russia with KamAZ I realised just how little I knew about this vast country and its people and I wrote nothing. Perhaps my lack of understanding was one of the reasons that encouraged me to go back to Russia with the Know How Fund. I was fortunate to be able to travel extensively, often alone, visiting many parts of the country and meeting with a wide cross-section of people over a period of several years. Even now more than ten years after the events described, I am definitely not a Russian expert but despite my imperfect knowledge I wanted to share my experiences and memories of this intriguing country. In many ways, Russia is silent and deaf both to its past and its present. The vast empty spaces of provincial Russia seem too great to contain any memories and for many, the problems of day to day living are too pressing to think of other things. In the winter any harsh recollections are masked by thick blankets of snow and ice; in summer the warm balmy days bring softer thoughts, easing the mind into a gentle forgetfulness. As the Russians say 'We all have memories but it's largely up to us whether they are good or bad.' I have to admit that overall, my memories of my time in Russia are pleasant ones.

11 Brad Newsham – All The Right Places

www.ingramcontent.com/pod-product-compliance
Ingram Content Group UK Ltd.
Pitfield, Milton Keynes, MK11 3LW, UK
UKHW020132250726
13967UKWH00002B/598